BRANDO

WITH HIS GUARD DOWN

ROGER C. VERGIN

CABOT RILEY PRESS

Brando With His Guard Down

Roger C. Vergin

Published by:
CABOT RILEY PRESS
287 Devon Way
West Chester, PA 19380-6821

Library of Congress Catalog Card Number: 97-091616

Book Design: Carrie J. Gamble, Inc.
Front Cover Photo Courtesy of: Photofest

PROLOGUE

Actor celebrities occupy a special position in American society. While they enjoy benefits and glory not available to other people, the price is life in a goldfish bowl. Their position is difficult and they may justly complain when those to whom they have spoken privately use such confidences for a public purpose.

But, by putting themselves on display, whether as athletes, actors, or politicians, famous people invite public appraisal. By exercising the impulse to, as H. L. Mencken said, "flap their wings in public," they are stepping into an arena where their ideas, their performances, their bodies are projected as more interesting than those of the average person. For this, they receive adulation, but they also suffer inspection and criticism. Should the burden become too large, there is always the alternative of leaving the scene and taking a more secluded path.

This book deals with Marlon Brando - hardly the ordinary actor celebrity. Many have called him the greatest American actor. He transcends his profession. He is to actors what Everest is to mountains. It was his performance on the stage and screen that first captured the public's imagination. Beyond that, his behavior off the screen transformed him from an exceptional actor into an extraordinary public figure.

This is a slice-of-life biography of Brando, set in the early 1970s; I do not attempt to provide a complete picture of his entire life and career. This period, though brief, was one of the most action filled and newsworthy periods of Brando's career. It included his appearance in two of the most influential movies of the 1970's, THE GODFATHER and LAST TANGO IN PARIS, the taking of his oldest child, Christian, from his home by force, his rejection of the Academy Award, his punching of a photographer on the streets of New York, his development of the island of Tetiaroa, his gifting of mortgage-encumbered land to a group of Native Americans, and his involvement in numerous lawsuits, including tempestuous battles with his two ex-wives. It was also a time when he had decided that he would never act again and had determined to devote his remaining productive years to ecological and humanitarian causes.

He stated that he was going to direct all his future attention to developing his South Pacific island of Tetiaroa into "an ecological paradise where people can go one on one with nature, where scientists can go to discover new ways to feed the earth's masses from the abundance of the seas, and where we can develop new and more humane ways to survive in a cruel, inhumane world." The development was also supposed to throw off a profit sufficient to support Brando for the rest of his days so that he would never again be forced to, as he told me, "slave in that ridiculous posture of standing in front of a camera mouthing somebody else's idiotic words."

This book describes that ill-fated endeavor and chronicles Brando's life during that time.

However, this book is as much my story as Brando's. It describes how an ordinary person was plucked from a university professor's workaday existence and thrust into the life of a giant of the twentieth century. My life was suddenly transformed from a routine of grading papers, fixing kitchen leaks, and stretching the family budget to a world of movie stars, Beverly Hills mansions, chauffeured limousines, high-priced Wilshire Boulevard lawyers, and exotic South Sea Islands.

This is also a management book, written by a management professor. It describes how I tried to apply the management methods I had taught in universities and had applied in other conventional business settings in an exotic and very unconventional environment in which the ultimate Board of Directors was Marlon Brando, the fictional Godfather himself.

Since very early in his career, Brando has given only a handful of interviews. On the few occasions that writers and reporters have caught him in a talkative mood, they came, hoping for interviews filled with gossipy accounts of his romances and his opinions of fellow actors and directors. They left with what he gave them - his philosophical homilies on life, his expressed dedication to the American Indian cause, and his plans and accomplishments for creating a small-scale utopia on Tetiaroa. Those interviews were transformed into the articles that have appeared in the magazines and newspapers.

As seen herein, Marlon Brando is fully as talented at acting out life as he is accomplished in acting on the screen. His performance in the 1990 movie, THE FRESHMAN, was a parody of his own triumphant role in THE GODFATHER. So too are his interviews with reporters a most skillful portrayal of how he wants the public to perceive Marlon Brando.

This book, however, is Brando with his guard down. It shows a different side.

A reporter wrote, "Brando electrified those he encountered. When he walked into someone's psyche, he left his mark forever."

And so it was with me. The day I met him began one of the most exciting periods of my life. It would also eventually prove to be the most frustrating. Though many years have passed since my time with him, he has not disappeared from my mind. That mark with the name Marlon Brando will indeed remain forever indelibly imprinted on me.

So, I have undertaken to present my own picture of this most complex man and my time with him.

TABLE OF CONTENTS

CHAPTER ONE

BRANDO COMES TO THE DESERT

The Boeing 727 touched down gently, tires gripping the concrete runway, blue smoke wafting upward from the burned rubber. It was a shirt sleeve March day in Tucson. The air was clear, the sky cloudless and of the penetratingly clear blue seen only in the high, dry desert.

We stared through the glass at the plane, *WESTERN* in six-foot high muted orange letters along the silver fuselage, hoping that Marlon Brando was on board. Although he had reservations on the noon flight eighty-two from Los Angeles, there was reason to question his arrival.

"Do you think he is on it this time?" I asked, chattering idly to cover my nervousness.

"Who knows, who knows?" replied Dr. Wallace Heath. "Last year, I had a meeting lined up in New York for him to meet with some people from the Ford Foundation. I practically lived at the airport for three days waiting for him."

"What happened?" I asked.

"He'd say he was coming, so I'd go to the airport to pick him up. His plane would land but he wouldn't be on it. I'd call him at home and he'd tell me he was leaving the house to catch the next plane. He never did show up. I finally canceled the meeting."

We were starting in the same pattern. Earlier, we had waited for his scheduled arrival on the morning flight only to be disappointed when he had not deplaned. Heath's call to Brando had brought a promise to be on flight eighty-two.

"He'd better be on it," added Taylor A. (Tap) Pryor. "I want to get back to Hawaii. I need to get this money situation settled right away."

"I hope so too," I said. "If he doesn't come in today, this whole trip will be a waste of time for me. I have to fly back to Vancouver tomorrow. This is the last week of the semester. There's no way I can skip my classes."

I had flown to Tucson the previous night. It was the spring of 1973. The Academy Award ceremonies were just a couple of weeks off and the predictions were unanimous that Brando would be presented the award for best actor for his portrayal of Don Vito Corleone in THE GODFATHER.

After several years when he could hardly find work in the movies, Brando's career was again in ascendancy. LAST TANGO IN PARIS had just been released, breaking box office records in Paris. Audiences were lining up around the block at theaters in New York and Los Angeles. Pauline Kael, the influential film critic of THE NEW YORKER, had heralded Brando's explicitly sexual and agonized performance and cited it as "altering the face of an art form."

The TIME magazine I had picked up on the airplane had Brando's visage staring back at me from the cover. He had just been featured in the cover story in NEWSWEEK as well.

Having grown up in an era before television, the movies had been my fantasy land, showing me what life might be like outside my small Minnesota hometown. Although long removed from that small town environment, I still had a childlike fascination with the movies. And, at that particular moment in 1973, there was no bigger star or more fascinating actor than Marlon Brando.

Heath and Pryor had both known Brando for several years and they were now working with him on an aquaculture research project investigating raising lobster. They hoped it would lead to a commercial venture on Brando's South Pacific island of Tetiaroa. Pryor was director of the project. Heath was serving as a part-time consultant on biological matters.

Brando was providing all the money for the project and it was floundering. That is why I was there.

Brando had put two hundred thousand dollars into the project over the previous months. The money was gone and there was little progress to show for it. Pryor was budgeting a somewhat slower pace for the Hawaii based operation requiring twenty thousand dollars a month. Brando was apparently disappointed with the progress to date and balking at the size of the budget. Although Brando was providing the money, Pryor was to receive half the profits from the venture, besides drawing a liberal monthly salary and expenses.

Pryor was in his early forties and wore the dark tan of a year-round resident of Hawaii. He wore a deep open neck Hawaiian print shirt, light weight khaki slacks, and leather loafers, without socks. With his project in trouble and his life and finances in disarray, his uncertain future was weighing on him. Fatigue etched his face.

Heath's regular job was director and chief biologist of the Lummi Aquaculture Project, a commercial operation raising trout and oysters in Bellingham Bay, on the Lummi Indian Reservation near Bellingham, Washington. He had met Brando several years earlier when Brando, who had long had an interest in the welfare of the American Indian, had shown up one day at the reservation to look over the fledgling aquaculture operation.

Heath was a tall articulate man in his middle thirties with a lean, athletic build. He had descended from a familial line in which the male children inherited a strange anomaly, an extra link or joint in each thumb. The articulated thumbs matched the fingers in length. Anthropologists regard the opposing thumb as one of man's most significant evolutionary advantages over the animal kingdom. Heath's extra long and supple thumbs, in turn, provided him an advantage in dexterity, reach, and power over his fellow man that was an athlete's dream. He, however, preferred scholarly pursuits to athletics. He had been a university professor before joining the Lummi aquaculture project.

He had taken on his position on the Lummi project because of his concern for the welfare of the native Americans as well as his interest in aquaculture.

It was Heath's belief that Brando's lobster project was not being managed efficiently. He worried that his friend's funds were disappearing with little promise of eventual return. Because of this, he had invited me to evaluate the project from a management perspective.

My credentials included effective management consultancy positions with several large corporations and the successful "turn-around" of a few small businesses of my own. I was a professor of business administration on a leave of absence from the University of Washington in Seattle. I was currently a visiting professor at Simon Fraser University on the edge of Vancouver, British Columbia.

Heath and I had met only a week earlier. He had been sharing his consternation about the management of the lobster project with a friend, who was another professor at Simon Fraser University. The friend had recommended that Heath talk to me about the project. Our subsequent conversation resulted in Heath inviting me to the Tucson meeting.

Flight eighty-two finally taxied in. We waited in the terminal as the passengers entered. They disembarked from the plane. There was no sign of Brando.

I had read often of the pattern of behavior of some movie stars, which kept people waiting until they were ready to make their "entrance." Brando had a reputation for difficulty on the set. His absences and delays in filming MUTINY ON THE BOUNTY had allegedly resulted in millions of dollars in cost overruns and almost brought MGM to its knees. He moved at his own pace.

But now, there was an additional reason to wonder if Brando would show up. Brando's closest and dearest friend had recently died. Wally Cox, Mr. Peepers of television fame, had succumbed to a heart attack on February sixteenth at the age of forty-eight.

Cox and Brando had been boyhood friends as they grew up together in Evanston, Illinois. They had lost contact when Brando moved to Libertyville, Illinois at the start of his high school years. Later, Brando had moved to New York in 1943 at the age of nineteen to begin studying acting. Meanwhile Cox was studying industrial arts at New York University. Purely by chance, they ran into each other in a grocery store on Seventh Avenue one day. They again became inseparable companions and shared an apartment as both worked to establish acting careers. They had remained best friends throughout their adulthood as both had achieved fame and success far beyond any boyhood dreams.

Now, with his closest friend and contemporary dead, there must have been chilling thoughts of his own mortality running through Brando's mind. Just days before, he had chartered an airplane and flown over the Mojave Desert, scattering Cox's ashes. Heath said that Brando had been devastated by the loss.

So, it was not surprising when Brando did not step off flight eighty-two. It appeared that I would not meet him.

We searched out a phone for Heath to call Brando's home for an update. Just as my nervousness at the anticipation of meeting Brando was subsiding, two figures walked toward us, somehow looking lost in the wide, empty airport corridor. It was the man whose countenance had graced my copy of TIME, with a slim young woman by his side, looking like father and daughter.

The scowl on Brando's pallid face produced a furrowed brow that implied he was not looking forward to the meeting. His hair was thinning at the top and graying around the temples and hung over his ears. He wore baggy corduroy pants and a shapeless velour pullover shirt that could not disguise the thickness through his middle. His slack posture and his dead eyes provided external evidence of his internal bereavement. Whatever magnetism the camera could capture was not evident in the man before me.

I found out later that Brando was often the last to leave the plane. He waited for the other passengers to clear out to avoid the annoyance of their attention to him in a crowded public place.

Heath introduced me to Brando and his companion, Jill Banner. Brando mumbled through the introductions. They had only a single carry-on bag, too small to hold even one change of clothes for the two, so we quickly left in our rental car. Our destination was the University of Arizona to meet with Dr. Carl Hodges, Director of the Environmental Research Laboratory, and members of his research group.

Hodges was heading a research group that investigated and developed commercial hydroponic gardening operations for raising vegetables in desert climates. Brando was planning such a development for his island of Tetiaroa. That project was also on the meeting agenda. Hodges was a leading authority in hydroponics and his group had consulted on several commercially successful operations in water scarce desert areas as diverse as Arizona, Mexico, Israel, and Abu Dabai. The vegetables were grown in a green house environment. Using hydroponic technology, the vegetables grow in liquid nutrients, instead of normal soil. Inside the closed greenhouse environment, the evaporated water does not escape to an open atmosphere. So, water consumption is less than a tenth of the usage for normal farming operations.

There was little conversation during the drive; the atmosphere seemed strained. Brando had not been told why I was there and he may have assumed that I was another of the many biologists who had been consulting on the lobster and vegetable projects. I sat in the back seat, with a morose Brando on the left and the slim, attractive Banner, clad in jeans and high heels, with straight sandy hair brushing her shoulders, just as quiet in the middle.

A fifteen minute drive brought us to the University of Arizona research center. I met Hodges; the rest of the group, including Banner, already knew him. Several of the higher ranking members of his research staff were also introduced. Brando's presence brought all work to a halt as the female members of the clerical staff were all hoping for an introduction to the actor. You could read the disappointment on their faces as he walked head-down through the reception area, avoiding their eyes.

After the introductions, Hodges took us through the research facilities. There were several acres of plantings under a greenhouse roof. Walking through the airlock was like being transported into a tropical rain forest. While Tucson was hot and dry, the greenhouse was like a mild steam bath. A profusion of vibrantly colored tomatoes, beans, peas, and other vegetables was growing to impressive size. This was more than a research facility, it was also a successful commercial operation.

Hodges' enthusiasm about the future of hydroponic farming could be read on his face and in his energetic, arm waving descriptions of his operation. He was a tall, gangling man in his late thirties with thinning pale red hair. Even though he had grown up on a farm, he had earned a Ph.D. and was now a leader in agricultural research. While he wore a suit and tie, you had the feeling he would be more comfortable kicking the dirt in boots and Levis.

After the tour, we gathered in an office to begin our meeting. Banner had remained silent throughout the tour, walking a pace behind Brando. Now, as chairs were being drawn round, she tugged at his sleeve, saying, "Marlon, you promised," through clinched teeth and eyes cast upward.

Brando looked at her for a moment, befuddlement on his face. Then the meaning of the message sunk in. "Oh, yeah," he responded, looking toward Hodges. "Can someone take Jill to a motel so she won't have to sit through this?"

A secretary was dispatched to drive her. It was an assignment accepted with deference. Glancing out the window, I noticed that they did not chat like two newly introduced young women might as they walked across the lot to the car. Rather, you could see the secretary hang back, as though the aura of Brando had rubbed off on Banner.

The meeting got under way. Hydroponics disappeared from the agenda as Pryor quickly focused on the lobster project and kept the discussion there. The project had begun just a few months earlier, in December when Brando had received a profit distribution check for THE GODFATHER. During the subsequent four months, Pryor had pushed the project forward. He had commissioned an economic feasibility study by the Stanford Research Institute, had rented space near Honolulu for experimental research on the breeding, feeding, and growth patterns of the lobster, and had hired personnel and begun the research.

A great deal of money had been spent on consultants and on travel. Indeed, Heath had explained that Pryor had crisscrossed the Pacific Ocean and the continental United States several times, even making his way as far as Paris. On most of his trips, the recently divorced Pryor had brought a young Hawaiian woman along as traveling companion.

In addition, many of Pryor's acquaintances from the biological sciences had also enjoyed sojourns in Hawaii, Tahiti, and Tetiaroa. Some of the biologists had produced brief consulting reports on lobster farming following their trips, but others had gone for a pleasant Tahitian vacation without producing anything tangible.

The information on the biological aspects of the project was not encouraging. Two factors were particularly disturbing. First, in cold water habitats, lobster are rather inactive crustaceans. So, much of the food they consume is converted to growth - to that delectable white meat that is so superb with melted drawn lemon butter. However, in the warm water of tropical Hawaii - and Tahiti - the lobster constantly moved around. Thus, a large portion of the food consumed was converted to energy rather than to growth. It appeared that it would take an excessively long time for the warm water lobster to reach a marketable size.

The second problem concerned the way the lobster would have to be corralled. In the ocean, the lobster were content to explore and search for food individually and leave their fellow lobster pretty much alone, other than a male lobster cornering a female lobster on a warm sandy ocean bottom on occasion. But, whenever the lobster were kept within a confined area, as they would have to be if raised commercially, they turned cannibalistic. So, it appeared that you could give the evening feeding to your pen full of cute little baby lobster and tuck them in for the night and then return in the morning to find just one very big lobster sporting a satisfied smile.

Throughout the meeting, Brando's lost enthusiasm for the lobster project could be seen in his body posture and read on his face. He said little and let the discussion revolve around him. Most of the time he just sat silently with pensive face and downcast eyes, his mind perhaps more on his departed friend Wally Cox than on the problems of nurturing hyperactive cannibalistic crustaceans.

Our laboratory host, Hodges, demonstrated an impressing breadth of knowledge. Even though aquaculture was outside his primary field of expertise, his comments showed that he understood the status of research and development and the problems that were being encountered in the field. Heath had extensive experience in the Lummi aquaculture development and knew of the many unpredictable problems and delays attendant to developing new biologically based operations. Both Hodges and Heath spoke apprehensively of the difficulties that lay ahead. Pryor, by contrast, seemed to dismiss their objections and forecast major breakthroughs on the horizon.

The meeting continued for three hours through the afternoon. From time to time, I would comment on the financial and managerial problems that were presented. My comments were few. I mainly asked questions. The project was still new to me and it would have been premature to make detailed recommendations.

As the discussion progressed, it became apparent that the project itself may have been premature. The work was more in the nature of pure research than applied development toward a commercial operation. Until research was done to more fully analyze the basic behavior of lobster in warm water and in confined space, it would be impossible to determine how to set up a lobster aquaculture operation or even decide if one would be economically feasible.

This was the type of research for which government funding grants could be obtained and the kind of research customarily carried on by universities and governmental agencies. But, government grants take a good deal of time and effort to obtain, and university research programs often progress at glacial speed.

Such avenues would do nothing for the depleted project budget. Pryor kept bringing the discussion back to the budget and pressing Brando for a commitment on the level of financing he would provide. Without Brando's provision of funds, the project would be suspended and Pryor's salary terminated. Pryor had recently been displaced from his executive position in Hawaii when the organization he was heading went into bankruptcy, leaving him with no source of financial support and here sat Brando, his money the key to Pryor's project.

Brando continued to put aside Pryor's entreaties. He would either mumble a noncommittal answer, change the topic, or, more often, say nothing at all and wait until someone else picked up the conversation.

As the scope of the project, the biological problems, the fast rate at which money had been spent, and the lack of significant progress to date became clear, I gradually entered the discussion. I suggested the possibility of seeking governmental or university cooperation on research, an economic development grant from the Tahitian government, or other private sources of investment capital, rather than being funded entirely by Brando.

After more talk, Brando seemed to draw himself up from his normal posture of sullenness and dejection when I spoke. He would lift his eyes from the floor and, with his head cocked to one side, he would concentrate on my words. As the meeting wore on, his negative expression began to melt away.

Then, after I had drawn a scenario illustrating the possibility of obtaining an investor to provide joint venture financing, a massive transformation in Brando's demeanor took place, surprising in its suddenness. He became positively alive. He sat up straight, eyes ashine and a luminous smile on his face, he said, "Roger, where have you been all my life? All my life I've needed someone exactly like you."

Turning his head toward Heath, he asked, "Wally, where did you find this guy?"

Well, after that comment, if Brando's smile and expression were incandescent, you should have seen mine - a good one hundred and fifty foot-candles brighter. Until that moment, I thought he did not even know my name. While a few hours earlier, I had fretted about not even getting to meet Brando, it suddenly began to show promise of being an interesting trip, after all.

I quickly put on my best "Ah shucks, it's nothing" look and we went on with the meeting. From that point on, Brando began to enter the discussion, often following my statements with a positive comment or a question of his own.

However, nothing specific was settled, and as the day grew late, we adjourned with a promise to reconvene the next morning.

Then, Brando, Heath, Pryor and I picked up Banner from her motel room and went to Carl Hodges' home. Hodges' wife welcomed us with a pitcher of chilled martinis. After the tension of the day and the exhilarating effect of Brando's comments, my first martini disappeared like rain into the dry Arizona sand.

Our conversation soon left behind the problems of the Tetiaroa projects. We engaged in cocktail party talk and I had the opportunity to get acquainted with Brando and with the others. Among other things, Marlon and I talked about wives and kids. He had an eclectic collection of both.

He mentioned that Christian, at fifteen his oldest child, had just begun living with him. He had a thirteen-year-old son Miko, who lived with his mother, and visited Brando on occasion. Then he talked about a third son, nine-year-old Teihotu, and a daughter, three-year-old Cheyenne both of whom lived with their mother Tarita on Tahiti. He said that he would stay with Tarita and visit with his two younger children on frequent trips to Tahiti.

He did not mention the mothers of Christian or Miko. Christian's mother was Anna Kashfi, Brando's first wife and Miko's mother was Movita Castenada, his second wife. Both were actresses who had only a few minor movie roles during their careers.

In his chronology, Brando also mentioned another daughter. However, in contrast to the others, he did not state her age, mention any interaction with her, or even her name.

Even though Brando was thirteen years older than me, our children were of similar ages. My three sons were thirteen, eleven, and five. Though he had been a father for a long time, living with a child seemed a new experience for him. Yet, while he expressed a specific pride in the number of children he had sired, he did not show any real interest in the process of raising a teenage son.

When we first arrived at the Hodges' home, Banner had been drawn into conversation with Heath and with Mrs. Hodges. But, she only provided short answers to specific questions - "Yes," "No," or "I guess so." Though she had been alone all afternoon, she soon excused herself, retreating to a bedroom to make long distance phone calls.

The combined effect of the icy martinis, the thirst brought on by the desert climate, and empty stomachs led to a quick relaxation of minds, bodies, and tongues. I could see the tension melt away from Brando with every icy sip from his long stemmed glass. In the midst of our conversation, he ambled over to the piano. He sat and played a passable rendition of an old tune, MY DARLING CLEMENTINE. A while later, he went back to the piano and played the same song again, and again.

Someone brought the conversation around to extrasensory perception. Hodges, Heath, and I, closed-minded Ph.D.'s all, expressed our skepticism, while the others stated varying degrees of belief. Each believer narrated a personal experience that had helped validate his or her view. Brando exhibited the strongest conviction of the existence of ESP.

Following several such examples, Brando suggested a simple experiment to see if the present group could demonstrate any sign of ESP. One person would write down a number from one to ten and then concentrate on it to see if the others could pick up his or her brain waves. We would then each write down the number we perceived.

Hodges, stating that he possessed no ESP, volunteered to pick the number. He wrote it down and we sat for a few moments in intense concentration. With a brace of martinis, combined with the intoxicating effect of Brando's earlier flattering comments, I was picking up all kinds of messages from the great beyond. Unfortunately, none of them were numbers.

Each wrote down a number. One by one, each showed his or her number. They were all different. This was hardly a demonstration of extraordinary ESP. Finally, Hodges opened his paper and revealed a seven.

One other person also had a seven - Brando. With six of us picking numbers, there was a greater than even chance that at least one would pick the correct number. It did not seem to be an evening for telepathic transmission.

We were about to give the experiment as much attention as it seemed to justify - very little - when I picked up Hodges' paper. The seven had been written strangely, with a meticulous horizontal

European slash through the center. I commented that one seldom saw a seven written in that manner. Thereupon, Brando showed us his paper. His seven also had that same extra line. Closer comparison revealed a remarkable similarity of size and shape. Brando said that he normally wrote a simple traditional American type seven and he did not know what had compelled him to add that strange slash this time.

ESP? I was not convinced. Nonetheless, it was an intriguing prelude to the evening.

We soon left for dinner at Pinnacle Peak Restaurant, an authentic cowboy restaurant and a landmark in Tucson. Neckties were definitely not required. Indeed, they were not welcome. If you wore a tie, before your meal was over, a waiter would swoop by with a scissors, snip it off, and add it to the colorful collection hanging from the ceiling.

I had been curious about the response of people when they saw Brando out in public. At the airport, nobody had seemed to have noticed him. But then, hardly anyone had really seen him. When he had emerged, the gate was deserted and we had not walked through trafficked areas of the terminal. When we had entered the Environmental Research Laboratory, all secretarial eyes had been on him, but furtively and from a distance.

I expected a constant parade of autograph seekers at the restaurant. Actually, although the place was waiting-list full, the only turned head was mine - to see if any other heads were turning. They were not.

A hostess seated us. A waiter took our drink order and brought drinks. Brando had a Coors; I switched to Wild Turkey, straight up. A waitress took our food order. Clearly, nobody noticed Brando's presence. Our dinners were eventually served - thick, pink steaks, befitting the cowboy atmosphere. After my initial pondering about how people would behave when they observed a "movie star" in their midst, I quickly forgot about it and enjoyed the evening as anyone would with new friendly acquaintances.

Brando sat across the table from me, rhapsodizing on the epicurean magnificence of the meal, "God, these baked beans are out of this world. I could sit here all night eating them." He clearly preferred the beans to the beef. He washed them down with the house Burgundy. He gave me his full attention, pointedly ignoring Pryor, who tried to enter the conversation from time to time. Banner only nibbled at her dinner and laconically answered questions. Her answers revealed that she was an actress who had been in a few movies. She again spent most of her time absent from the group on the long distance phone.

Almost an hour after we had been seated, I noticed that a quietude had settled over the dining room. People had lowered their conversations and many were stealthily glancing in our direction. While no one had noticed Brando initially, eventually someone had and the word must have then quickly spread, carried by the employees.

Soon, a cute dimpled waitress, no more than eighteen years old, walked up behind Brando. She leaned over and asked him very politely if she could give him a kiss. He rolled his eyes upward, leaned back with a bored grimace, and tilted his head to expose a cheek. After she gave him a peck on the cheek, a thank you, and quick retreat, he looked at me and with a sideways shake of his head, said, "What an absurd society this is. Can you imagine that happening to a fat middle-aged lumberman from Portland?"

"I suppose not. I know it sure doesn't happen to a skinny young professor from Vancouver," I replied, "At least not until final grade time."

For the rest of the evening, most of the eyes in the restaurant were at least occasionally turned, if not constantly focused, in our direction. But, except for two other waitresses who later gathered autographs, no one else approached the table.

It was my first lesson in how people respond to celebrities.

While Banner was along as Brando's companion, they did not seem to exchange a single word from the time she emerged from the motel until finally she returned from the phone and said to Brando, "I'm tired, can we go now?"

That provided the signal for the end of the evening.

The next morning, Heath and I picked Brando up at his motel to take him to the resumed meeting. He was wearing the same baggy clothes of the previous day. On the drive, he leaned over the front seat and, in a confessional tone, said that he was not in good shape financially. In fact, he said, "If my health was like my bank account, I'd be ready for the last rites. I don't know what to do about Tap (Pryor), the way he keeps pushing for more money."

It seemed a startlingly revealing statement to make to a new acquaintance. It was as though he was searching for a confidant and a confederate.

The same group regathered at Hodges' office around nine o'clock. The discussion went somewhat further afield this day. Time was spent considering the hydroponic vegetable project as well. Again, however, Pryor kept intruding to bring the discussion back to financing the lobster project. Having heard Brando's earlier explanation of his financial condition, I tried to move the conversation away from funding.

At noon we broke off the meeting and went to a reserved private room at the Tucson airport for lunch. Heath, Pryor, Brando and I were all scheduled to fly out in the early afternoon, in various directions. Through lunch, discussion of the projects was put aside. Pryor played with a sandwich, exhibiting a hummingbird appetite. When the waiter cleared the plates, Pryor again attempted to get a commitment on financing the lobster project. He asked Brando point blank how much he was going to provide per month and said he wanted to stop at Brando's accountant in Beverly Hills the next day to pick up a check.

Brando finally quit evading the question and gave a specific answer. His response must have surprised Pryor. It absolutely astonished me.

I can still picture the look of concentration on Brando's face and how he evasively used his table knife to toy with the crumbs from a consumed dinner roll on the white tablecloth in front of him as he spoke, and can yet hear the quiet and halting cadence of his voice, as though he was painfully dredging up the lines from a long ago, half forgotten script. His words are indelibly etched in my memory.

Brando said, "I would like Roger to look into the project. I haven't spoken to him about it yet, but I hope he can find the time to do that. I'm not going to make a decision on the lobster project today. It's just going to have to wait until Roger has had a chance to go to Hawaii to evaluate what has been done, if he's willing to do that."

It was a slow speech, but no one was going to interrupt. He continued on, "I'd also like him to look at the other Tetiaroa projects and my other investments. I've been impressed with some of his insights over the last couple of days. In fact, if he's willing to take it on, I'd like him to give up his job and take complete charge on my financial interests."

Like the fictional Godfather, Brando had made an offer that he thought I could not refuse.

Refuse? I could not seem to move my lips to accept either. I sat there as dumfounded as Charley McCarthy without Edgar Bergen as every eye in the room turned toward me, waiting for a response. Expressions of surprise filled the room. It was as though everyone was waiting for an off-stage director to call, "Action." Even the waiter seemed frozen in the act of filling a coffee cup over Pryor's shoulder.

Though every word of Brando's speech remains in my head, I have absolutely no memory of my response. I must have muttered something indicating assent, for the others were soon surrounding me, asking questions and offering their good wishes. I could not have been very responsive to them, for my mind was filled with a compulsion to get out of the room before Brando changed his mind.

As we filtered out into the hallway, I looked back to see Pryor, still sitting at the table, looking like he had just been hit by a Muhammed Ali right cross.

That is how I came to be Marlon Brando's financial manager.

Other duties were to be added to the job description.

CHAPTER TWO

NAME YOUR TERMS

B rando, Banner, Heath and I walked through the airport terminal to catch the same flight to Los Angeles. Heath and I were transferring there to return to Vancouver.

We were all ticketed in the coach section, in nearby seats toward the tail end. A few miles out, Brando asked Banner to exchange seats with me.

Our relationship had changed dramatically in the last half hour. As I settled into the adjoining seat, Brando said, "Roger, I hope you're good at juggling. You're going to have a lot of balls in the air. When it comes to this money situation, I'm up to my ass in alligators."

A man in the row ahead had recognized Brando. He was leaning toward his right, with his head turned, to try to pick up our conversation through the crack between the seats. Brando noticed, lowered his voice and bent his head toward mine.

He talked more about his financial condition. The Beverly Hills accounting firm of Brown Kraft and Company had handled his day to day finances for the previous decade, paying his bills, calculating his taxes, and providing him with monthly cash flow statements. Brando made it clear that, although they also gave him financial advice, he made his own investment decisions and Brown Kraft did not function as his business manager.

He said that, from a cash standpoint, he was essentially broke. He had received a check from Paramount for a million and a quarter dollars in December, just three months earlier, from THE

GODFATHER and the money was already gone. There had not been enough funds withheld to cover the taxes on the income. A big tax bill was due April 15 - only a month off.

Pryor had tried to convince Brando that the reason he was not wealthier was that Brown Kraft must have been embezzling from him for years. There have been numerous cases of business managers mismanaging or actually stealing their show business clients' money. In recent times, stars such as Doris Day, Cher, Carol Burnett, and Billy Joel have sued their managers for fraud.

Pryor had arranged for the eminent accounting firm of Price Waterhouse to audit the Brown Kraft books. Price Waterhouse had recently sent Brando a financial statement that showed that he had a net worth slightly less than a million dollars, the major portion of which was his investment in his island of Tetiaroa. However, they had not yet made either an oral or written report on the results of their audit of Brown Kraft. Brando did not seem the least concerned about Brown Kraft's honesty, but appeared to have gone along with the audit primarily to placate Pryor.

Brando acknowledged that he had lost a lot of money on bad investments over the years, but put the blame for his present relative lack of affluence on his father's poor handling of his son's money. On the plane, he spoke of Marlon Brando Sr. buying non-existent cattle, salted gold mines, and magical divining rods that could cure everything from arthritis to cancer. He spoke of his father as a living presence, but I later discovered that Brando Sr. had died some eight years earlier.

Price Waterhouse's valuation of his net worth was less than the amount of the GODFATHER check he had received only three months earlier. GODFATHER had not only revived his career, it had put food back on his table.

When I inquired where all the GODFATHER money had gone, Brando said that some had gone into the lobster project and some into the development of a tourist resort on Tetiaroa. He also mentioned that $100,000 had gone into a tax shelter cattle investment and that he still owed more money on the cattle. That left a lot of money still unaccounted. Brando exhibited a sense of bewilderment that it was all gone so quickly.

He wanted me to go to Hawaii as soon as possible to evaluate the lobster project. Also, Pryor had found a house on Maui that he was trying to persuade Brando to purchase as a place to stay when Brando came to Hawaii to deal with the lobster project. Brando wanted us both to look at it. However, he was even more anxious for me to go to Tetiaroa and evaluate the development of his island for tourism.

I had to return to Vancouver to teach my next week's classes. I made plans to return the following week to Los Angeles to meet with Price Waterhouse and with Brown Kraft to get a more complete picture of Brando's financial position. After that, Brando and I planned to go first to Hawaii and then on to Tetiaroa. With only one week of classes remaining in the semester, my time would soon be completely free.

As we talked, Banner would repeatedly look back from her seat a couple of rows ahead and across the aisle. It seemed that she would have been more comfortable next to Brando than visiting with Heath.

Brando spoke about how much I would enjoy Tetiaroa. He talked about the warmth of the sand, the clearness of the water, and the quiet and serenity of the island. He said that on Tetiaroa, you were "one on one with nature. If you are hungry, you fish. If you are tired, you sleep." If that sounded suspiciously like something I had read, it was. It was essentially Brando's quote repeated from the TIME magazine article which I had read two days before. He spoke in a quiet, unexpressive voice so that his recitation reminded me of remembered lines from a script, not of currently experienced thoughts and emotions.

"The Tahitians are the most laid-back people on earth. I think the world could fall off its orbit and they'd never know the difference."

"Nobody gives a damn about me down there. I can walk around among the natives and I'm just another asshole on the beach. That's about the only place in the world where people leave me completely alone. That's what I like best about it."

As we made our travel plans, I mentioned that there was a time conflict involved. At the time we were talking about being on Tetiaroa, the Academy Awards ceremony was to be held. Brando had been nominated for the Best Actor Award for his performance as Don Corleone in THE GODFATHER and the predictions were that he was a shoo-in.

"There doesn't seem to be any doubt that you are going to win the award," I said. "Shouldn't we plan on leaving a few days later?"

Brando's arms had been reposing on the arm rests, hands dangling limply beyond the ends. To my comment, his two hands lifted, thumbs pointed upward, he cast his head to one side and pursed his lips, his gesture implying that he knew the award would be his, but that it was a matter of no importance. His "Ah, shucks" look was better than mine, but that was hardly a surprise. I did not mind coming in second place to Marlon Brando.

He lowered his voice further, keeping his eye on the man still trying to eavesdrop from the front. He bent his head toward me, and in a conspiratorial tone said, "No, we can leave. Keep this quiet; nobody else at all knows about this, but I've got a plan for the Awards. You know, Roger, the movies have always portrayed the Indians as mindless savages. Those people that make movies don't have the slightest idea of what an Indian is really like. All they care about is how many tickets they can sell. This country has destroyed the Indian culture and all but annihilated the Indians themselves. I'm going to turn down the award and use the forum as a chance to draw attention to the Indian cause. I've got a friend lined up to read a speech about how the movies have portrayed the Indian, so we can go to Tetiaroa as we're planning."

That should be interesting, I thought. Maybe I should stay home and watch television.

Our time together on the plane was too short for the many things there were to discuss. As the plane neared Los Angeles, Brando asked me how quickly I could be released from all my university obligations. I suddenly realized that I had been too absorbed in finding out about his projects and financial situation to give any thought to my employment conditions.

Despite the irresistible nature of Brando's employment offer, I suggested a more cautious course of action. I proposed to make the trip to Los Angeles, Hawaii, and Tetiaroa to evaluate his projects and financial situation. Then, we could discuss whether or not he would really want me to work for him for a longer period. I added that would give him a little time to evaluate me personally, and that for his own peace of mind, he might want his attorney or accountant to check out my background. He had, after all, just met me and I was even a comparative stranger to Wallace Heath, who had brought me to the meeting. In reality, Brando knew little more about me than what he had absorbed from our conversations of the last twenty-four hours.

Brando replied, "No, we don't have to wait for that. I'm a very intuitive person. I like to go with my own feelings about people. What other people say about someone doesn't mean much to me. I like to talk to people, watch their mannerisms, see how they express themselves, try to figure out what makes them tick. I've got a good feeling about you. I know I can trust you and you're going to be able to handle this."

I was eager to get started on this challenge and said it would only take a couple of weeks in Vancouver after we returned from Tetiaroa to close accounts, pack up my family, and be in Los Angeles, ready for full time work.

"Well, maybe you should think about moving your family all the way to Tetiaroa," he said. "That's where the action is going to be. I think our top priority should be to develop the island. We can get it opened up for tourists and use the profits to support some of these other activities. I don't want to go back to work. I plan to spend most of my time on Tetiaroa and I'd like you to be there too. You can fly to L A whenever you need to handle things here."

"That sounds interesting, all right. But, don't forget, we've got three school age kids. I can't take them there just to play in the sun. They have to go to school."

He acknowledged the problem and said, "How about if you move there until fall, anyway. By then the resort should be finished and operating. You could move your kids back to L A to start school then if you want.

"But, I think they might really like it there. What I'd really like to do is build a little school down there for the Tahitian kids. I'd like some families to live on the island. Maybe you can get that built this summer, then your kids can go too. It's not like building a school in the U.S. With the climate down there, you don't need much of a building - just a little one-room schoolhouse. If you get it built, you can hire a teacher from anywhere, from the U. S. if you want - whatever your kids need."

His long term plan was not very appealing, but the opportunity to bring my family to Tetiaroa for the summer was intriguing.

Then, Brando made another proposal, in a way even more astounding than had been his original job offer. He said, "I really appreciate how you're willing to give up your job and uproot your family in order to help me. I know those university jobs can be a pretty soft life and here you're going to have a full plate. There's something I'd like to do for you to take care of your future."

"I'd like you to build a home on Tetiaroa that you would be comfortable with. You can pick out any site on the island you want. If you're short of cash, I'll lend you the money to build it. Then when you move back to the states, you can rent it out in conjunction with our tourist program. You should be able to get a thousand bucks a week for a nice bungalow."

I sat fascinated, unable to speak.

"I want you to set up travel agents in the states to organize tours and handle reservations for the resort," Marlon added. "You should be able to keep your house rented all year round. We'll have the resort handle maintenance and cleaning. You can keep all the income."

It kept sounding better and better.

"I'll even deed the land to you and you can keep getting the income for the rest of your life, even if you aren't working for me anymore. It can be the second unit rented all the time. I've promised Bernie - he's an architect I've got over there - that he could build a house there too and that his would always be the first one rented, so yours will have to be second."

This was as surprising and as exciting as his original offer. The house could bring an income of $50,000 a year. Since my 1973 university salary was only $24,000, I was suddenly being propelled into a position of comparative affluence - before even starting the job.

I could not believe my good fortune. I quickly made a mental commitment to work day and night, to cast aside my own business interests, and commit my total effort to getting this generous and benevolent man back on his financial feet.

My mind wandered to the scene of the Academy Award ceremony a year into the future, one in which Brando would win a second consecutive award, this time for best actor for his performance in LAST TANGO IN PARIS. My day-dreaming vision saw him, "give my special thanks to Roger Vergin (pronounced ver jeen') for bringing me financial stability for the first time in my life . . . "

I was jerked back from my reverie when Marlon asked me, "How much salary do you want?"

Usually reluctant to name a high figure in such a situation, it was a question I hated. "Why don't we ask Brown Kraft to set a figure? They should have an idea of how much somebody like me should make."

"No, just name your terms. I trust your judgment."

"I don't know. How about $30,000?" That was more than my university salary, but that represented only an eight month per year work schedule and I would now be forsaking consulting and business income. It was probably less than Brown Kraft would have recommended, but if Brando's house income offer would actually be achieved, I would have been willing to work the first year free.

"Sounds good to me," Marlon said. "Now, you've got to earn it."

Too quickly, we entered the glide path to LAX, the Los Angeles airport. Returning to my seat, I apologized to Banner for monopolizing Brando's time. She did not respond to my apology. I felt her silent recrimination. The plane landed. Heath and I said our goodbyes to Brando and Banner and deplaned to make arrangements to catch our connecting flight to Vancouver.

After checking the departure schedule, Heath and I had some time on our hands so we walked outside around the air terminal to enjoy the California sunshine and get some exercise. As we circled the terminal, we again saw Brando and Banner. He was sitting on an outside metal-grated stairway, casually reading a newspaper as they waited for a ride. She was standing by herself at curbside watching the traffic flow by. Passers-by hurriedly went about their business. Clearly, none of them noticed Brando; there were no double takes or prolonged looks. It had seemed impossible that someone so familiar to the public would pass unrecognized in Los Angeles, yet here he sat unnoticed.

A short while later, we boarded the plane for Vancouver, to return temporarily to a life I hoped to soon leave behind forever.

CHAPTER THREE

THE LIFE AND TIMES OF
MARLON BRANDO

Following that spring day in Tucson, I began working closely with Brando. During that time, I met many people who had been associated with him over his life and career who shared with me their stories of Brando.

Many actors, producers, and directors have written about Brando's development as an actor. In their own memoirs, they have written about their interactions with him and his influence on them and on the acting profession.

Most of the prior biographies on Brando have been written by authors who never met him, and did not even do very exhaustive research on their subject. Consequently, their books were filled with accounts of his movies, often repeated anecdotes, many of them pure fiction, and many "facts" that are simply incorrect.

While this book covers only a short period in his life, it comes from a different perspective than other sources, that of a business manager; not someone from the entertainment business. But, my relationship went far beyond that of someone just overseeing financial matters for a client. Brando and I shared a friendship as well as a working relationship. We traveled together. While in the U.S., I lived in his Beverly Hills home. During the times I was on Tetiaroa, Brando was usually there also, occupying his own bungalow just a stone's throw away from my own family's lodgings. He befriended my children and I befriended his. Indeed, there were periods when he left Christian or Miko in the care of me and my wife on Tetiaroa while he went back to Beverly Hills for a couple of weeks. Thus, this account provides a view of Brando's activities and character not seen elsewhere.

The first published report on Brando of any significant depth was a 1957 profile by Truman Capote in THE NEW YORKER. Capote had visited Brando in his hotel room in Japan during the filming of SAYONARA and had plied him with more and more shots of vodka to the point that Brando had lost his normal obsession with privacy. Capote got Brando to talk about his upbringing. He spoke freely about his mother's alcoholism and his father's womanizing and domineering behavior and his complex feelings toward them. In the interview, which went through the night and on into the next day, Brando's inebriated commentary revealed details and feelings about his life and his acting. He also expressed highly critical opinions about many people in the movie profession with whom he had worked. From this conversation and from interviews with people who had worked with Brando, Capote produced a scandalous profile. Capote's article revealed much of the Brando psyche and life that had been previously unknown.

Subsequently, several "movie star" biographies were written about Brando. Most failed to add anything very new and a review of them shows that most of the "personal anecdotes" were drawn directly from the Capote article - without credit given to the source. It was not until 1974 that the first book appeared that was written by someone with first hand knowledge.

BUD; THE BRANDO I KNEW, written by Carlo Fiore, provided a portrait of Brando's early years in acting with an emphasis on his personal life. It particularly dwelled on Fiore's and Brando's woman chasing. Fiore was an actor of limited achievement. He unsuccessfully fought a life-long addiction to cocaine and heroin, which eventually killed him. Brando frequently found minor roles for Fiore in his movies and tried to help him rid himself of his addiction. The book contained a few interesting stories about Brando, but was largely devoted to the author playing up his own furious sex life and his self described contributions to Brando's career. The unbelievable nature of many of the anecdotes casts doubt on the credibility of the whole rather unflattering portrayal.

A second personal portrait of Brando was provided in the 1979 book, BRANDO FOR BREAKFAST, written by his first wife, Anna Kashfi, and co-author E. P. Stein. Kashfi's 1951 marriage to Brando survived only a few months of cohabitation, but had produced their son, Christian, who became the focal point of continual battles between father and mother, both in and out of court, over the next two decades and who was to become involved in his own tragedy when he shot and killed his half-sister's boyfriend, Dag Drollet, in 1990. Kashfi endured a long battle with drugs and alcohol and spent periods in both jail and hospitals as a result of those problems.

Her book is largely a vitriolic portrayal of Brando as a sadistic monster bent on driving her insane; the vitriol supplied by Kashfi and the writing by co-author Stein. Consequently, the book is a combination of stories repeated from earlier books, almost word for word, and Kashfi's stories of their marriage and conflicts. From my own firsthand knowledge, I know much her portrayal to be factually incorrect and regard the whole book with suspicion.

The first broadly researched account is the 1987 book titled BRANDO, THE UNAUTHORIZED BIOGRAPHY, by Charles Higham. Higham employed several researchers and interviewers who collectively interviewed over sixty people who had known Brando, from childhood days on. Higham's book provided a broad new biographical picture of Brando's life, filled with detail. The interviews provided information of Brando's life and character that should dispose of many of the apocryphal myths and impressions that somehow found their way into print - often based on Brando's own facetious story or account to a newspaper reporter or magazine writer - which were perpetuated as each succeeding biographer took much of his material from earlier writers.

While Higham's biography was thoroughly researched, it was still a second hand account. Higham did not interview Brando for the book - although he did point to having had "conversations" with Brando on a movie set some twenty-two years earlier. Consequently, the portrait drawn is necessarily limited. While it does show Brando, warts and all, it still has much of the "movie star adoration" found in most such biographies. Despite the research, much of what Higham wrote about Brando's development of

Tetiaroa, his support of scientific research, his rejection of the Academy Award, and other matters during the period of my involvement with Brando was simply incorrect.

So, to set the background for the remainder of my story, consider the life and times of Marlon Brando before I met him.

Marlon Brando was born in Omaha, Nebraska on April 3rd, 1924, the only son in the family. His sister Jocelyn was four years older and sister Frances was one year older.

His father, Marlon Brando, Sr., was then twenty-seven years old and worked as a salesman for Western Limestone Products. The Brando family had been in Omaha for several generations. Brando, Sr. had been educated at Shattuck Military Academy in Minnesota, where he had been on the swimming and football teams. He had a distinctly military bearing as he walked to work every morning in his homburg, dark suit, white shirt, plain tie, and patent leather shoes. He was known around Omaha as a well mannered teetotaler and church attendee.

However, behind that pious facade, he was an altogether different person. He was a regular in the brothels and the speakeasies of the cities where he made his business trips.

His wife, Dorothy Pennebaker Brando (Dodie) was an attractive, lively woman who dabbled in amateur dramatics and had ambitions of becoming a professional actress.

Brando, Sr. was able to provide his family with a comfortable standard of living, although his work required several changes of residence. In 1930, he obtained a better job, with the Calcium Carbonate Company of Chicago, and the family moved to Evanston, Illinois.

Marlon, Jr. was always called Bud within the family. He was mischievous and strong-willed as a child. His sympathy for underdogs was apparent at an early age and several times he brought home human derelicts including, one time, a drunken woman. He was also fond of animals and went around collecting stray pets and exotic wild animals such as raccoons and possums. He became so attached to each animal that he objected to any dead cat or bird being buried. When his pet chicken died, Dodie buried it and young Bud dug it up and refused to allow it to be reburied.

He often got into fights with neighborhood kids. He was full of pranks like pulling the fire alarm and watching from a hidden vantage point as the red fire trucks come screaming down the street. Wherever he lived, he was remembered as the center of attention, the star of the neighborhood block. Bud and his sisters went to the movies on Saturdays and Sundays. Bud especially loved the Westerns with cowboys and Indians and cheered loudly when another Indian bit the dust. He would dress up in a cowboy outfit and entertain the neighborhood with his imitation of Hoot Gibson or Hopalong Cassidy.

His early teachers remember him as being mischievous and "full of pep and life" and as spending a lot of time in the hallway to prevent him from disrupting classes in session. At the age of ten, one of his classmates was the frail little Wally Cox, who was often picked on. The bigger Bud protected him by entering a fight that some boy had started with Wally.

When the children were small, mother Dodie's passion was the Omaha Community Playhouse. She was the biggest name in the Playhouse, with great style and presence on the stage. Besides acting, she was also a major force in production and direction at the Playhouse. Despite her successful work at the Playhouse and in raising three young children, Dodie had a weakness, her fondness for the bottle.

An oft quoted opening line from Tolstoy's ANNA KARENINA is, "All happy families resemble each other. Each unhappy family is unhappy in its own way." Yet, so many unhappy families share a common denominator - the specter of alcoholism.

Research and clinical observation have demonstrated that children who grow up in families where one or both parents are actively alcoholic are profoundly affected by the experience. They commonly adopt dysfunctional behavioral characteristics and patterns that follow them into adulthood and which, if not addressed, lead to chaotic personal and social lives. They often suffer from low self-esteem, have trouble with authority figures, have difficulty to trusting people and in intimate relationships, and even in just having fun in life.

While the causes of alcoholism are complex, certainly her husband's philandering added to Dodie's turmoil. When the family moved to Evanston, she suffered the loss of her acting career. Her drinking, which had been a problem before, now grew worse.

To outsiders, the Brandos appeared to be a happy family. Indeed, the early Brando biographies describe Bud growing up in an easy-going and ideal family environment. When Bud was twelve, the facade was shattered when his father came home from Chicago with his underwear smeared with lipstick. Dodie drunkenly screamed at him. In response, he brutally beat her. Bud threatened to kill him. Similar scenes were repeated many times in the succeeding years.

By the time Bud was fourteen, Dodie's drinking had become such an embarrassment in Evanston that the family moved again. Brando, Sr. changed jobs and bought a small farm near Libertyville, Illinois, a rural area close to Chicago. Bud entered the tenth grade at Libertyville Township High School. His high school career was a near disaster. He played the snare drum in the band, but showed little interest in his studies. He displayed some ability at track, but was dropped from the team because he repeatedly skipped practice. His interest in dramatics was limited to a session as a backstage hand. Bud flunked typing and his absenteeism and interruptive behavior kept him in constant trouble with the teachers. He would run away from home and then phone home collect for money to return after a few days of wandering.

Bud's screaming arguments with his father went on. He constantly rebelled. One day he lit a fire in one of the classrooms. On another occasion, he kicked the band teacher and was banished from the band. Bud had become a chubby teenager. His father bought him barbells and kept after Bud to use them. Under this prodding, his physique began to develop.

Unable to discipline his child at home, Brando, Sr. eventually decided to send Bud away to his own alma mater, Shattuck Military Academy in Minnesota. There he developed considerable athletic promise and was popular with his fellow students. Athletics were compulsory and Bud was on the swimming, football, and track teams, but is remembered as having a lack of discipline. He did demonstrate an interest and ability in dramatics and acted in school plays. His performances drew praise though he tried the patience of his dramatics teachers by changing the lines as he saw fit. He continued to duck out of assignments, classes, and duties. He was put on probation for missing classes and pretending to be lame. When he was given a final warning to appear at inspection or go the hospital, he just went downtown. He had broken probation and was immediately expelled.

The other cadets were disturbed at the dismissal and petitioned the headmaster to reinstate Brando. He did relent and offered to allow Brando to return the following summer. Brando, however, had no interest in doing so.

That was the end of his academic schooling. He never did earn a high school diploma.

It was now the middle of World War II. He took the draft physical exam and was pronounced 4F. Brando has said that he pretended to be psychologically disturbed, convincing a psychiatrist to excuse him from the draft.

He worked as a day laborer for a while, but quickly tired of that. His sister Jocelyn was in New York and had made some progress as an actress and Frances was also there studying art. Brando decided he would go to New York and try to work his way into the theater as an actor. It was the only thing for which he had shown any aptitude or interest. Brando, Sr. ridiculed his son's decision, contending acting was a job for "queers or fairies." His father's opposition undoubtedly served to confirm Bud's decision.

Brando arrived in New York in 1943, just past his nineteenth birthday, moving first into Frannie's rented apartment in Greenwich Village. It was a transformation and he loved being on his own, away from the restrictions of home and school. Greenwich Village was filled with artists and intellectuals and they gathered in smoke filled rooms to talk philosophy, art, music, politics, and literature. If Brando had learned little in school, his education now began. He listened and he absorbed.

He settled comfortably into the flow of Village life. Even then, he closely studied people, their dress, speech patterns, manners and movement, gathering material he would later use. He became a master at mimicry and could speak with any kind of accent.

He worked briefly as a street corner lemonade salesman, a pool attendant at the Henry Hudson Hotel, and as an elevator operator in Best's department store. He soon enrolled in the Dramatic Workshop at the New School for Social Research. The Workshop had been established in 1940 and was under the direction of the great Erwin Piscator. Among the students of the mid-forties were such future stars as Walter Matthau, Rod Steiger, Tony Curtis, Harry Belefonte, Shelley Winters, and Ben Gazzara.

There, he came under the influence of Stella Adler, the most distinguished drama coach in America. Brando would later say that Adler had the deepest influence on him in both his personal and professional life. Of him, she said, "I taught him nothing. I opened up possibilities of thinking, feeling, experience, and I opened the doors, he walked right through. He never needed me after that. He lives the life of an actor twenty-four hours a day. If he is talking to you, he will absorb everything about you, your smile, the way your teeth grow. His style is the perfect marriage of intuition and intelligence."

His life away from class was spent going to movies, eating hamburgers and hot dogs, and chasing - and bedding - girls, often joining with fellow classmates Darren Dublin and Carlo Fiore in these pursuits. That summer, Dodie separated from Brando, Sr. and moved to a small Manhattan apartment. Embarrassed by her drinking, which was as heavy as ever, Brando would only occasionally see her.

By October, 1943, Brando was appearing in Drama Workshop shows. The classes were long and hard. He appeared in more than a dozen Workshop plays over the next six months. Brando was still undisciplined. The records of the Workshop showed seventeen days of absence in thirty-four days of class in March and April, and Piscator was disturbed at his frequent class-cutting.

Agent Maynard Morris of the Music Corporation of America (MCA) was impressed by Brando's presence and sexual magnetism as Sebastian in the Workshop's presentation of Shakespeare's

TWELFTH NIGHT and took him on as a client. Mayer Mishkin, who was in the talent department at Twentieth Century-Fox pictures was also impressed and arranged for Brando to meet the casting chief, Joe Pincus. They arranged a screen test. Like many theater actors, Brando professed a contempt for Hollywood. He acted bored and disinterested at the test. He started playing with a yo-yo. As he would pull one prank after another at each take, Pincus became exasperated and threw the test out without sending it to Hollywood.

In the summer of 1944, Brando headed for the Drama Workshop's three month Summer School at Sayville, Long Island. Brando and Carlo Fiore selected a barn as their residence. It came with hayloft and a ladder that could be drawn up, rendering it inaccessible to intruders when girls were lured up there. Brando continued to appear in Workshop plays, but did not seem to take his studies very seriously. Dodie, who was paying his fees, showed up to visit Marlon. She chewed him out for his laziness and threatened to send him back to work for his father in the feed business if he did not shape up.

His performance improved for a while. Before long he was caught in the barn with Blossom Plumb, one of the female students, on top of the bed just holding hands according to her account. Piscator expelled them both despite their protestations of innocence. Blossom was heartbroken, but Brando shrugged and left.

Back in New York, Brando spent long hours in Maynard Morris's office hoping for jobs to make some money. He moved in with his mother at her apartment on West End Avenue. Dodie would disappear for days at a time on drinking sprees. Sometimes she would return by herself, other times Brando or his sisters would find her drifting or in some bar. She would maintain sobriety for a while and then fall off the wagon again.

Brando had little confidence in his talent. Edith Van Cleve of MCA and Stella Adler persuaded him to audition for the Broadway play, I REMEMBER MAMA. He thought the material was sentimental rubbish. Though his audition failed to impress producers Richard Rodgers and Oscar Hammerstein II, playwright and director John Van Druten decided to cast Brando as Nels, the fifteen-year-old Norwegian immigrant son.

The play was a great success, playing for over a year on Broadway. Brando received good reviews. However, he disliked the tedium of repeating the same performance and developed a lifelong habit of changing words and movements, greatly irritating the older members of the cast. Periodically, director Van Druten would find it necessary to redirect Brando's performance when his concentration would trail off.

After it closed on Broadway, the play went on tour through the country. Brando was by then completely bored and was the only member of the cast who did not go along. Dodie had gone back to Brando, Sr. for a time, but now returned to New York. A few days after I REMEMBER MAMA closed, she fell down drunk at Marlon's feet. Embarrassed and ashamed, he left her lying there and moved out of the West End Avenue apartment.

Over the next couple of years, Brando appeared in three Broadway plays - TRUCKLINE CAFE, CANDIDA, and A FLAG IS BORN. Though the play runs were all short, Brando got generally good reviews for his performances. It was during this period that he again ran into his childhood friend Wally Cox. Although they had not seen each other for fourteen years, their friendship blossomed at once. They would sit by the hour discussing every topic under the sun. It was Brando's encouragement of Cox's natural comedic talent that led Cox to leave his small jewelry crafting business and embark on an entertainment career.

Brando still lacked confidence in his talent and exhibited little of the typical actor's drive for stardom. He would appear at auditions and either give indifferent readings or leave before his name was called. He preferred to spend his time discussing life and chasing girls. It was common for him to be going with several girls at the same time. For over a year, he did not appear on the stage.

In 1947, a new play by Tennessee Williams, A STREETCAR NAMED DESIRE, was being cast. MCA agents Edith Van Clive and William Liebling tried to persuade Brando to read in front of director Elia Kazan for the part of the brutish and violent Stanley Kowalski. Brando did not like the character and begged off, but finally, after hanging onto the script for a week, broke and hungry, he agreed to read for Kazan. Though the reading was unimpressive, Kazan felt that he might be able to generate a powerful performance from

Brando. He sent Brando to meet Williams, who thought he was the perfect Stanley.

During the rehearsal period, Brando was tortured by doubts about his ability to play Stanley. Also agonizing over the self destructive behavior of his mother and his hatred of his father and his own sexually compulsive behavior, he began going to a psychiatrist, Dr. Bela Mittelman.

Brando was to continue to regularly seek psychiatric help over the next two decades. Later, in the 1960s and 1970s, an understanding of the results of parental alcoholism began to occur. Today, there is a large body of literature which describes how the effects of parental alcoholism on children results in dysfunctional behavior patterns that remain beyond childhood. The term Adult Children of Alcoholics (ACOA) has become commonly used in the past decade to describe such individuals. By the time therapists began to understand these effect, Brando had stopped his analysis and so many aspects of his adult behavior strongly demonstrates that he is one of the ACOAs who was never able to escape the dysfunctional results of his childhood alcoholic environment.

The gentle and thoughtful Brando struggled, under the conflicting pressures of Kazan's coaxing and berating and Dr. Mittelman's support, to become the selfish and crude Stanley Kowalski.

On December 3, 1947, A STREETCAR NAMED DESIRE opened at the Ethel Barrymore Theater in New York. On that evening, Marlon Brando's life changed forever. Some would say that he changed the face of acting in America forever.

Williams' play displayed a graphical reality and sexuality beyond anything previously seen on the stage, or the then heavily censored movies. There were excellent performances by Jessica Tandy, Karl Malden, and Kim Hunter. But it was the young unknown Marlon Brando who captured the attention of the crowd from first moment to last. From the opening scene, when Brando entered in tight jeans, carrying a blood-stained butcher's package, the audience was transfixed. When he shouted his line "Hey, there! Stella, baby!" and threw the meat at her, it was obvious that a new and different stage presence had arrived.

Writer Sidney Stern described this as "the moment that revolutionized acting."

The audience was astounded by Brando's Stanley, as the brutal, unfeeling, ill-mannered slob who pitilessly exposes his neurotic, fantasizing sister-in-law Blanche DuBois, and drives her into madness. Brando acted with an intensity and passion he had never before achieved. The muscular Brando exuded an animal-like quality, arousing women with his sexuality. When the final curtain fell, the audience applauded and shouted wildly. The newspaper reviews of his performance ranged from enthusiastic to positively ecstatic. The next day, the line at the box office went around the block. Overnight, Brando had been propelled to the top rank of theatrical stardom. He was twenty-three years old.

Brando was receiving a salary of $550 per week, the equivalent of perhaps $2,500 today. But, instead of finding comfortable living quarters, he moved into a drab and ugly one-room flat on Fifty-second Street, sharing a filthy communal bath with other residents. He furnished it with only a couple of mattresses and pillows, a hi-fi, and a set of barbells and a workout bench. He would take his girlfriends out on a motorbike. Despite his animosity toward his father, he sent all but $150 of his salary to him for investment. Most of it went to his father's cattle feeding operation, Penny Poke Ranch in Nebraska - which operated at a loss.

Before long, Brando grew weary of STREETCAR and his performance periodically lagged. Despite the unevenness, it remained sufficiently engrossing that the young Walter Matthau went to the Barrymore one hundred and fifty times, after his own evening's work was done, to catch Brando in the third act. The play finally closed in mid-1949. Brando refused to go on tour with the rest of the cast and went to Paris by ship.

Brando never returned to the New York stage.

With his success in STREETCAR, Brando had been receiving movie offers from all the studios. He had instructed his agents to reject them all. He then spent several months in France and Italy, staying in inexpensive pensions and spending his evenings in sleazy cafes and bars. When his agent Maynard Morris happened to be in

Paris, he was accosted on the street one night by a figure in shaggy clothes, accompanied by a group of beggars. It was Brando.

He was still vacationing in Paris when he received an outline of a movie about the postwar problems of paraplegic servicemen that Stanley Kramer was planning. It was a film with social significance and Kramer was a Hollywood producer whose work Brando admired. He signed a contract to head the cast of THE MEN for a fee of $40,000.

Though he looked forward to working with Kramer, Brando despised Hollywood. He showed a sullen indifference to even the basic standards of behavior for public figures. His entire wardrobe consisted of one suit with holes in it, three pairs of blue jeans, three T-shirts, and socks with holes. He told reporters that he ate gazelle's eyes for breakfast, was born in outer Mongolia, that Hollywood was notable for putrid glamour, and the only reason he was there was that he did not have the moral courage to turn down the money. When reporters would ask about his mother, he would reply, "She's a drunk."

THE MEN proved only a modest success with the public, but it did serve to establish that Brando's magic as a stage actor also came across on the screen.

Warner Brothers wanted to make a movie of A STREETCAR NAMED DESIRE. Both Brando and director Elia Kazan were unhappy with the changes in the script from the theatrical version required because of the heavy censorship then in force in the movies and had been reluctant to take on the screen version, but eventually were persuaded to do so. Brando signed for $75,000. Vivian Leigh was cast to play Blanche DuBois, since Jessica Tandy was not considered to have box office appeal. Once production began, Kazan and writer Tennessee Williams were forced by the Breen office to make change after change, eliminating much of the sexual content from the play. The movie turned out to be a pale version of the original play, substantially changing Williams' characterizations. Whatever respect Brando might have had for the Hollywood establishment vanished at this point.

Nonetheless, STREETCAR was both a box office and critical success. Brando received an Academy Award nomination. (The

Award for Best Actor was won by Humphrey Bogart, for AFRICAN QUEEN.) Vivian Leigh, Karl Malden, and Kim Hunter all won Oscars - Leigh for best performance by a woman in a leading role and the others for best supporting actor and actress.

Brando went on to make his third movie, VIVA ZAPATA for $100,000 and earned salary increases in subsequent years until he received one million dollars for THE FUGITIVE KIND in 1960. Along the way, he won the Academy Award in 1954 for best actor for his role as longshoreman Terry Malloy, in ON THE WATERFRONT, the movie about corruption on the New York docks. Brando was less than happy with the film. He said, "The first time I saw WATERFRONT in a projection room with Gadge (director Kazan), I thought it was so terrible I walked out without even speaking to him." He thought the film dishonest and evasive and could not understand how the world could award his performance in such a mediocre film. The film actually won a total of eight Academy Awards including Best Picture.

The films following ON THE WATERFRONT did not broaden Brando's scope. In many, he appeared to just walk through his part. Several were both box office and critical failures. He also developed a reputation for difficulty on the set. He would argue with writers and directors, and demand script changes. If they did not agree with Brando's interpretations, he would insist that the writers and directors themselves be replaced. He would fail to show up for meetings, insist on endless reshooting, refuse to learn his lines and generally disrupt production unless he was completely satisfied with everything.

In 1960, Brando went to Tahiti to begin acting in MUTINY ON THE BOUNTY. The experience was to have a profound effect on both his personal life and his career. From it developed a life long love for Tahiti that led to a Tahitian wife and two children and to the purchase and habitation of his own South Pacific island, Tetiaroa.

The making of MUTINY was to be plagued by endless delays, illnesses, foul weather, and accidents. The final budget more than doubled from about $10 million to over $20 million and the movie was a colossal failure. MGM attributed many of the delays to

Brando, who had insisted on numerous rewrites, fought with director Lewis Milestone from the beginning, forgot or bungled his lines, and was late on the set again and again. Because of the delays, Brando received over a million and a quarter dollars in overtime fees, in addition to his half million dollar salary.

Over the next decade, Brando appeared in such box office disasters as MORITURI, THE CHASE, THE APPALOOSA, A COUNTESS FROM HONG KONG, REFLECTIONS IN A GOLDEN EYE, CANDY, THE NIGHT OF THE FOLLOWING DAY, and QUEIMADA. With his difficult behavior and his string of box office failures, demand for his services had almost vanished by 1970. The work he did find was for a small fraction of the fee he had commanded a few years earlier.

When THE GODFATHER was being cast, director Francis Ford Coppola wanted Brando for the title role. Paramount Pictures board of directors unequivocally told him it was out of the question. Coppola did not give up. He convinced Brando to take a screen test. Coppola and a cameraman went to Brando's house in the Hollywood hills and with makeshift makeup applied at home, Brando sat for a short screen test. With the test film, Coppola was able to convince Paramount to cast Brando. THE GODFATHER was to became the top grossing film of its time. Brando was universally acclaimed for his performance.

Before THE GODFATHER was released, Brando finished LAST TANGO IN PARIS. As I began my work with Brando, it had just been released and had created an immediate and overwhelming international sensation with its explicit sexuality.

Brando was again recognized as one of the foremost actors in the world.

Brando always concealed from the press any discussion of matters pertaining to his private life and personal affairs. He had a contempt for the movie columnists and either resisted their personal questions or made up outrageous responses. He called writers "irresponsible, cruel, vicious and exploitative," arguing that the public had no right to inquire about his private life. Early in his movie career, he was coaxed into interviews with the high priestesses of Hollywood gossip, Hedda Hopper and Louella Parsons. He dressed slovenly for their interviews and would mumble incomprehensibly, hardly concealing his contempt for them. Louella Parsons wrote of him, "As far as I'm concerned, he can drop dead. He has the manners of a chimpanzee, the gall of a Kinsey researcher, and a swelled head the size of a Navy blimp, and just as pointed." Yet, his protestations and his penchant for privacy only made him more interesting and it was the renegade in Brando, combined with his talent, that made him an appealing figure in an age of conformity.

Brando gradually came to terms with his success, but he still managed to remain an individual, never succumbing to Hollywood social life or partaking of publicity schemes. He averaged only about one film a year, far less that the usual output for a star. He spent a lot of time in New York and traveling in Europe. While he avoided discussing his romances with the press, he remained actively involved with many women. Although his affairs with actresses, such as Rita Moreno, Marilyn Monroe, France Nuyen, Nancy Kwan, Joan Collins, Barbara Luna, and Shelley Winters, would make the newspapers, he was more frequently involved with waitresses, would-be actresses, movie extras, students, and secretaries.

His affairs all had one thing in common, non-exclusivity. He would often be romancing three or four women at the same time. Brando would make no commitment in these relationships. If his girlfriends expected anything serious to result from these liaisons, they were inevitably disappointed. Many of the relationships were nothing more than one night stands, yet others lasted for years. Brando would drift into an affair, drift out again, and return to the woman months or years later, his charismatic personality usually overcoming her apprehension at resuming the relationship. Any kind of emotional demands would drive him away permanently.

On March 31, 1954, Brando's mother passed away at the age of fifty-five. Dodie had been suffering in the hospital for weeks, her kidneys and liver almost gone.

At that time, Brando began a serious relationship with Jossane Mariani-Berenger, a twenty-year-old French governess. Although he was continuing to romance other women, Jossane's parents announced her betrothal to Brando on October 29, 1954. Reporters swarmed around and for once Brando cooperated with them, posing with Jossane. Within days, however, he was seen with another woman and by the beginning of 1955, the gossip columns were filled with reports of his affairs with a black cabaret dancer and with Rita Moreno. The romance with Jossane soon ended and they parted amicably.

In the fall of 1955, Brando met Anna Kashfi, a woman who was to bring him to the first emotional commitment he had ever known. Anna was a beautiful dark skinned woman who was making her first appearance as an actress in films. Over the next two years, they had an intermittent tempestuous romance. Although their romance had been marked by almost continual fighting, when Anna became pregnant, they decided to marry to legitimize their child. They were wed on October 9, 1957. Anna was drunk during the ceremony, according to her own account.

Within weeks, Brando was disappearing from their home for days at a time. He had resumed his romance with France Nuyen. By the time their son was born on May eleventh, seven months after their wedding, they were already separated. Brando showed up at the hospital more than a day after the birth to see her and the baby. They named him Christian Devi, Christian after Brando's friend Christian Marquand and Devi after Anna's father. Thereafter, Marlon always called his son Christian; Anna always called him Devi. Brando and Anna were divorced in 1959.

In 1960, Brando went to Mexico and married Movita Castenada, a movie extra whom he had met some nine years earlier when filming VIVA ZAPATA. She was some six to sixteen years older than Brando, depending on what biography you believe. They had periodically lived together over the intervening nine years. Several months after the wedding, Movita gave birth to a son, Miko. The couple lived together only a few days after their marriage, although they were not officially divorced until 1968.

People having grown up with an alcoholic parent often marry either alcoholics or people with other chemical dependencies and generally have difficulty in intimate relationships. Brando's marital history falls within this pattern.

At the end of November, 1960, Brando went to Tahiti to begin production on MUTINY ON THE BOUNTY. He soon became romantically involved with a young Tahitian woman named Tarita, whom he selected to play his girlfriend in the movie. It was to become his first long-term continuing relationship with a woman. They were married in the way of the island, not legally, but with a native ceremony. Seven years later, Tarita was to bear Brando a son named Teihotu and three years after that a daughter, Cheyenne.

CHAPTER FOUR

CALIFORNIA HERE I COME

This was the Marlon Brando who was asking for my help, but I knew much less about him then. My knowledge was limited to information found in a few magazine articles and newspaper reports over the years and what I had learned in Tucson.

It was clear that Brando needed someone to manage his finances. I had confidence in my ability to handle the job, not so much from my university background but rather from my business and consulting experience. I had purchased failing small businesses and turned them profitable; as a management consultant, I had transformed departments, divisions, or entire businesses. The consulting client companies varied in size from a dozen employees to firms as large as Ford Motor Company and the Boeing Company. From my brief exposure to the Brando business ventures during our Tucson discussions, it was apparent there was so much room for improvement that it would not require a management genius to produce substantial results.

Heaven knows, this would be more interesting than showing a construction company how to sharpen its cost estimating, improving quality in a machine shop, teaching linear programming to an undergraduate class, or sitting through another tedious tenure committee meeting. The opportunity was enticing to a thirty-five year old university professor who had grown a little bored with academic life.

I was born and raised in northern Minnesota, in a Midwest small town environment not too different from what Brando had encountered as a child. It was a time before television, when kids developed their own entertainment. Most kids spent a lot of time playing with the kids next door. Living in an apartment over my father's auto parts store, there were not any kids next door. Our next door neighbors were a bakery and a bar.

But, there were the movies. Just up at the next corner were the town's two movie theaters, the Brainerd and the Paramount. Tickets were nine cents for children. The movies changed frequently. The longest run to ever hit town was four days, many showed for only two. Double features were as common as single bills.

I saw them all. From the age of six, I rarely missed a movie - Western, comedy, drama - whatever came to town. Only when a 1940s polio epidemic closed the theaters to children was I forced to miss my fantasy land. Then, guess who was first in line when the ban was lifted?

Money was no problem; nine cents a ticket and I had a paper route. At a profit of two cents a paper and always at least thirty customers on my route, there was even plenty of money for a Milky Way or a box of Nibs.

Nor was there reason to worry about being allowed into an R-rated or X-rated movie. There were not any. In that era, every movie was, if not completely understandable to a child, at least permissible for a child to see. Nudity? Never saw any - though I kept hoping. Foul language? Seeing a half dozen movies a week for ten years, the only single four letter word ever coming from the screen was Gable's "Frankly, my dear, I don't give a damn." And believe me, that word caused some discussion around town.

So, it was the movies that were both my escape from a crowded downtown one bedroom apartment and my first view of the outside world.

The one place in the world that called to me was California. From an age barely old enough to understand the geography of the United States, my heart belonged in California. It is bewildering to consider what causes lasting impressions on young minds. Like the sled name ROSEBUD imbedded deep in the mind of Charles Foster Kane, there were two photographs that left an indelible imprint upon my brain. They were brought back by an aunt and uncle from a trip they had taken to California right after World War II. Though they have been tucked away in a yellowing scrapbook for forty years, the memory remains.

The first was of the young couple they had gone to visit in Los Angeles. They were posed between a palm tree and an orange tree - an honest to God orange tree in their own backyard. You would have to have lived in Minnesota to imagine the impression that an orange tree in the backyard could have on a youngster. Minnesota is a land of the Northern Lights, of forty below zero mornings, of frozen cars, frozen fingers and frozen toes, where the cold seems never to go away. Sinclair Lewis said of the Minnesota cold, "Winter is not a season, it's an occupation." And everyone knew the oranges only grew in exotic tropical lands, and palm trees only existed in the movies. It was not only my heart that was drawn to California; my frozen body yearned for it as well.

The second photograph was taken when they had seen Burt Lancaster and Joan Fontaine on location at Griffith Park in Los Angeles. After shooting a scene, Lancaster had smiled and waved at my aunt as she snapped his picture. To an impressionable nine year old in a small town, that was even more amazing than oranges growing in your backyard. To think that one of those people from the movie screen was actually waving to my aunt was difficult to even comprehend. That grainy black and white photograph of Lancaster was the first solid revelation that my fantasy world of the movies was not entirely imaginary. There really was a bigger, more intriguing world out there beyond the frozen Minnesota jack pines and maybe those movie people really were not so different than regular folks. Maybe even eventually I could grow up and do some of the amazing things hitherto experienced only through the movies.

By the age of twenty-five, I had earned a Ph.D. in Business Administration from the University of Minnesota and fulfilled one childhood ambition of moving to warm California by taking a position as assistant professor at the University of California at Berkeley. Three years there were followed by five at the University of Washington. During this time, I built apartment buildings as an investment, purchased and managed two restaurants and cocktail lounges, as well as serving as a management consultant.

At the time of my trip to Tucson to meet Brando, I was on a leave of absence from the University of Washington, serving as a visiting professor at Simon Fraser University, located on the edge of Vancouver, British Columbia.

A career change appealed to me. I had sold the restaurants. Consulting assignments were interesting, but sporadic. Learning and research for their own sake seemed less stimulating than they once had and university life had grown tedious. A management position in the real world was more intriguing.

So, if Brando had really needed someone like me all his life, I too needed somebody like him, and the opportunity he was presenting.

Following Brando's job offer, my phone calls home, prior to catching the return flight to Vancouver, had gone unanswered. So, my news was still fresh when I walked into the house. While I had accepted the job without a family conference, it was not without prior discussion, for we had been planning for me to seek alternative employment and to return the children to schools within our native United States.

My wife, Toni, greeted my report of Brando's offer with disbelief, thinking I was merely teasing.

"Sure, and Paul Newman asked me out for a date while you were gone, too," was her response.

Having been one of the millions of teenage girls who had swooned over Brando when he was in THE WILD ONE and been a fan since then, she seemed afraid to believe it was really true. When I finally convinced her, she welcomed the news with a hundred percent enthusiasm and got on the phone right away to tell everyone she knew.

The children, who were not movie fans, particularly not movie actor fans, were not impressed with dad's new job. Actually, twelve-year-old Gregory, would be leaving a future movie star, though he had no way of knowing it, for one of his Canadian classmates was Michael J. Fox.

Upon returning to Simon Fraser University, I told the Dean of my new plans and resigned. Although my enthusiasm was running over,

I forced silence upon myself, knowing that word would quickly circulate through the department without my help. It did and much of my day was spent dispelling the disbelief of my colleagues.

Professor Cal Hoyt had an evening class in which he was lecturing on communication in organizations. He asked permission to use the news of my job in an exercise he always conducted when presenting this topic. The exercise was to give a short piece of factual information to just one class member. That person then whispered the information to a second class member; the second to a third; and so on until it had passed step by step through the class. The purpose of the exercise was to illustrate how information gets distorted as it passes through the informal communication channels in an organization. The statement Hoyt started with was, "Roger Vergin has gotten a job as business manager for Marlon Brando." After the statement had passed to the fourteenth and last member of the class, it had been twisted to, "Virgil got a patent on a new brand of milk."

This distortion occurred within a group of business managers located in the same room who were engaged in a straightforward communication exercise. Perhaps it was a portent of the kind of miscommunication that I was to experience later when dealing with people who did not speak a common language, across distances of thousands of miles, and with people who often had self-serving agendas and whose only understanding of the word straightforward was as a direction, not as a standard of behavior.

Brando phoned everyday, anxious to discuss plans for our trip. His secretary would place the call. When Toni answered, she would hurriedly thrust the phone into my hands, fearful that Brando would come on the line to engage her in conversation. Though my travel plans were quickly established, Brando kept calling, seemingly just wanting to visit. It was like a courtship, an introductory prelude, with a promise of more to come. It was as though I was suddenly the most important person in his life. It was easy to comprehend his well publicized success with beautiful and famous women - or 140 pound professors!

It was fortunate that it was final exam week, for a bad case of "short-timer's disease" toward my university job set in. Though I barely spoke to anyone about my new job, word spread far beyond the university. Meanwhile, Brando was in the news daily, with stories of the upcoming Academy Awards. Phone calls from newspaper and radio reporters began coming in, requesting interviews with me. I declined them all, shuddering to think about Brando's reaction if he were to hear of me shooting off my mouth about him.

With my wife busy arranging passports and shots and planning for the sale of our furniture and our move, the week passed in a flash and I was soon back on an airplane headed for Los Angeles. A taxi brought me to Brando's home at 12900 Mulholland Drive in Beverly Hills, just off Coldwater Canyon, where he has lived since 1958, except for a short interval.

Mulholland is a winding and picturesque road that runs near the top of the ridge of hills that separate Van Nuys, Studio City, North Hollywood, and the rest of the San Fernando Valley from Hollywood and Beverly Hills. My first introduction to Mulholland Drive had been on the old Jack Benny Show, where a running gag was for Jack to tease Mary Livingston about parking there with her Saturday night date. I had heard about it for thirty years; it was like a trip back through time to now see it. I imagined myself watching for a Maxwell, with Rochester driving and Benny looking out a back window, trying to spot Mary on one of the secluded, tree lined side trails.

After a half hour drive, the taxi pulled off Mulholland into a narrow driveway. I was not expecting a spacious Beverly Hills mansion since Wallace Heath had described Brando's house as fairly modest. As the taxi approached the end of the driveway, the broad expanse of the San Fernando Valley was visible far below with the San Gabriel Mountains on the distant horizon. We passed two other homes on the driveway before going through an open seven foot high wrought iron gate. Brando's home was tucked into a small grove of madrona trees at the end of the curved driveway.

It was the kind of day for which southern California was famous; the temperature was perfect in the mid-seventies, the sun was shining, and the sky blue with only a hint of smog hanging in the valley below. The climate in Vancouver had not been bad, but California was warmer and dryer and exhilarating.

In front was a single story home in typical California stucco and wood trim, with a slight oriental flavor. In the undistinguished facade, the location of the front door was not immediately discernible and I knocked on what turned out to be a side door leading to the small office used by Alice Marchak, Brando's secretary. We were somewhat acquainted, having spoken on the phone several times in the previous week.

She had sounded officious on the phone and I had unsuccessfully tried to visualize the person behind the voice. Alice answered the door. She was about forty years old and carrying a little more weight than was appropriate for her medium height. Her short dark hair was surrounded by a narrow scarf running around the back of her head and tied over the top, that reminded me of the Gidget era. She somehow managed to transform the haughtiness I had perceived in the telephone voice to the look she now gave me.

"Hello, I'm Roger Vergin," I said, anticipating a cordial reply.

Instead, she coldly scolded, "You shouldn't have come in here. You should have come in the front door."

To break the ensuing silence, I somehow found myself apologizing. She did not bother to introduce herself.

That was the beginning of a working relationship that was never openly hostile, but never turned much warmer.

Alice escorted me through the kitchen into the living room and called Brando from his bedroom. He walked into the room with a lot more energy than he had displayed in Tucson the week before. He seemed relieved to see me, asking, "How are you, Roger? Did you have a good trip? Are you hungry? Thirsty? Is there anything I can get for you?"

The questions came so fast I could scarcely squeeze answers in between. After I assured Brando of my comfort, he told me that he had scheduled a meeting with Norton Brown and George Pakkala of Brown Kraft and Company to provide me with a more complete picture of his financial condition.

As Brando and I sat in the living room talking, his German shepherd demanded my attention, trying to make friends. I had never been fond of dogs, particularly large aggressive dogs that salivate all over my pants, but tried to act as though I was enjoying the attention, patting and talking to the dog, thinking my manner convincing.

Brando, who liked to watch people's actions as he interacted with them, in order to pick up little snippets of behavior which he might later use to enhance his own acting performance, closely observed my stilted performance with the dog.

Finally, he said, "Roger, you don't really like dogs very much, do you? You're trying very hard to be polite, but it's pretty clear that you'd prefer that he'd just go away."

I readily admitted that he was right. Still, he did not send the dog away and seemed amused at my discomfort.

I asked Brando if he was going along to the meeting with Brown and Pakkala at their Wilshire Boulevard offices.

Until the point he answered my question, I had not fully realized how different business relationships were going to be for me as Marlon Brando's representative - Brown and Pakkala were coming to the house to see me.

Brando opened a document of about an inch thickness on his coffee table. It was a plan for the development of his island of Tetiaroa for tourism. He had commissioned an architect, Bernard Judge - the Bernie on his island whom he had referred to earlier - from a Los Angeles company called The Environmental Systems Group, to put together a conceptual design for the whole island.

Judge had created a comprehensive three-phase plan for development. A map showed the geography of Tetiaroa. The island actually consisted of thirteen small islets scattered inside a coral reef. Phase one of the plan called for construction of the airstrip for access and a primitive style tourist village on an islet named Onetahi. Phase two was a luxury class village with fifty bungalows on a second islet. Phase three was a high rise hotel with two hundred rooms on a third islet.

Brando said he wanted to continue construction until phases one and two were completed. The timetable for phase three was to be dependent on the commercial success of phases one and two.

The plan mentioned some of the difficulties of constructing tourist facilities on a small island in the middle of the South Pacific. An entire infra-structure, including transportation, electric, water and sewage systems, had to be developed before tourists could be served.

Brando said that Judge had been working at Tetiaroa for over a year and that an airstrip had been completed on Onetahi. He went on to talk about some of his plans for development. Brando wanted to generate electricity from the sun, the wind, and from methane gas from the sewage, to harvest the fish from the sea and grow fruits and vegetables on the island to feed the tourists, and to create a community for artists and scientists to study ecology and to study how life itself could better be lived - a modest agenda.

It was intoxicating to listen to his enlightened and ambitious plans. I was filled with excitement to be able to participate with him. There seemed to be the opportunity for priceless advances in human knowledge.

While waiting for Brown and Pakkala to arrive, we wondered around the house, Brando introducing me to Blanche, the black, middle-aged cook, saying, "If you ever get hungry around here, just tell Blanche what you want. You take good care of Roger, Blanche. He's going to have a lot of work to do around here."

Blanche had a friendly smile and a promise to keep me well fed.

Marlon's fifteen-year-old son Christian came walking head down through the kitchen to the refrigerator, took something out and turned around to leave. Marlon said, "Can't you see we've got company? Aren't you going to say hello?"

"Yeah, hello?" he answered as a typical bashful teenager in the presence of a strange adult.

As we went about the house, I had a chance to observe Brando's style and taste.

The original house had a spacious master bedroom and a second small bedroom, kitchen, a combined living/dining room, and a small office. Later, the large garage had been converted into a general purpose library/sitting/guest room. The house encompassed about two thousand square feet, including the converted garage. The garage had never been replaced, so Brando's automobile was kept outside.

There was a swimming pool outdoors with a small lawn around it. The rest of the property was landscaped with lush plants and ground cover in the southern California style. A pool man and the inevitable Japanese gardener came once a week.

The living-dining room had a Japanese flavor. There were two couches in a soft white fabric on a bare teak floor, black lacquered coffee and end tables, and a fireplace with a polished stone facing. The black dining room table had eight chairs and there was a small black upright piano along one wall. The walls were covered with a dark grass cloth.

The front door entered directly into the living room. Two wall length windows flanked the door, overlooking a small rock landscaping pool in an exterior courtyard that added to the Japanese flavor of the home. The courtyard was screened from the parking area by a solid wooden fence, which was why I had earlier missed the main entry. The wall opposite the entry door was mostly floor to ceiling glass and overlooked the outdoor pool, which was thirty feet away and set at a lower elevation. The background beyond the pool displayed the area known as the Hollywood Hills, which were golden brown most of the year, but were now still green from the winter rains. Although Mulholland is a busy street, the house was set far enough back so that one heard little traffic noise, and there was a pleasant, uncluttered ambiance to the room.

Brando's bedroom was about twelve by twenty-four feet, furnished with a bed, chest, small table and two chairs and a television. A bathroom was at one end of the room and a large set of drums was mounted on a stand at the other end. A few small shelves were filled with books near the head of the bed. The walls were dark brown and although there were large windows in the room, the drapes were drawn, and one had a feeling of entering a sanctum. The door to the closet was ajar, but there were only a few articles of clothing on hangers, a half dozen pullover shirts, three or four pairs of slacks, and a couple of sport jackets. Brando had very few clothes.

There was no display of art or of anything pertaining to the movie business. The room had a cluttered, lived-in look. I would later discover that a Mexican cleaning woman came in twice a week to clean the house.

Christian's bedroom was the size of a second bedroom in a typical tract home, with room for a bed, dresser, desk and not much more. It had an attached bathroom. There was a single rock-group poster over the bed and the room was quite tidy. The German shepherd would follow us throughout the house, but then retreat to Christian's room when it tired of the activity.

The kitchen was bright, with white walls and pale yellow cabinets and counter tops, and ample natural illumination from windows and skylight. It had a long Pullman orientation with refrigerator, stove, sink, and cabinets along one wall and a center food preparation island. There was room for a small table and four chairs in the yellow and white motif at one end. A dispenser with an inverted five gallon jug to provide cool spring water was along one wall.

The small office off the kitchen was where Alice Marchak worked. It contained her desk and chair, and a visitor's chair. Behind louvered bi-fold doors were three filing cabinets with wall hung cabinets above. The only bathroom for day visitors or overnight guests was awkwardly located off this office. A medical office type balance scale was parked next to the shower.

The converted garage was the only spacious room of the house. It contained a second fireplace. One wall had built-in bookshelves that were filled with an eclectic collection of a few hundred books ranging from anthropology to zoology with a liberal sprinkling of fiction, and with almost nothing pertaining to the movie industry. The opposite wall had large windows that overlooked the San Fernando Valley far below. This room was sparsely furnished. There was a platform along the windowed wall on which lay a fabric covered three-quarter size mattress with pillows along the back. This served as a couch during the day and sheets and blankets could be added to convert it to a guest bed. This was to become my normal quarters when I was in Los Angeles. The view from this room was panoramic, diminished only by the haze of the brown San Fernando Valley atmosphere during the day. At night, the myriad lights penetrated the smog and covered the horizon as far as the eye could reach.

Despite the eminence that Brando had achieved as an actor, there was nothing on display in the house that would give any indication of the profession of the owner. I would later discover the Academy Award Oscar statuette that Brando had been presented for Best Actor in 1954 for ON THE WATERFRONT lying face down in a bottom drawer of one of the filing cabinets in the office. According to Alice Marchak, that had been its permanent place of residence.

The house had a history that belied its modest appearance. At one time, it had been Howard Hughes' hideaway. Although several Brando biographies state that Brando purchased it from Hughes, that was not the case. There had been an intervening owner, Robert Balzer. Brando rented the house from him in 1958, just after his marriage to Anna Kashfi.

When the lease expired and the owner inspected the house, he was dismayed at the condition of the interior. As an adult, Brando had not lost his childhood penchant for keeping animals. However, he had little interest in training them or in cleaning after them. His large dogs and raccoons had done their best to tear the place apart, and had scratched, torn and destroyed carpets, walls, and doors. The owner did not want to take the house back in that condition and threatened to sue for damages. Brando, who, like Hughes, had been in many legal battles but was averse to appearing in courtrooms, bought the house from Balzer. The price, according to recorded documents, was $40,700 - not quite a million dollar Hollywood mansion.

Despite the concern for privacy of both Hughes and Brando, the property itself had never been fenced. There was a wrought iron gate across the driveway that connected to a fence that extended a few feet along the drive. However, I was to see it locked only once - when Brando was dodging a process server. The gate, if closed, would deter a car, but the connecting fence provided no real obstacle to someone on foot - only a detour of a few feet. Despite Brando's often expressed opinion that the public has no right to know anything about his private life and his awareness of the public's insatiable curiosity, he had done little to secure his home.

I would discover that he would often neglect to lock the exterior door, whether he was home or when leaving the house empty. Even if the door would be locked, the swinging dog entry door, for the German shepherd that roamed the house, was large enough for all but the fattest intruder to pass through. The dog itself was not much of a deterrent, unless an intruder would be afraid of being licked to death.

Fortunately, Brando's address was not commonly known. On the lists of movie stars' addresses that are sold by street corner vendors in Hollywood, the address given for Brando's home was for a house he had occupied more than fifteen years earlier.

The part of the house easily visible to passing traffic on Mulholland was Brando's bedroom. Thus, while hundreds of thousands of tourists have purchased the address lists and driven by a home perhaps now occupied by a plumber or retail clerk and wondered what Marlon Brando was doing inside, millions of passing motorists have looked upon his bedroom without any awareness of its famous occupant.

As I was absorbing my new work environment, Brown and Pakkala arrived for our meeting. For the next couple of hours, they presented a detailed and comprehensive picture of Brando's finances, with a history of his income and personal expenditures, a complete description of existing investments - their projected revenues, costs, cash flows and tax implications, a list of lawsuits that were pending against him (and the lawsuits did require a list) and their possible financial effects, and a description of the immediately pressing financial problems.

Brown was about five feet, five inches tall, dressed in a rumpled brown pin striped suit. He spoke in a manner that made it clear that, while there were two names in the corporation title, he was the man in charge at Brown Kraft.

Pakkala was in his late thirties, perhaps twelve years younger than Brown. He wore a perpetual smile and spoke slowly and softly with a trace of Finland still in his speech after twenty years in California. I wondered if they might question my competency, or resent a stranger usurping some of their duties.

There was absolutely no reason for concern. From the first introduction, they became Norton and George and treated me as though I was there as the result of a nation-wide recruiting drive by a top executive head-hunting firm rather than an almost spur of the moment whim of Brando's.

The major problems became defined. First, there was no cash to continue supporting the lobster and hydroponic vegetable projects. Second, there were income taxes due of over $140,000 and again no resources with which to pay them. Third, construction had stopped on the resort on Tetiaroa when the contractor left because his $30,000 bill was unpaid. Fourth, there were fairly large monthly outlays of cash for the normal running of the household, alimony, child support, private school tuition, and salaries of employees. There were four employees at the Mulholland Drive home - Marchak, the part-time cook, the part-time cleaning woman, and a young man who had recently been hired to help care for Christian - plus at least a dozen employees still on salary on Tahiti and Tetiaroa, and my salary. Fifth, Brando was having a home built for Tarita on Tahiti and construction had been stopped on that because the contractor had not been paid. Sixth, Brando had paid $100,000 on a cattle purchase in December, but the contract acknowledging the purchase had never been delivered. Another $157,000 payment was due shortly.

Each of the above problems required fairly immediate action. In addition, we discussed Brando's other investments, which consisted of an apartment building in Anaheim, forty acres of land in Ventura County, both heavily mortgaged, and some oil and gas partnership shares.

Brando sat quietly through the presentation and ensuing discussion, adding little. While he was quiet, he sat totally absorbed in a manner that suggested he was learning as much as I was. An infrequent question suggested that he indeed was unaware of much of what was affecting his financial life. For example, he wanted to know what the neighborhood was like around the Anaheim apartment and how far away was his Ventura County land. The cattle investment was a deal that Brando had negotiated himself. Pakkala and Brown were confused by it and asked Brando several questions. The only answer they would get was a shrug of the shoulders.

Brando's actress sister Jocelyn came to the house shortly after we started. Without being introduced, she sat with legs crossed on the floor throughout the conference without saying a word. Pakkala was to suggest the next day it was likely that Brando had invited her there to evaluate me.

The cash problems might not have been too critical if Brando had a large income or even good credit. Unfortunately, he had neither. There was no more money to come from THE GODFATHER. Even though it was still generating millions of dollars a month in box office receipts on its way to becoming the largest grossing movie of all time, Brando's five percent share of revenues had stopped after a million and a half dollar cap. (Other biographers claimed his profit share was much larger with figures ranging as high as sixteen and twenty million dollars. Had that truly been the case, the world might well have seen the end of Brando, the actor.) The only one of his older movies still providing any revenue was MUTINY ON THE BOUNTY and that brought in only a pittance. The only investments to provide positive cash flow were the oil partnership shares and that similarly was small.

There was one major prospect for income on the near horizon, LAST TANGO IN PARIS. LAST TANGO was drawing well in France. It had opened in only two theaters in the United States, but was drawing record breaking crowds in those New York and Los Angeles theaters. Brando's $300,000 salary for making LAST TANGO had also already been spent, but he had a ten percent share of the distributor's gross revenue coming, without a cap. GODFATHER was projected to hit close to one hundred million dollars. Even with LAST TANGO's record start, however, it was difficult to predict what it would do at the box office. To begin with, it was an X-rated film, which cut out most of the teenage audience. Second, its vivid treatment of sexual activities would also keep away a substantial portion of the adult movie going public. Third, there was an ominous problem on the horizon that had surfaced in Italy. The Italian courts had declared the film obscene and had prohibited it being shown. In fact, Brando, along with co-star Maria Schneider, director Bernardo Bertolucci, producer Alberto Grimaldi, and distributor Ubaldo Matteucci had actually been tried for obscenity and sentenced to two months in jail - Brando and Schneider in absentia, the others present at the trial. There existed the possibility that similar prohibitions against the film could occur elsewhere in the world, even in the United States. Given the variable factors affecting receipts, the projection that Brown and Pakkala made was a gross of between ten and thirty million dollars, which would mean one to three million to Brando, less the $300,000 he had already received.

With his history as a money maker and that expected income, it might seem that it should have been relatively easy to borrow the requisite funds. Such was not the case. Pakkala had been dealing with Brando's bank. The bank had already advanced funds for construction of the Tetiaroa resort and would not make an additional loan. Brando had earned substantial money in the past. However, his banker asserted that he could not effectively manage his money and therefore a further loan was a larger risk than he was willing to accept. And, the LAST TANGO money was anything but certain.

Given the need for money, Brown and Pakkala urged Brando to take on a role in another movie. After GODFATHER and LAST TANGO, he was at the peak of his demand. He could demand and receive both a large salary and a percentage of the gross revenue. This suggestion was met with stony silence on Brando's part. Brown again approached the money problem obliquely, inquiring if he should initiate contacts to see what kind of movie offers could be obtained. In response to this suggestion, Brando stared out the window.

A few months before, Brando had terminated relations with his long time movie agent Hal Kanter, saying he did not intend ever to act again. However, since he had obtained his last several roles directly, rather than through Kanter's efforts, he may have just been making the break in order to save the agent's commission on future work.

By the time our meeting was finished and Brown and Pakkala departed, the house staff had also left for the day; Christian was gone too. Brando and I were alone. He mentioned that Christian Marquand had been staying with him for a few weeks. Marquand was a French actor and director who was in Los Angeles trying to obtain financing on a movie project at the time. He had directed the disastrous movie CANDY in which Brando had acted.

Brando apologized that since Marquand was occupying the only guest bed, there was no room for me to stay in his home. It bothered him that he was unable to accommodate me. He kept apologizing and assuring me that he expected me to stay there in the future.

Brando suggested I stay at the exclusive Beverly Hills Hotel. He was, of course, paying my expenses and was selecting perhaps the highest priced place in town. If a large company had been paying my expenses, I would have delighted in such luxurious accommodations. However, this hotel bill would be coming directly out of Brando's pocket, which was virtually empty. I said that a less expensive hotel would be just fine, couching my suggestion in terms of closeness and convenience, rather than expense. He reluctantly selected the nearby Sportsman's Lodge.

We decided to go out for dinner. Marlon poured us each a generous Cutty Sark, straight up. After twenty minutes of conversation, we had finished our drinks. He fixed me another and excused himself, saying he needed fifteen minutes to shower and change and then we could be on our way.

While waiting, I browsed through the books on the shelves and, when he did not come out for a while, started reading a short novel. I read on and no Brando; read, in fact, the whole book and still no Brando. I had another Cutty Sark and was sixty pages into a second book before he stepped back into the room. With a shower of such duration, he fairly sparkled!

Three generous sized drinks on an empty stomach slows the mind. After getting into the car, I discovered my eyeglasses missing. Brando left his driver's seat, saying he would find them for me. He went back into the house and returned, saying he could not find them. But, there they were, my glasses precariously perched on his face, right lens over the left eye, left lens dangling in midair, like the old Milton Berle television shtick. But, this was live entertainment! Who said that Brando could not do comedy?

He drove down Coldwater Canyon to Ventura Boulevard in the valley. Using his credit card, Brando checked me into the Sportsman's Lodge. The clerk must have found it intimidating to deal with him, for he keep his eyes down and did nothing to indicate he was aware of who Brando was, addressing him as "Sir," rather than "Mr. Brando."

We went on to dinner in the hotel dining room. When I had asked for a Cutty Sark, straight up, Brando had also had a Cutty, straight up. When I now ordered a sirloin, medium rare and a Caesar salad, he now ordered a sirloin, medium rare and a Caesar salad. Was he trying to make me feel comfortable or did he need help even more than I had thought?

We enjoyed a fine California cabernet sauvignon with our steaks. After only a couple of days with Brando, I was beginning to feel like a character in an old black and white movie from the forties - I always seemed to have a drink in my hand. I began to expect a cigarette to show up between my fingers at any moment and envisioned myself in white dinner jacket and black bow tie.

The dining room was not busy and we got into a conversation with the maitre d'. He had been a grade school teacher for several years but had grown weary of teaching and had left the profession.

Brando told him about his plans to build a school on Tetiaroa, and before the evening was over, ended up inviting him to come there to view the island and consider teaching in the school. He made the invitation without any knowledge whatsoever about the man's character or his competence as a teacher. I had not detected any particular abilities in the man that would have caused me to seriously consider him for such a position or to spend a thousand dollars bringing him to Tetiaroa to view the island. If anything, he seemed at a loss for what to do with his life and in no hurry to find out.

That cast a different light on Brando's decision to hire me. Maybe I had not done anything overly impressive in Tucson after all. Perhaps he was just in the habit of befriending lost souls in the same manner that Elvis had given away Cadillacs. Well, whatever his motivation, I determined to make his decision to hire me a good one.

After dinner, I retired to my room for the night. There was a busy day ahead.

CHAPTER FIVE

BRANDO'S MAN IN CALIFORNIA
DAY ONE

There were three meetings on my "first day" agenda; with George Pakkala to review Brando's financial records; with Brando's banker; and with a representative of Price Waterhouse. Pakkala would not hear of me taking a taxi and so he sent a car to pick me up.

A very attractive blond in her mid-twenties, a real California dreamin' girl, showed up wearing a bright red mini-dress and driving a bright red convertible, to chauffeur me to the meeting. Yes, I was definitely glad to be back in California.

Pakkala and I spent a couple of hours going over Brando's financial records and getting acquainted. He apparently recognized some professional competence in me and quickly shared his years of frustration in dealing with Brando and trying to keep him from throwing his money away on bad investments. He made it sound like my interpersonal skills were going to be vastly more important than my financial skills when it came to dealing with Brando.

After our meeting, we drove down Wilshire Boulevard to the Beverly Hills National Bank to meet with Lewis Horowitz, who handled Brando's account.

Horowitz's office was on the top floor of the bank building, removed from the daily traffic. It had a large anteroom with two walls covered with eight-by-ten glosses of actors, directors, and producers, all signed with their expressions of friendship and gratitude for Horowitz. Horowitz dubbed himself "the banker of the stars."

He sat in his inner office behind a large, bare desk, before a walnut paneled back wall with more glosses, this time of studio heads and other top level industry executives. Horowitz was a large man about forty years old whose long disheveled graying hair around the ears did not disguise the thinning on top.

Pakkala had earlier discussed with Horowitz the possibility of borrowing $250,000 to cover Brando's income taxes and provide some money for restarting construction on Tetiaroa. Horowitz had been refusing to make such a loan because of his concern about repayment.

We continued this discussion and explored alternatives that might provide some assurance to the bank. I suggested an assignment of the first $250,000 that Brando would receive from United Artists, the distributor for LAST TANGO, for his revenue share from the movie. From reading the newspapers, it seemed clear that he would be getting at least that amount. An assignment is a simple financial arrangement whereby Brando and United Artists would agree that the $250,000 check would go directly to the bank, rather than to Brando.

However, this did not satisfy Horowitz. He wanted to go one step further. He wanted United Artists to guarantee that there would be at least that amount coming from the movie. This seemed to be the only way to satisfy him, so we decided to explore that possibility with United Artists.

This loan guarantee requirement seemed a minor inconvenience at the time. A few months later, it was strangely to become a matter of grave importance.

During the meeting, Horowitz mentioned that he would be very pleased if Brando would sign a photograph for him that he could place in a prominent position on the wall behind his desk. He even spoke somewhat wistfully of the possibility of meeting Brando some day. Although he had been handling Brando's account for years, he had never laid eyes on him. All the personally inscribed photographs around the two rooms indicated that he likely knew all of his other major clients.

As the business of our bank meeting came to an end, Pakkala, with a twinkle in his eye, asked Horowitz, "Do you suppose you have one of your little tricks for Roger? He had a long hard day with Marlon yesterday and could use a little entertainment."

"What's this?" I thought. It sounded like he was asking Horowitz to provide me with some female companionship - a lady of the evening. Perhaps it had been some kind of evil omen that Brando's guest room had been occupied and that Pakkala knew that I now had a room alone. It looked like the published reports about the morality in the movie industry were really true, but I had hardly expected it to pervade the banking aspects as well. True, the question was phrased a little awkwardly. The customer was supposed to be the trick, not the girl. But then, what could you expect from an accountant?

It was a situation as far removed as could be from university life. I had a wife and family; it was not the kind of thing I did. Yet, undeniably, there was the momentary temptation - the vision of an aspiring actress entertaining a stodgy professor. My mind was confused, in gridlock waiting for the next move.

"I think I can arrange that", Horowitz replied, with what appeared to be a conspiratorial grin towards Pakkala. Thereupon he opened his top drawer and rummaged through, searching for something - perhaps a telephone number?

Instead, he pulled out three sponge rubber balls. He then proceeded to demonstrate a little slight of hand. He was an amateur magician, with emphasis on the word amateur. His rather transparent slight of hand was not quite the trick that had first entered my mind.

Following the meeting at the bank, Pakkala dropped me off in downtown Los Angeles for my meeting with the Price Waterhouse accountant in charge of the audit of Brown Kraft. In a brief meeting, the accountant told me that the audit had turned up no discrepancies or problems with the Brando account and he spoke highly of the Brown Kraft firm. Ironically, the only problem that Price Waterhouse did point out was inadequacies in Pryor's documentation of expenses for Mona Mona Inc., the corporate entity that was the umbrella for the lobster project.

Brando had not seemed too concerned about his lack of cash. He was used to seeing money come and go. Compared to my own standard of living, however, these were major sums and major deficiencies, and I was determined to cut down on his expenses. Earlier in the day, I told Pakkala that it was not necessary to pay my salary until Brando's cash flow improved. Now, leaving Price Waterhouse, I tried to save a few more dollars by taking a bus, rather than a taxi. There being no bus route to the house, I decided at least to take the bus ten miles out Wilshire Boulevard to Beverly Hills before catching a cab.

Seeing no taxi when getting off the bus, I decided to walk a few blocks further toward Mulholland. My knowledge of Los Angeles geography was limited. I soon found myself in a plush residential area of Beverly Hills. The streets were ghost town empty and no taxi in sight. It was said that nobody walked in Beverly Hills; I was now seeing it. After two or three miles of walking, the Beverly Hills Hotel appeared like a pink oasis in the tangle of residential streets, and I finally found a taxi to take back to Brando's house.

We discussed the day's business over a ham sandwich and a Budweiser. Marlon was indifferent to the news that Price Waterhouse had given Brown Kraft a clean bill of health. It was clear that he had not shared Pryor's suspicions.

I told him of Horowitz's request for a signed photograph. The manner in which Horowitz proudly displayed his autographed photos and the important location he had reserved for Brando's led me to believe that providing the photo might result in the loan being granted.

My suggestion did not go over well, not well at all. Brando's vehement reaction was not aimed at me, fortunately, but at the absent Horowitz. He fairly bristled in reaction to Horowitz's request and lectured on the absurdity of the public adulation given to him just because he stands in front of a camera. He next launched a diatribe on Horowitz's motives, stating that the only reason he wanted the photograph was to use it as an endorsement to promote his business.

Horowitz's request had not struck me as an endorsement, but it was redolent of the fawning admiration that Brando deplored. He could have made hundreds of thousands of dollars promoting commercial products and services and had always declined to do so. What seemed to me as merely a friendly gesture, Brando saw as an endorsement, so it was not unreasonable for him to decline.

Despite his reaction to the photograph request, I made another proposal, "Why don't I bring Horowitz up to the house for a cup of coffee when we get back from Tetiaroa. You could spend fifteen minutes telling him about your development plans for the island. When he hears directly from you what you're planning to do there, I'll bet he approves the loan in no time. Hell, if you just sit and visit with him for a while, he'll probably okay the loan."

Brando said nothing.

I was quickly beginning to learn his favorite conversational ploy. Whenever a topic came up with which he was uncomfortable, he simply would not discuss it. Like the lyrics in the song, *"she wouldn't say yes, she wouldn't say no,"* Brando wouldn't say anything. Even a direct question would fail to bring a response. If he did not want to make a decision, there was no way of dragging one out of him. The silence would hang in the air and inevitably the other party to the conversation would become uncomfortable and go on to another topic.

In this case, I was the other party; so, I got uncomfortable and went on to another topic. We forgot about business and spoke of other things - of seas and ships and sealing wax, of cabbages and kings.

As the evening grew later, Brando apologized that we could not spend the evening together. He said, "Jill's pissed cause I'm going over to Tahiti with you. She doesn't want me to go. I better see her tonight or she'll be pouting when I get back. Ah, the things you have to put up with when you get to be an old man."

After a while, Christian Marquand returned and I left for my hotel. Marlon and I were scheduled to start our trip by flying to Hawaii in the morning.

The Academy Award ceremony was three days off.

Chapter Six

Two To Tahiti, One Comes Home

B rando knocked on my door early in the morning, a half hour earlier than we planned. He was wearing a T-shirt, light-weight powder blue slacks with an elastic waistband and flip-flops on his feet. His clothes accentuated his overweight frame.

His early arrival was a sharp contrast to his usual pattern of missing a plane or two. He was driving his car to the airport. It was a middle of the line Ford station wagon with a small dent in the left front fender. Since it always sat outside, the California sun had turned the light brown finish to a faded drab color even though the car was only two years old. Dirt covered the windshield, hindering vision.

After grabbing my bags and carrying them to the car, he drove out of the parking lot. Although he had been living only two miles away for the previous fifteen years, he was uncertain of how to get to the Ventura Freeway. After one abortive attempt, we found the right street. He was driving in the right hand lane. At the last minute, he saw that the westbound freeway on-ramp required a left turn, from the left lane. Without so much as a glance to side or rear, he abruptly pulled left across the three lanes of traffic onto the ramp. Brakes screeched. We made it unscathed, narrowly missed by a car traveling our direction in the next lane and another which skidded sideways in one of the oncoming lanes. Brando breezed along undisturbed. I fastened my seat belt.

He cruised erratically along the freeway, changing lanes at whim, speeding and slowing to a rhythm only he understood. I tried my best to maintain a conversation, but my head kept turning distracted with worry that somebody's Mercedes would wind up in my lap at any moment. We managed to slip from the Ventura Freeway to the San Diego Freeway unharmed, but the exit off the San Diego was almost a repeat performance of our earlier dramatic entrance. With an abrupt last second dash from the middle lane, Brando cut off a screeching car on the right.

A third close call near the airport involved two other cars. In the earlier freeway incidents, we had left the offended drivers behind and Brando had taken no notice of the havoc he had created. This time, two irate drivers were shaking their fists and mouthing unheard obscenities. Still, Brando seemed unaware.

To my relief, we finally arrived at the airport. Brando pulled up to the United Airline check-in area. Since he had told me the night before that our tickets were on Continental, I said that we were at the wrong spot. He insisted we were flying United. He double-parked in the no parking zone and we went into the terminal. I asked him to let me look at the tickets to clarify the airline. He pulled them out and stared at them for a while, seemingly unable to comprehend. Then, without giving me a chance to look, he walked up to the ticket counter, his thongs slapping against his sockless feet, thrust the tickets in front of a clerk who was busy handling another customer and asked for the departure gate. The clerk, recognizing Brando, left his customer standing, looked at the ticket, and politely explained that the tickets were for Continental.

The lines at the United counter stretched almost to the entry door. This was one time that Brando was noticed. His barging to the front of the line assured that he would be. A gray haired man in the middle of the line said loudly enough so that Brando would hear, "Look at him. He thinks just because he is somebody, he can do anything he wants. He can't even read his ticket. Nine o'clock in the morning and he's drunk."

Everyone else in line heard and all eyes were on Brando. However, he himself appeared not to have heard the man and his manner made me think that he had not. He walked back to me, smiled and said, "I'll have to listen to what you say from now on. You remembered from last night and I had the tickets in front of me and I still didn't know where to go." He seemed to be truly amazed at my mental powers over such a triviality.

This incident proved to be totally out of character. In our subsequent travels, he customarily was polite in public and considerate of others and did not take any liberties because of his position.

I began to wonder if he actually was drunk. That would explain the erratic driving. However, there had been no smell of liquor on his breath and I sat next to him for most of the next six hours on the plane without detecting any. He spoke with perfect lucidity on the plane. He did not take drugs, so that was not the cause of his abnormal behavior.

I was to discover that his driving was often breathtaking and the morning drive had not been extraordinary. There was only the one brief moment of abnormal and inexplicable behavior at the United counter. Apparently, the evening spent with a girlfriend half his age had left his brain a little slow the morning after.

It demonstrates how a brief encounter can create a completely erroneous impression. The eighty or so people standing in line who observed Brando's behavior undoubtedly formed an opinion that he is an inconsiderate, obnoxious drunk. It is an opinion that many people there would in turn pass on to others. Yet, that was a totally inaccurate picture of his normal demeanor.

We eventually found the Continental check-in area. Brando had a carefree way of dealing with some of the everyday activities of life. For example, taking a taxi to the airport would have been simpler than his driving. Now, he handed the car keys to a skycap, told him to park the car, and that someone would come by in a day or two to pick up the car. Alice Marchak was then faced with the problem of hiring someone to find the keys, find the car, and deliver it to Brando's house. This was Brando's normal way of getting to the airport. More than once, it took Alice multiple efforts and even on occasion the creation of a new set of keys since those Brando so casually gave away could not be found.

Our seats were in the first class section of the Boeing 747. A day earlier, Alice had told me that Marlon always traveled coach class but that he told her to order first class tickets for us because "he *must* want to impress you." The disapproval was clear in her voice. If that was his reason, he was successful. I was impressed.

The service we received from the stewardesses was far more attentive than any I had previously experienced, more due to my traveling companion than the class of ticket or to any charms of my own. A couple of hours out, Marlon mentioned that he was tired but had always found it impossible to sleep in an airplane seat. He asked a stewardess for a pillow and a few blankets, promptly put them down in the aisle, lay down and went to sleep. He spent the next two hours lying there like a beached whale. Fortunately, there were two aisles on the 747, because his bulk proved an immovable roadblock on the one he occupied.

This time, the passengers certainly recognized Brando in their midst. His action almost demanded attention. Yet, their behavior seemed almost as strange as his. It was similar to how most people pass the downtown homeless lying on heat grates in the middle of winter. They simply did not allow their eyes to look at him - at least when I was around.

The guppy like protrusion at the top of the 747 was a lounge for first class passengers. It was up a flight of stairs above the first class seating section. While Brando enjoyed his siesta, I wandered upstairs.

Gwen, a stewardess, came up to the lounge to chat. She had the kind of figure that wins bikini contests, sun bleached long flaxen tresses, and clear blue eyes. She had been molded into a tight Hawaiian sarong, blue with a pattern of white hibiscus. It was slit up the right side, revealing long suntanned legs when she sat down. Gwen displayed a fascination with my life and hung on my every word. Never before in my flying experience had a stewardess showered me with such attention as she did over the next hour.

Although we had the lounge to ourselves, Gwen sat as though saving space for all four hundred other passengers. The cocktails were complimentary, but the company was more intoxicating.

With a voice like warm, mellow wine and a hand on my arm, Gwen said that she and another stewardess had the evening free in Honolulu. It was amazing how popular I was becoming.

Most plane rides are too long. This one was too short. The plane landed. We had to get off.

In Honolulu, the passengers deplaned down a stairway and then walked to the terminal, rather than into the now familiar jetway. When Brando and I reached the tarmac, we found an airline representative waiting with a van to drive just the two of us to the terminal, directly to the baggage claim area - fame does have its privileges.

It was not something we prearranged, just a benefit provided by the airline for its special customers. In my next life, I plan to be a handsome and famous actor.

There had been no disruptions or requests for autographs on the entire trip - and to think I had been practicing my signature all week.

The purpose of our trip to Hawaii was to provide the opportunity for me to evaluate the Mona Mona lobster project. Traveling across time zones, we had picked up two hours on the clock and it was still early in the day. Brando rented a car at the airport. Since he still seemed half asleep, I drove the few miles to Makapuu Point, where Tap Pryor was renting offices and working space for the project from the Oceanic Foundation. The Oceanic Foundation operated the Sea Life Marine Park, a major Hawaii tourist attraction. Pryor had served as president of the Foundation. Sea Life Park was where Brando had met Pryor. He had visited the Park one day, had been impressed with the concept, and had asked to meet the person in charge, who turned out to be Pryor. From that meeting began an acquaintanceship that led to the creation of the lobster project. Although the Park provided enjoyment to thousands of tourists, it was a failure financially and the Foundation had lapsed into bankruptcy. Pryor had been replaced as president and as a member of the board of directors.

Ironically, a few months before, Brando had been nominated by Pryor and had been elected to the board. However, he never attended any of the meetings or showed any interest in the operations while I was with him.

Pryor was waiting for us at the project offices at Makapuu Point. He showed us through the facilities and described the recent work and his plans for the future, adding nothing to what we had already heard at the Tucson meetings. His plans were extensive, but there was scant evidence of real accomplishment. Almost two hundred thousand dollars had been spent and Pryor now waved a thick stack of additional bills payable at Brando. The effects of the financial pressure seemed to have added frown lines to Pryor's darkly tanned, round face.

The most impressive thing in sight was a set of clear Lucite panels that had been constructed to form individual pens for small lobster in order to thwart their cannibalistic nature. It was like a miniature lobster condominium, and like many condominium projects, it was empty.

The lobster condo had been constructed by Joel House, a young American friend of Brando's who had moved from Tahiti to work on the Hawaiian project at Brando's request. Other than House and Pryor, the place was deserted.

Unlike most biological research scientists who might expect to work months or years on a major research problem, Pryor was expecting major progress on his experiments within the next week.

Brando paid little attention to Pryor's tour and report. He was far more captivated by three dolphins that were swimming in a holding tank on the grounds. Down on his knees and leaning over the tank, he greeted each dolphin with a shake of its bottlenose snout and a rub on the side. Each impatiently lined up for its turn, nosily greeting him like a friend too long unseen. Brando and the dolphins chirruped back and forth, seeming almost to converse.

Brando and I soon left to share a room at a small resort on the beach. Our evening meal was memorable only because Brando did not invite anyone to move to Tetiaroa.

The next morning Marlon decided to show me around the island of Oahu. He seemed to have dismissed the lobster project from his mind. Pryor had wanted to schedule a meeting to provide progress reports from some of the people on his staff, but Brando vetoed it. It was apparent that he did not want to continue with the project and he was not about to waste a gorgeous today on yesterday's business.

Brando took the driver's seat in our rented car. This drive was less hectic than the earlier one in Los Angeles only because it was shorter. Being even less familiar with directions in Hawaii, he made a few wrong turns. Not to worry. If he was on the wrong street, he would just turn around - no wasting time until the lanes cleared or he reached an intersection. Median barrier in the way? Up and over. Hertz would not mind. They sell their cars in a year anyway.

We were so engaged in conversation about Hawaii that Marlon seemed to not even notice the presence of the other cars nor did he acknowledge that there was anything unusual about his driving. Ten minutes of this and I insisted upon driving, telling Marlon that since he knew his way around Honolulu and it was my first time there, it would be more efficient if he watched for landmarks and directions while I drove. Life had turned kind of interesting lately, and I did not want it to end just yet. From then on, whenever we went anywhere together, I made sure to be buckled in behind the steering wheel before Brando ever entered the car.

We spent the day as almost typical tourists; Brando wanted to avoid the high pedestrian traffic areas, so we steered clear of Waikiki and Honolulu. He had been to Hawaii many times and was an informed guide to the many spots of natural beauty on the island. One stop was at a high mountain pass near the center of Oahu on the Pali highway running from the north coast to the south coast. It had an all encompassing view of the mountains surrounding, the island below, and the ocean beyond. While we were bathed in warm sunshine, a rainstorm was visible far beneath us. The topography produces a steady strong wind at the Pass as the ocean winds funnel through the valleys and up the mountains, even on a still day below. I could not stand at this site without visualizing the Japanese fighter planes and bombers coming through these mountains on December 7, 1941 on their way to strafe and bomb the United States fleet at Pearl Harbor. How helpless one would have felt standing there watching the death and destruction far below.

Again, no one seemed to recognize my famous tour guide throughout the entire day. However, one incident at the pass probably caused a little puzzlement for one elderly tourist couple at a later time. They asked a passerby to take their photograph with the panorama of the mountains in the background. We were standing just to the side and rear of the couple as they posed. From the distance between the couple and the camera, it was clear that we would be in the frame of the picture. As the recruited photographer asked the couple to say, "Cheese", Marlon mischievously and uncharacteristically gave a smile of his own and thrust his head forward and to the side to get further into the picture as the photograph was snapped. While he normally hated to have his picture taken by a stranger, this was apparently different since the photographer was not aware that he was taking "the famous Marlon Brando's" picture.

I could picture this couple showing their vacation slides to their children, grandchildren, and neighbors later back in the snow of North Dakota.

"Say Fred, who is the guy just behind you there, someone you met in Hawaii?"

"No, I don't know who that is. Just some guy who likes to get his picture taken, I guess."

"You know, he kind of looks like that actor, what's his name, Marlon Brando?"

"It's not though. Maybe it does kind of look like him, but we would have noticed if he was there, wouldn't we, Mabel?"

"I'm sure we would have, Fred."

"Yeah, besides, if that was Marlon Brando, he'd be traveling with some good looking woman - one of them starlets - not that skinny bald guy standing next to him."

We returned to our room that evening. With the indecision of the lobster project now behind us, Brando was curious to find out more about what made me tick and also in a mood to talk about himself. The discussion concentrated on our common mid-west upbringing. Brando was candid in discussing his father's tough and unloving treatment of him, his mother's drinking, and the disharmony and fighting that went on between his parents and between he and his father.

A few months later, when I first saw LAST TANGO IN PARIS, there was a scene about halfway through the movie that could have been almost filmed from Brando's conversation with me in the room that evening. In the movie, Brando's character Paul has been carrying on a sexual relationship with a twenty year old girl, played by Maria Schneider. Their alliance is so one-dimensional that they do not even know each other's names. Suddenly, Paul begins to tell the girl about the unhappiness of his youth in America. The character talks about his father's whore chasing and the embarrassment of discovering his mother arrested - naked and drunk. He talks of the humiliation of having to milk the cow before taking a girl to a basketball game and then discovering cow manure still on his shoes.

In that movie scene, it was not Paul, the fictional character of the movie. It was Brando talking about himself.

The next morning, we were lying around the bedroom we were sharing, engaged in an ambling conversation. Brando was wearing the same clothes from the previous day. The conversation drifted around to the topic of religion. Brando thought the organized church bodies concentrated too much on financial matters while ignoring problems of poverty and broken families. There was a strong anti-religious fervor in his voice.

Marlon suggested we fly to Maui to view the house that Pryor had proposed that Brando buy. However, without any money to pay for it and the likely curtailing of the lobster project, there seemed little point in looking at it. Brando could not come up with a reason to buy the house, but still wanted to go to Maui, primarily because he wanted me to see the island. So, we decided to catch a flight there.

We were scheduled out the next day on the Pan Am flight to Tahiti.

Marlon was lying back on the bed. From his reclining position, he picked up the phone and called an airline, presumably to schedule our day-trip to Maui. Suddenly, he sat up as though surprised by something and started asking the airline representative when he could get a plane back to Los Angeles. One was departing in less than an hour. He put down the phone, started throwing the few clothes he had brought into his cloth bag and asked me to drive him to the airport.

"It would be better if I'm back in Los Angeles for the Academy Awards tomorrow," he explained. "With my statement about the Indians being read there, it might not look good if the newspapers find out I'm on Tetiaroa. There'll be a lot of publicity and they'll make it look like I'm down there vacationing and I really didn't care enough about the cause to stick around."

"If you're going back, what do you want me to do?" I asked.

"You can fly to Tahiti by yourself and look everything over. Then we'll talk about it when you come back to Los Angeles."

There was a project manager and a dozen more Brando employees on Tahiti and Tetiaroa. Since he had not phoned ahead, nobody there was expecting us or even knew I existed. I pointed this out and suggested he telephone Tahiti when he got back to Los Angeles and explain that he had put me in charge of his financial interests, so they would not think I was just some inquisitive interloper.

"Don't worry," he said. "Just tell them I sent you and you're in charge of everything. They'll listen to you."

It was nice that he had so much confidence in my aura of command. However, there were still a few questions. "Where do I stay when I get to Tahiti? Who do I see to arrange to go to Tetiaroa?"

"Go out to Tarita's. Tell her you're a good friend of mine. You can stay at her house. You'll figure out what to do when you get there."

"Well, what's Tarita's address?" I asked.

"I don't know. I think I might have her phone number somewhere, though." Marlon searched through his belongings and found it.

I had felt comfortable and confident traveling to Brando's island with him along to guide the way. Now, I was to go off by myself, unable to even speak the language of the country, to take over an organization in which no one had ever even heard of me, and I was supposed to begin by barging in unannounced to spend the night in the home of a woman to whom I was a complete stranger.

My hope had been that this job was going to be more interesting than a tenure committee meeting. I was not being disappointed.

I drove Brando to the airport and played tourist for another day.

The next morning I repacked my clothes and laid out my airline ticket and freshly minted passport. Since it would be my first use of a passport, I took pains to make sure neither it nor the plane ticket was misplaced. I drove to the Honolulu airport and returned the rental car to Hertz, leaving it only a little the worse for wear from Brando's brief kamikaze driving stint.

This leg of the trip was on Pan American, so I went to that ticket counter to check in. My ticket was in order, but my passport had vanished. I searched vainly through my clothes, luggage, everywhere. It had simply disappeared. The Pan Am representative said he would not allow me on the plane because the French immigration authority would not allow me to deplane in Tahiti without a passport.

My memory said that I had laid the passport with the airline ticket when loading the trunk of the car, but it clearly had not been there when I unloaded. I ran back to Hertz and combed through the car again, even removing the spare tire and rubber trunk floor mats - it was not there.

I telephoned the resort to see if the passport was still on the dresser in the bedroom. It was not.

Again I returned to Pan Am, searching the streets and sidewalk along the way. The next plane to Tahiti was an intolerably long three days off. I tried to talk my way onto the plane, citing Brando's importance to tourism in Tahiti and how the French would allow me to me stay for a few days once my presence there was a *fiat accompli*. The Pan Am rep was not dissuaded.

Takeoff was minutes away. It appeared that my first major assignment for Brando was going to end in dismal failure. There was only a week available before my scheduled final exams in Vancouver and I could not even get on the plane to Tahiti. Without a passport, they would not allow me on the next plane either. My career as Brando's business manager was slipping away as abruptly as it had begun. If I could not even handle getting to Tahiti by myself, how could Brando believe I could handle the job?

My mind still told me that the passport had been on top of my plane ticket in the trunk. I ran back to the Hertz office again. By now they had removed the car from in front of the office and parked it with other vehicles. The clerk reluctantly handed back the car key and pointed in the general direction of the Hertz parking area.

I found the car and began searching the trunk once more, again removing the spare tire and trunk floor mats.

This time I noticed an almost imperceptibly small crack, no more than the thickness of a pocket comb, at the front end of the trunk, with a black void beyond.

Finding a long thin twig, I climbed into the trunk, awkwardly put my eye to the floor, and squeezed the twig into the crack, probing as gently as an arthroscopic surgeon searching for bone chips in a star quarterback's knee. The twig touched an obstacle. Far ahead, underneath the back seat of the car was the thin green book, the passport to my new world. Obeying Newton's first law of motion, it must have slid easily on its smooth glossy surface into the crack when the car braked.

Delicately, I drew the passport back from the void. I threw the car keys to a parking lot attendant and then sprinted like O. J. Simpson in the old Hertz television commercials, dodging people and hurdling luggage as I raced toward the Pan Am counter. The ticket agent, who, by now, was more familiar with my problem then he ever cared to be, saw me waving the passport from a distance. He dropped what he was doing and phoned to the gate.

The plane had left the gate.

He persuaded the pilot to hold, invoking Brando's name. He put me on a van and drove to the plane, calling over the radiophone as he drove to have a stairway rolled up.

I was moving up in the world, at breakneck speed. It had taken thirty-five years to get my first special airline treatment. Now, only three days later and there was more of the same.

It was an honor I hoped never to have to receive again. After getting seated on the plane, it was easy to see why the pilot had waited. There were a dozen passengers and a hundred and forty empty seats. I was thankful that there were not a hundred and forty-one empty seats.

Though there were almost as many stewardesses as passengers on this flight, my newly acquired charms seemed to have vanished almost overnight. For all of the attention they paid, I felt as though disguised as one of those empty seats.

Well, I had my memories anyway. I reclined my seat, closed my eyes, and dreamed of Gwen's devoted attention.

After the six hour flight due south to Tahiti, it was just turning dark when the plane landed at Faaa (pronounced with two syllables - *fahh ahh*) airport at Papeete (*pah paa a' te*), the capital of French Polynesia and only large town on Tahiti.

Stepping off the plane, I felt a strange atmosphere surrounding me. The warm air was so heavy you could weigh it on a scale and so moist that my luggage was wet to the touch. This Minnesota boy felt a wind chill factor of eighty-five degrees. The perfume of bougainvillaea, magnolia, and night-blooming jasmine lay heavy on the evening air.

I passed through customs, my passport only cursorily glanced at. I changed some dollars to South Pacific francs and telephoned Tarita's number.

No answer.

My phone calls remained unanswered over the next hour. All the other passengers left the airport. There were no other flights that evening. There was just a janitor and me, with one lone taxi outside. The lone stranger at the deserted foreign airport; it was a familiar scene from an old movie.

Finally, it seemed necessary to try the taxi before it too left. Having no address, I said to the Tahitian driver, "Marlon Brando's house?" That was sufficient; he knew where to go.

He drove a few miles along the coast over a narrow winding road, lush tropical vegetation walling the sides, and pulled into a driveway. The taxi driver had found the right place; there was a partially constructed house near the road. The original home was some hundred feet from the road, and no more than thirty feet from the ocean. No one was home and the house was dark.

The door was not locked. In fact, it was not even closed. The empty doorway was an open invitation to walk in and relax after a long day. Still, I hesitated. Scenes from a dozen old movies flashed through my mind - the open door, the foreign patsy walking in, the body in the bedroom, the blood smeared knife in the back. No, I was not going into that house by myself and then have to try to explain my presence without being able to speak the native tongue.

I meandered around the yard and along the ocean shore in the moonlight for an hour. Finally, I pushed the movie scenes from my mind and went in.

No bodies in sight.

Now inside, I looked around. The home had a large living-dining room with a window wall overlooking the ocean. There was a wooden dining table and chairs. The sofa and chairs were rattan with upholstered cushions.

The walls were completely bare except for a solitary walnut plaque about eight inches by ten inches with a brass legend which bore an inscription showing that it was a Golden Globe Award for Best Newcomer to the movies, which had been awarded to Tarita by the Foreign Press Association for her performance in her single career movie role in MUTINY ON THE BOUNTY. The kitchen was large, with electric stove and refrigerator of a design from thirty years earlier. The place invoked a vision of Bogart and Bacall in KEY LARGO.

There were two bedrooms off one wing from the living room and a single bedroom off another wing, each wing having a bathroom. The single bedroom was being used as an office for Tetiaroa business. The room was completely filled with a bed, filing cabinet, and small desk.

I waited patiently in the living room for Tarita to return home. Her response to finding a strange man in her home was unpredictable, so it seemed best to stay awake to meet her outside whenever her car drove up. But, the long plane ride, jet lag, and a burn from the Hawaiian sun began to take their toll and my eyelids grew heavy. Finally, late into the night, it began to appear that Tarita would not return that evening, so I decided to go to bed. Most women would be badly frightened to walk in and see me there. I wrote a note explaining my presence, not knowing how effective it would be, since Tarita had limited English capacity.

I could imagine being shaken awake in the middle of the night staring into the barrel of a policeman's gun. French or Tahitian would not make any difference - one could kill you just as dead as the other. My god, one week with Brando and I was starting to sound like Philip Marlowe.

I brought my luggage into the office/bedroom, got undressed and crawled into bed with trepidation. Gwen might have been preferable, but trepidation was all I had.

Despite my apprehension, I fell into a dreamless sleep, the gentle lapping waves of the nearby Pacific proving the perfect sedative.

Sometime later my dreams mixed with a pleasant physical sensation. Trepidation was gone. In its place, soft, soothing fingers were running gently through my hair, a warm hand rubbed my bare shoulder. Maybe Gwen was back. Rolling over, through sleep-swollen eyes, I saw in the dark the silhouette of two dark-haired women, one rather short seated on the edge of the bed, the other a head taller standing alongside. The Tahitians were a friendly people and Marlon had said it would be all right for me to stay there, but this was an unexpectedly affectionate reception. Half asleep, for a moment I hallucinated being back in one of those 1940s movies after all.

Pushing the cobwebs from my brain, I sat up and mumbled something like, "Hello, I'm Roger, I'm a friend of Marlon's. I've just come from Los Angeles. He said it would be all right if I stayed here. I'm sorry for just barging in like this. I tried to stay awake to ask if it would be okay, but I finally couldn't keep my eyes open any longer..."

From the shorter of the two woman came the reply, "Oh, okay. We thought that you were Christian. Well, good night."

Oh well, maybe it was not going to be as affectionate a reception as it had first seemed, but I had not been kicked out either.

CHAPTER SEVEN

ON BRANDO'S PARADISE ISLAND

The next morning, I made a more intelligible introduction to my two night visitors. Photographs of Tarita Teriipaia from 1961, the time of MUTINY OF THE BOUNTY, had revealed a pretty nineteen-year old girl. Tarita was now thirty-one and in the subsequent twelve years had been transformed into a beautiful woman. Had she chosen to continue her brief, but successful movie career, and leave the South Pacific, her mature beauty would have commanded the attention of American casting directors. Though she might have longed for such an opportunity, Brando was opposed to her leaving Tahiti and it was not in the nature of a Tahitian woman to make such a move on her own.

Tarita was tall, with gleaming white teeth that seemed to almost glow when contrasted with her dark Tahitian skin and eyes. Straight, black hair covered her bare shoulders. Wearing a green and white print pareau, a sarong-like garment popular in the islands, she was the embodiment of a travel magazine's perfect Tahitian maiden.

The shorter of my two midnight visitors was Reiko Sato, a Japanese-American in her late thirties. Reiko had once been a dancer and actress and had a half dozen minor speaking roles over a fifteen year movie career. She had met Brando when he showed up unannounced at her apartment one night after the day's shooting of a movie on which they were both working. According to Reiko, he lay down on the couch, promptly fell asleep, and remained sleeping there through the night. They became lovers and friends and Reiko had now worked for him on and off for almost two decades in a variety of positions, as secretary, caretaker on Tetiaroa, and now primarily as a companion for Tarita and baby sitter for three-year-old Cheyenne. Although it had been many years since Reiko had danced, she still maintained the dancer's slim figure, the residue of her training still visible in her shapely legs and muscular calves.

It might seem unusual to find two of Brando's romantic interests living together, but I was soon to discover that he seemed to enjoy the subtle intrigue that resulted from mixing present and past wives and lovers.

Tarita served breakfast consisting of thick, delicious coffee and a magnificent lime colored fruit called pamplemousse - French for grapefruit. Though a member of the grapefruit family, it was richer, sweeter, and juicier than any grapefruit I had ever tasted and so delicious that it was to become a part of my breakfast almost every day in the South Pacific.

Tarita did not use her English in my presence, although I would eventually discover that it was more than passable. She would speak softly in French to Reiko, who would translate to English. Both women were happy to welcome me to Tahiti and seemed not the least bit surprised to have found me in bed the previous night. It apparently was not the first time Brando had sent over a stranger unannounced. Since their days and nights contained many unfilled hours, they were glad to have company.

Brando's seven year old son, Teihotu, was having breakfast. He was dark skinned like his mother. He looked healthy and energetic as he went out in plaid shorts and short sleeved shirt to catch the bus to public school. Cheyenne was careful to keep her mother between herself and this stranger in her house. She was also a bit of a flirt who liked to peer around her mother's skirt with a big smile. The Brando genes were apparent in her golden skin and light, almost blond hair.

A walk outside produced my first look at Tahiti by the light of day. The hot sun beat down with a searing intensity, even early in the morning. Coconut palms soared above the house, keeping it shaded from the heat of the equatorial sun.

From the small dock, small exotic fish, every color and combination of colors of the rainbow, could be seen swimming in the shallow water. The water sparkled with a clarity I had never before seen, a clear almost transparent hue. The large submerged rocks, scattered here and there, stood out with stereoscopic three dimensionality. The ocean was calm, the waves pale imitations of the roaring breakers of the California coast. Ten miles in the distance could be seen the high volcanic island of Moorea. Low lying Tetiaroa was below the horizon, some twenty-six miles away.

Tarita's new house near the road was about sixty percent complete. It presented a sharp and incongruous contrast to the older Tahitian house, looking more like an inexpensive Southern California subdivision rambler than something appropriate for the South Seas.

The Tetiaroa staff had been using the office/bedroom of the main house as a base during the previous year. Now, I met them as they showed up throughout the morning. Bernard Judge, the architect from Los Angeles, was in charge of the development of the tourist facility on Tetiaroa. Ivan Failsich, an experienced restaurateur from Switzerland, was in charge of planning the restaurant facilities and operations. Yvonne Chung, a Chinese, was secretary and an administrative aid in many areas. Michelle Darr, a young American who had lived most of her life in Tahiti, was a gofer for Tetiaroa. Klaus Rober, a German and former member of the French Foreign Legion, the mechanic who spent most of his time on Tetiaroa, even showed up. It was truly a multinational group. However, there was one nationality missing. I wondered where the Tahitians were.

I told them that Marlon had put me in charge of his business and financial interests, including Tetiaroa. They all unquestioningly accepted my word. Each, with the exception of Bernard Judge, had a list of problems that needed solving. Failsich, the only one with any experience in the tourist business, forecast disaster for the operation. Judge optimistically said that everything was going "swimmingly." Visions of paradise on Tetiaroa flowed from his descriptions of the island and the development he had designed.

As they told me individually about their duties and about the project, each also had a long list of complaints. Most could be boiled down to two factors - money and direction. There had not been enough of either.

They focused their complaints about the lack of direction more on Judge than on Brando. Judge was the man on the scene in direct charge of the operation, whereas Brando had appeared only sporadically to look over the island development and had not provided direct instruction to anyone other than Judge. A measure of the dissatisfaction of the staff was that they were anxious to pour out their complaints immediately to this complete stranger. Their chief complaint against Judge was that he went blithely about his work without ever explaining to them what was going on, discussing the overall plans, coordinating activities, or giving directions.

There had been a Tahitian contractor on Tetiaroa, a middle-aged man by the name of Tapituri. After going unpaid for several weeks, he had pulled his entire crew off the island. Tapituri's son was also a contractor and had similarly pulled his own construction crew from the partially completed house in Tarita's backyard because of not being paid.

With construction stopped, no one on the staff knew if the project would continue. There had been a vacuum of leadership. Brando had given little direction to any of them for the development of Tetiaroa and had not communicated his financial difficulties. They were all looking to me for answers. I did not even know the real questions yet. I was anxious to get to Tetiaroa. Yvonne Chung chartered a plane from Air Tahiti for the next day.

In the afternoon, Yvonne took me for a tour of Papeete and part of Tahiti. Yvonne was in her late twenties, tall and attractive, her jet black hair parted on the side and falling gently on her slim shoulders. She was the kind of high cheek-boned oriental beauty to whom Brando was so often attracted, and I wondered at first if that was why she was on the staff. It was soon clear that she was by far the most competent member of the existing staff, in fact, the only one who could be counted on to do her job and do it well. While Brando may have been first attracted by Yvonne's beauty, any interest she had in him was strictly business, not pleasure. She was quite content with her French airline pilot boyfriend and already complaining about Brando's inconsistencies.

Tahiti is the largest of the 130 islands that make up French Polynesia. It is in the same time zone as Hawaii, about the same distance south of the equator as Hawaii is north. The climates are similar. There are, however, major differences for the visitor.

French Polynesia is French - governed by the French, not the native Polynesians, and the French ambiance is everywhere, from architecture to language, customs, and food. Tahiti was far behind Hawaii in development of tourism. The 130 islands of French Polynesia had fewer hotel rooms in total than the Sheraton Hotel on Waikiki Beach. There were only a couple of modern hotels. Others ranged from the type of fifty year old downtown hotel you might find in an American small town to facilities that were downright primitive, by tourist standards.

No matter what the type of facility, they all seemed to be inhabited in varying population densities by small lizards and giant spiders. The lizards, varying from two to six inches in length would crawl about on the ceilings, often unnoticed until one lay in bed at night and stared upward, although occasionally one would lose its upside down grip and plummet to the floor or onto whatever or whomever was below. Sometimes their presence was less startling but equally distressing when, for example, their droppings would splash into the shrimp salad on your plate or into your spoonful of soup.

The spiders scampered up and down the walls and had a particular fondness for bathtubs and showers. Their distinguishing characteristic, other than size, was their speed and elusiveness. They always got away. Although both species were quite harmless, they were not always regarded that way by tourists.

The islands are visually beautiful. Dormant volcanic peaks are covered with lush tropical vegetation. Flowers are in abundance everywhere, with blossoms of blue ribbon size and vividness. Offshore, coral reefs protect lagoons where the water is warm and crystal clear. Temperatures rarely stray from the low eighties and the prevailing trade winds are a caressing breeze.

The Polynesians are gentle, sweet, and very shy. They have been blessed with a climate that requires nothing more than a coconut-frond roof for shelter. The sea provides an abundance of food. Clothing needs are satisfied by two square yards of bright print cloth and a flower for the hair. The native Polynesian neither has to, nor wants to, work - not when he can sail, swim or fish all day and still fulfill his every need.

American tourists do not see it quite that way. "*Service*" means "*this minute*" to an American; "*sometime today - if we don't forget*" to a Polynesian. While some tourists found the laid back nature of Tahiti captivating, others could not wait to leave.

We took the narrow two lane road into Papeete, passing small farms, with meager garden plots and cattle in the fields. Despite the verdant vegetation, the ribs of the cattle were clearly visible, suggesting they needed a good meal. Several small white painted churches lay along the route; Christian missionaries had found Tahiti to be fertile ground. Here and there small clusters of people stood alongside the road waiting for the truck - Tahiti's public transportation system - the women invariably clad in the printed pareau and the children in shorts.

Entering Papeete, we passed the government buildings. The white walled, green roofed French governor's house stood in stately splendor behind a broad expanse of lawn. The streets were narrow, filled with cars and trucks. People, far more Tahitians than tourists, bustled from one small shop to another. The were few new buildings and the tallest in the downtown was three stories. Along the waterfront passed the one wide, somewhat stately, drive with commercial buildings along one side and a wide lawn down to the water on the other. Sailboats of every size and description and bearing names of home ports like Bora Bora, Seattle, San Francisco, Auckland, and Paris were tied to the docks.

A center of activity was the market, two square blocks of small temporary stalls with locally grown fruits and vegetables on display -

mangoes, papayas, breadfruit, and bananas as far as the eye could see. Seeing the profusion of native grown fruits and vegetables at moderate prices caused me to wonder about the economic feasibility of Brando's hydroponic vegetable growing plan.

The next morning mechanic Klaus Rober and I flew the twenty-six miles north to Tetiaroa on a chartered plane. It was a dual engine nine passenger Dehavilland capable of taking off and landing on short airstrips. As we left Papeete, the high, volcanic island of Moorea filled the horizon a few miles away. Low-lying Tetiaroa, however, was not visible until we were in flight for several minutes. It first appeared as though it was just a change in the color of the ocean water. As we moved closer, the island began to take shape and the contrast in colors became dramatic. The Air Tahiti pilot passed over the island for my benefit before swinging back out over the ocean to turn and approach the landing strip. I began to appreciate Brando's descriptions of its beauty. A group of small islands in varying sizes formed a circle around a lagoon. From the air, there was a forest of green - the coconut palms - rimmed by broad white beaches. The lagoon was almost transparent, with a slight green hue, in sharp contrast to the dark impenetrable blue of the ocean. It was about three miles in diameter with the islets filling less than one-twentieth of its area. White capped rolling waves plied their way across the expanse of the Pacific, but as they arrived at the coral reef their energy was absorbed in a crash of white foam. In the lagoon, inside the reef, the water looked as calm as a small lake in a light breeze.

As we came in to land, the wings of the plane bobbed sharply up and down until we were below the tree line and almost on the ground. The swath cut through the trees for the landing strip seemed to provide a focus for the trade winds and the landing was too dramatic for my comfort.

Brando's paradise island of Tetiaroa is actually a group of thirteen islets that lie in a circular configuration ranging about fifty to two hundred feet inside a coral reef. Collectively, they are referred to as the island of Tetiaroa. Unlike Tahiti, whose volcanic peaks rise several thousand feet above sea level, Tetiaroa is a low island. The highest point is only five meters - sixteen feet - above sea level.

As Klaus and I deplaned, we were greeted by a handful of Tahitians who worked, and lived, on the island - a few general purpose laborers and a cook and her three year old son. They were to be my companions during the next three days of exploring, looking over construction and development, and just enjoying this South Pacific paradise.

Tetiaroa was formerly owned by the royal family of Pomare and the Tahitian royalty used it as a pleasure resort. Ladies of the royal family were sent there prior to marriage for fattening. In those times, the Polynesians equated beauty with stoutness - the bigger the better. Aimata, Queen Pomare IV, spent two months on Tetiaroa before her marriage, reportedly gaining forty pounds - about the same rate of gain as the average tourist on a South Pacific cruise ship today.

Tetiaroa had been regarded by the Tahitians as a holy place. Still scattered throughout the island are maraes - primitive rock wall shrines - where the Tahitian gods had been worshipped.

In 1904, the island passed to Dr. Will J. Williams, a Canadian dentist who later became the British consul in Tahiti. It was either sold or given to him by the Pomare family in exchange for extensive dental work on the members of the royal family. Like stoutness, gold fillings and crowns were also an esteemed sign of beauty. It was inherited by one of Dr. Williams' daughters, who sold it to Brando in 1966 for $250,000.

The acquisition of Tetiaroa had culminated a ten-year search by Brando "for a place on this earth to hang my hat." He had considered locations in Mexico, Bali, and Bangkok before settling on Tetiaroa, which he had first seen while filming MUTINY ON THE BOUNTY in 1961. His methodical search was based on a grim belief: "I'm convinced the world is doomed. The end is near. I want a place where my family and I can be self-sufficient and survive."

Although Tetiaroa is found on many world maps and globes, it is no larger than the average North Dakota family farm. The land area is approximately one thousand acres - about 1.5 square miles. The islets vary in size from approximately one mile by a half mile down to the size of a suburban house lot. They are spread unevenly around the lagoon. Onetahi (o nah tah' he), the islet being developed for tourism, is a little less than a half mile in diameter - about 130 acres.

The island was filled with trees - mostly coconut palms. For a period after Dr. Williams acquired the land, he operated a coconut plantation on Tetiaroa, the copra (coconut meat) used for oil. Across the lagoon from Onetahi was a large islet on which were still standing the sheds in which the coconut had been dried and an old house, which perhaps was used by the plantation manager. Nearby was the steel skeleton of an old pier, stretching some eighty feet into the lagoon. Fifty feet beyond lay the coral reef.

Somerset Maugham had visited Tetiaroa a half century earlier. He wrote that the "sand on the beach has really the silver whiteness that you read of in descriptions of South Sea islands, and when you walk along in the sunshine it is so dazzling that you can hardly bear to look at it. Here and there you see the white shells of dead crabs or the skeleton of a sea-bird. At night the beach seems to be all moving; it is at first quite strange, this perpetual, slight movement, weird and uncanny; but when you light your torch you see that it comes from the incessant activity of innumerable shelled things; they move hither and thither on the beach slowly, stealthily, but there are such vast numbers of them that the whole beach seems alive."

The beach remains as white as when Maugham was there, made from the ageless action of the sea breaking and grinding the coral and from the shells of innumerable crustacea. The tropical sun beats down from the high bright blue sky, unhindered by any trace of impurity in the atmosphere, with a burning intensity. An untanned, unprotected body will begin to sunburn within fifteen minutes of exposure. The sun, the water, and the sand combine to create a dazzling brilliance.

The crabs and other shelled creatures also remain in abundance. Gone, however, since Maugham's time are the cats that once roamed the island. Maugham wrote of the natural history of the island. During the time of the coconut plantation, rats from the ships which came to load the copra gained a foothold on the island. They multiplied profusely and began to destroy the coconuts in the trees. To control them, cats were brought to Tetiaroa. The cats successfully eradicated the rodent population. As their food supply became depleted, the cats adapted their hunting behavior by fishing in the lagoon, where they thrived on an abundant supply of fish.

No one seemed to know what had caused the cats to disappear. It was unfortunate they were gone because the rats were back, in great abundance.

The airstrip we landed on ran the full width of Onetahi and was covered with grass. Construction had begun over a year before and had been completed now for several months. Building it was simple. Heavy equipment scooped out the natural soil. The soil was then spread back down in layers and compacted with heavy rollers. Getting heavy equipment to Tetiaroa was not easy, but that is another story.

Bernard Judge, resident architect, designer, and construction superintendent, always insisted and his drawings showed that the airstrip was 800 meters - approximately 875 yards - long. I have always had a keen eye for weights, distances, and other physical measures, a residue of several college summers working on a survey crew. The airstrip did not seem that long, so I paced it off. It came to 800 yards, not meters. Measurement with a tape confirmed it - still 800 yards.

As construction of the airstrip had neared completion, planes started landing on it. One twin engine, nine passenger Dehavilland plane from Air Tahiti had difficulty stopping and ran into a pile of dirt at the end of the still uncompleted runway. No one was seriously injured, but a wing was torn off and the plane had remained there for months until a new wing was acquired and repairs were completed. Perhaps the pilot had been counting on another 75 yards of landing strip, which existed only on paper and in the architect's mind.

Fortunately, the airstrip was of sufficient length to land the nineteen passenger Twin Otter planes of Air Polynesia; the anticipated transportation mode for the tourists.

Upon deplaning, Klaus brought me to the "camp." The camp was one of three development areas on Onetahi. It lay a few yards off the airstrip on the north side and a few yards off the lagoon. This was the area where Brando, his visitors, and the non-Tahitian workers lived. One building was a small cook shack, about ten feet by twenty feet, with a lean-to roof over an eating area. This eating area was used only when it rained; most meals were taken outside on a couple of faded trestle tables, their color long ago bleached away by the tropical sun.

The other building was known as the "radio shack". This was larger, perhaps twenty-four feet square. In addition to housing the radio, the communication link with Tahiti, there were several beds, chairs, and a library consisting of perhaps fifty books - many on the culture and natural history of the South Pacific. This was both an evening gathering place and sleeping quarters for temporary visitors.

Running the length of one side of the radio shack and about ten feet wide was a storage area for food and other supplies. This was encased in chicken wire and had a padlock on the door. Construction of the buildings was from native material. Poles three to four inches in diameter formed the framework and the walls and roof were made from the coconut palm fronds that were woven together by Tahitian women. The floor was formed from planking that had been cut from the coconut palm.

Spread nearby at the edge of the beach were four small canvas tents which served as residences for Judge, Rober, and Brando, with one spare for visitors or Brando's children.

The tourist facilities, the second development area, lay directly across the airstrip. Spread over a wide area were buildings in various stages of completion. There were twenty huts or bungalows that the tourists would occupy, a large reception building, a dining room/restaurant, a bar, and a central public dressing room/rest room.

Judge had designed the tourist facilities and supervised development of the island up to this point. While he operated under the business name of The Environmental Systems Group, it was a small group - it consisted of Bernard Judge. He had spent most of the previous year living either in a tent on Tetiaroa or in a hotel room he kept in Papeete. Judge had said the previous day that he expected that the tourist facility would be ready for opening within two weeks of the time Tapituri's crew came back to work. Failsich, Rober, and Chung had each separately said, however, that Judge lived in a dream world and that the facilities were far from being complete.

They clearly were correct. Even two months was beyond the realm of possibility. Nothing was close to being ready. Some buildings consisted of nothing more than a roof supported by a few posts; a few had walls; all still had a lot of work remaining.

There were thirteen low huts and seven high huts. Even when completed, the low huts were to be simply walls, a roof, and a door - no floor, no electricity, no plumbing. The high huts were elevated about six feet off the ground and had a planked floor. Construction was of the same native pole and palm frond material as the radio shack.

The Reception was a large circular building sixty feet in diameter near the airstrip. Ten to twelve inch diameter palm tree posts spaced every twelve feet around the perimeter supported a soaring palm frond conical roof. It was a mere skeleton of a building - posts and a roof.

The dining room/restaurant was identical in size and shape to the Reception. It was in a more advanced stage of construction - it also had a concrete floor. Attached was the cooking area which did have walls but still no plumbing or electricity. Although the concrete floor was only a few months old, it was already crumbling. It was so soft that merely scratching your fingernails across it would cause it to crumble and would leave a scar.

Nearby was the public dressing/rest room building. It was of similar construction and state of completion. Separate male and female sections were established with stand-up pull chain showers, dirt floors, and plumbed latrines - only the plumbing and latrines had not yet been installed.

Perhaps the buildings could have been completed as designed in a few months. However, it was doubtful that tourists would have accepted such facilities. Brando's concept was to offer the tourist a chance to experience life in a more authentic Polynesian style than would be found in the typical Tahitian hotel or resort. However, the resort was planned primarily for the American tourist market and what was being offered was primitive even by Tahitian standards. Tahitians had bathrooms; the tourists would not. Tahitians had floors; the tourists would not. Tahitians had electricity; the tourists could stumble around in the dark. And, while the facilities would be primitive, the planned prices reflected a luxury market. A daily tariff of $100 per person with double occupancy, including breakfast and dinner, was the anticipated rate - and those were 1973 prices.

I tried to envision the typical tourist showing up at Tetiaroa. The vast majority of the tourists to Tahiti were Americans. Air fares were much higher than to Hawaii, so they tended to be the more affluent, and therefore older, visitors. Imagine a senior citizen couple getting off the plane. Ethel is disappointed that Marlon Brando is not waiting to welcome her. After all, she put on her new summer print dress and yellow open toed heels, so she would be attractive for him. They are shown to their "bungalow."

Fred has to go the john, but there is no sign of a toilet. Now he sees where he is going to have to stay; it's time for a drink. No ice around here, not even any running water. Ethel decides that she had better change her clothes before they go to the bar. She takes off her dress and looks for a hanger. No hanger, not even a closet. Well, off come the pantyhose and down go the perspiring feet into the sand. Ethel sits on the bed to clean her feet. Fred lies down to contemplate how much of their floor will be between their sheets by bedtime. As he lies there, a little ginkgo lizard plops down on his chest. Ethel screams and Fred jumps up. Now, both have to run to the toilet. Ethel throws on some shorts and a blouse. Fred does not want to leave their hut because there is no way to lock the doors and he has a new $300 Nikon deluxe in his suitcase. However, nature's call is urgent and they hurry the three hundred feet to the rest room where, with their feet in the sand, they relieve themselves.

Ethel meets Fred outside and says, "If we run, maybe we can catch the plane back to Tahiti before it leaves."

There was one frightening problem for those who did stay. The huts were constructed from fresh green palm fronds. Palm fronds did not stay green long in the tropical sun. They had about the same fire resistance as a dried Christmas tree sitting in your backyard until March. In other words, the huts were highly combustible. Many of the tourists would spend the night in the bar; there would not be much else to do after the sun went down. The only electrical lights would be in the restaurant and bar area. On nights without a moon, the bungalows would be as dark as the inside of a cave.

So, there would be tourists, generally old, often in some stage of intoxication, stumbling around in the dark trying to light kerosene lanterns in a tinderbox. I could envision a bungalow a week going up in flames and imagined it becoming a tourist attraction to sit on the veranda of the Tahara'a Hotel on Tahiti and enjoy a rum punch while waiting for the telltale display of flames along the horizon which would indicate that Marlon Brando had at least one tourist on Tetiaroa that night.

In reality, it might take only one such incident to wipe out the whole tourist facility. Even the green growing coconut palms were not very resistant to fire. During construction of the airstrip, a worker had negligently allowed a campfire to spread. It became a major conflagration, covering about a quarter of Onetahi. Only with the aid of a fortuitous rainstorm were the workers able to extinguish it.

Although Tetiaroa was under Tahitian law, the Tahiti building codes had been ignored. Judge had applied for a building permit, but had never submitted plans or drawings, and the building inspector had not yet visited the island. It is not uncommon for building inspectors in the United States to order construction halted or even buildings torn down if there are severe violations of the building code. Hotel accommodations in the United States would typically require walls with at least a two hour fire resistance. Seeing the Tetiaroa accommodations with walls having about one minute fire resistance, I was apprehensive about the response they would get from the building inspector's first visit to Tetiaroa.

Brando had asked me to bring back an evaluation of what it would take to complete construction and open for tourism. I knew now that he would not be pleased by my report. A major redesign of the facilities was necessary. The planned capacity of the resort was about thirty-five overnight tourists, with a similar number of day tour visitors. Perhaps that many could be attracted to primitive facilities at Tetiaroa, mainly because it was Marlon Brando's island. However, to satisfy anyone, it seemed essential to add floors, electricity, and bathrooms to the huts. Even then, it was likely that many would come and be vastly disappointed by their accommodations. Without such additions, I concurred with the Swiss restaurant planner Failsich's prophesy of disaster.

Even though the operation was small, there were two strong advantages that could make it profitable if more modern accommodations were added. First, all tourist accommodations in the vicinity of Tahiti were very expensive in comparison to other vacation spots such as Hawaii, so that we could also charge high rates and still be competitive. Second, Tetiaroa had the unique competitive advantage of being the island of "the famous and reclusive actor Marlon Brando."

The other developed area on Onetahi was the native village that the Tahitian contractor Tapituri had erected to house his workers. It was built on the leeward side of the island, while the tourist facilities had been built on the windward side. One major difference in construction was that Tapituri had used some commercial material such as plywood, two by four lumber, and glass windows. Those materials were mostly covered with the native woven palm fronds, so the facilities still had a very Tahitian appearance. In actuality, such facilities were vastly easier and less expensive to erect, more practical, livable, and durable, and still native enough for anyone's taste - with the notable exception of one Marlon Brando.

There was a strange anomaly in comparing the two villages. The native village, which Tapituri had constructed at his own expense simply to temporarily house his workers, had a permanent appearance and was complete. By contrast, the tourist village which Brando was paying Tapituri to construct, was primitive and looked haphazardly erected.

While the tourist development was disappointing, Tetiaroa itself was as lovely as anticipated as I spent the next days exploring the island and enjoying the sand, the sun, and the water.

While the days were enjoyable, the nighttimes were a little different. My choice of accommodations was either the radio shack or one of the small canvas tents. I selected a tent, knowing it would be difficult to sleep amidst the rats that rambled through the radio shack. Unfortunately, it turned out they could also somehow get into a seemingly impenetrable canvas tent.

The second day Klaus took me in the rubber Zodiac boat to some of the other islets. One could look down in the clear lagoon and see exotic fish everywhere. Even though we were in the middle of the ocean, much of the lagoon was very shallow. From the camp area, one could wade out perhaps eighty feet across a bottom covered by firm smooth sand, without a single rock or weed to impede a footstep. Varieties of brightly colored fish would scurry out of the way as one walked through the water. The water was warm, a perfect temperature for sensual enjoyment.

At one of the outlying islets, there was a small bay, perhaps a hundred yards across and half of that in depth, formed by the extension of an arm of sand into the lagoon. The water was very shallow, ranging up to a foot in depth. Here the sun would heat the water to a temperature approaching that in a hot bathtub. It was the height of pleasure to lie back in this bay, absorb the warmth, and watch the giant frigate birds fly over and the small red, yellow, and orange fish dart in and out, nuzzling up against one's legs as their curiosity brought them to investigate.

On the largest islet, there was another small camp inhabited by four Polynesians. William Franheim from the Marquesa Islands was the chief of this work crew. Their job was to run the turtle farm, another of Brando's projects. The giant sea turtle had been hunted throughout the Pacific for its tasty flesh and was on its way to extinction. The sea turtle spends its life in the ocean, but comes to shore once a year to lay its eggs in the sandy beaches. When the eggs hatch, the baby turtles make their way to the sea. They are easy prey for birds and fish and have a high mortality rate. Only a handful from a nest of a hundred may survive the first few days.

By putting the turtles into pens as soon as they hatched, the turtle crew had been able to carry more than eighty percent through the first few months of life. The immediate objective of the turtle farm was to increase the turtle population of the South Pacific. A secondary objective was to provide an attraction for tourists.

The turtle farm had been Bernard Judge's idea. He frequently cautioned the Tahitian workers to never mention its existence when they were off the island. He had not sought environmentalists' opinions of the efficacy of the farm and capturing the baby turtles was against the Tahitian law. He thought that if the operation could be kept unknown until the turtles were of a mature size, it would help in getting the project approved by the Tahitian authorities

CHAPTER EIGHT

BRANDO TURNS DOWN
THE OSCAR

While I was inspecting Tetiaroa, Brando was ensconced in his bedroom five thousand miles away in Beverly Hills and like forty million other Americans, he was tuned into the movie industry's annual celebration of itself, the Academy Awards. There was one difference between him and the others, however. He was going to win the Best Actor award for his role in THE GODFATHER. He knew it, everyone in the industry knew it, and the movie going public knew it.

Before the night was over, he would make the 45th annual Academy Award ceremony the most memorable ever, without even being there.

Now, hardly a week goes by without some kind of award program on national television - Emmys, Grammys, Slammies, Whammies and so on until they seem to blur together. This proliferation has diminished the distinctive appeal of the Oscar, although no other award comes close to it in news coverage or audience interest.

In 1973, the Academy Award telecast was one of the major television events of the year. Although it was little more than a night of self promotion for the industry, Hollywood took it very seriously and had convinced the public that it was important.

The industry did a magnificent job of creating interest in its two and a half hour free commercial. Newspapers carried stories of the nominations, stories on all of the nominees for best picture, actor, actress, director, producer, etc., polls on the expected outcomes, interviews with leading candidates, and anything else the publicists could convince them to run. It was unanimous in the polls and movie columns, Marlon Brando would be awarded the Oscar for Best Actor.

The stage was set for a triumphant evening for Brando and no one should have enjoyed such an occasion more. Seldom had anyone made the kind of comeback that this award would commemorate. THE GODFATHER role was his return from the dead in the industry. He'd had neither a commercial hit movie nor an artistically acclaimed performance in almost two decades. His reputation had become so tarnished by the disastrous cost overruns on MUTINY ON THE BOUNTY and by a long series of box office failures that he was becoming an all but forgotten figure in films.

While Clint Eastwood, Paul Newman, or John Wayne on the marquee almost guaranteed a good ticket sale, Brando had no longer been a box office draw. The Quigley Publications annually produces a list of the top draws from a poll of theater owners. Now, GODFATHER had brought Brando to sixth on the list, between Barbra Streisand and Newman. He had not been listed in the top ten since 1958. Moreover, a survey covering fifty-five countries now showed Brando and Elizabeth Taylor to be the most popular male and female actors in the world.

Many people gain a measure of fame and fortune and then too quickly find it gone. Few are able to regain the glory. For those who do, the return can be doubly fulfilling. When the returnee is an actor or similar public figure, the public cannot wait to show its adulation. Many watching the Award telecast and in attendance at the Dorothy Chandler Pavilion of the Music Center must have been particularly looking forward to Brando's appearance.

But, it was not to be. The evening proceeded through the parade of awards - best costuming, sound, cinematography, and on and on - the big awards, best picture, actor, and actress held for last. Finally, the list of nominees for best actor were announced. The camera panned through the audience to focus on the nominees. All that appeared on the screen when Brando's name was announced was his photograph in heavy-jowled Don

Corleone makeup. Liv Ullmann and Roger Moore opened the sealed envelope revealing the name of the winner - as expected, Marlon Brando.

Walking to the stage was an attractive young woman in Indian dress, her black hair parted in the middle and hanging in two strands in front down to her waist. She introduced herself as Sacheen Littlefeather, a member of the Apache tribe and of the Native American Affirmative Image Committee.

Miss Littlefeather said, "Marlon Brando regretfully can not accept this award because of the treatment of American Indians in the motion picture industry, on TV, in the movie reruns, and the recent happenings at Wounded Knee."

The audience responded with a mixture of loud booing and cheering, as the woman went on to say that Brando had written a lengthy speech that she could not read because of time limitations.

After leaving the stage, Littlefeather released Brando's eight hundred word speech to the press. Her verbal statement had not been an accurate reflection of Brando's written reasons for refusing the award. His statement castigated the entire nation for a two hundred year history of starving, murdering, and cheating the Indians out of their lands. It stated, "We starved them into signing fraudulent agreements that we call treaties that we never kept. We were not lawful, we were not just…We turned them into beggars…"

In a disjointed rambling sentence, he carried the indictment to a much broader horizon, "It would seem that the respect for principle and the love of one's neighbor has become dysfunctional in this country of ours and that all we have, all we have succeeded in accomplishing with our power is simply annihilating the hopes of the newborn countries in this world as well as friends and enemies alike that we are not humane and that we do not live up to our agreements."

The entertainment industry only came in for brief mention near the end of his statement as he explained why he was using this forum to call attention to the treatment of the Indian. He stated, "… the motion picture community has been as responsible as any for degrading the Indian and making a mockery of his character.

Describing him as hostage, savage and evil. It's hard enough for children to grow up in this world when Indian children watch television and they watch films and when they see their race depicted as they are in films, their minds become injured in ways we can never know."

Brando even went on mildly to defend the motion picture community as his next sentence stated, "Recently there have been a few faltering steps to correct the situation, but too faltering and too few so I as a member of this profession do not feel that I can as a citizen of the United States accept an award here tonight."

This Brando directed performance at the award ceremony reflected so many aspects of his complex character. The concern he felt for the Indian was genuine. Greed, inhumanity to the downtrodden, and indifference to their circumstances always disturbed him. Some can drive through an impoverished neighborhood and be unmoved. Brando could not.

His criticism of the movie community was a frequent theme. He had little respect for the acting profession and particularly for those who regarded it as an art requiring unusual talent. He had even less respect for those who decided which movies would be made and was disturbed at how commercial objectives, rather than artistic considerations, ruled the studios.

He had certain fixed ideas he accepted and would ignore contrary evidence. The movie treatment of the Native American as savage, unreasoning villain, which Brando criticized was largely of the distant past. In previous years movies like A MAN CALLED HORSE, JOURNEY THROUGH ROSEBUD, and TELL THEM WILLIE BOY IS HERE portrayed the Indian in as realistic and sympathetic terms as the movies ever portray anyone.

He had a keen sense of the dramatic and compelling, and of what would benefit Marlon Brando. Certainly, the award ceremony with all its splendor is trivial when measured against the hunger, poverty, and the other legacies of Indian history. But then anything artistic is rendered trivial when compared to such abrasive realities. Brando's gesture itself was so movie like - the grand dramatic stroke on the screen. It was almost as if the happy ending should follow as it so often does in the movies, although seldom in real life. But what was the lasting impression he created? It was not sympathy for the plight of the Indian; no outpouring of concern or activity followed. Rather, the lasting impression was of Brando's concern, of how Brando was somehow better than everyone in the Dorothy Chandler Pavilion because he knew enough to put aside such trivial matters as Academy Awards for the things that should be of importance to all humanity. Because of the award night gesture, two decades later the public remembers not the hardships of Native Americans, but rather, Brando's concern. This is not to suggest than he was not truly concerned. But, hidden not too deeply beneath his primary motivation - maybe even side by side - was an awareness of what this would do for the image of Marlon Brando. From his early movie days when his refusal to cooperate with the influential Louella Parsons and Hedda Hopper brought him far more publicity than normal polite, informative interviews would have, Brando learned that any publicity was good publicity in his line of work. Vinegar - riling the movie establishment - drew more publicity than honey.

He vastly preferred an occasional dramatic gesture to a regimen of hard honest work. This incident and his whole history of involvement with the Indians has been an intermittent series of hit and run appearances. His involvement was the involvement of the protest march and the fish-in, not the sustained involvement of improving education, housing, and job opportunities - spasms of moral support and publicity, not long-term commitment.

Brando avoided direct personal confrontation. He would two months later slug a photographer on the street in New York, indicating that he had a boiling point, but his more normal style was to avoid a confrontation. If he had a disagreement with someone, he would just refuse to talk to him - for weeks, months, or perhaps forever. Had he appeared himself, certainly there would have been reporters asking questions and perhaps other attenders wanting to argue with him. The way to avoid that was to stay away.

With Brando, honesty was not always the policy. The final paragraph of Brando's statement said, "I would have been here tonight to speak to you directly, but I thought that perhaps I could have been of better use if I went to Wounded Knee to forestall in whatever way I can the establishment of a peace which would be dishonorable as long as the rivers shall run and the grass shall grow." Wounded Knee, South Dakota was concurrently the scene of a confrontation between Indians and federal officials. Miss Littlefeather said that Brando was on his way there.

In reality, he was holed up in his bedroom only a few miles away in Beverly Hills, watching the telecast. In fact, Alice Marchak told me he was still working on his speech there when the telecast started. She had become very nervous because he kept changing it and she was concerned that she and Littlefeather would not get to the theater in time for the award announcement.

The next days, he remained in his home while newspapers and even the national television news reporters speculated on his whereabouts. Meanwhile, Alice declined to tell an outright lie to reporters that he was on this way to Wounded Knee, saying only there would be "no statement of any kind."

It was not clear how welcome he would have been at Wounded Knee. Aaron DeSersa, a member of the American Indian Movement, said Brando was on his way there. Meanwhile, Tribal Chairman Richard Wilson, president of the Oglala Sioux Tribal Council declared he would want to see Brando first and learn whether Brando supported the dissident American Indian Movement group. "If I determine that he is pro-AIM, then he's off the reservation," said Wilson.

It is difficult to say if Brando ever intended to go to Wounded Knee. When he jumped off the bed in Hawaii and asked me to take him to the airport, he could have had that in mind. But, his stated reason had been that news reporters might question his sincerity if they found him in Tahiti that night.

Perhaps the real reason he returned was to write his statement. He had apparently started off to Tetiaroa with me, having neglected to write it. The way he had suddenly jerked up in bed in the midst of his conversation with the airline representative in a panicky manner had given me the impression that he had suddenly remembered something.

In any case, Brando was pro-AIM in his support and with the Tribal Chairman announcing that he would bar Brando from the reservation, there was no question that he would stay away. To be turned away by the Indians at the reservation gate after his public statement would have been intolerably humiliating.

Reaction of members of the Academy to Brando's Oscar refusal was primarily negative. Master of ceremonies Charlton Heston said, "It was childish. The American Indian needs better friends than that." Daniel Taradash, president of the Academy, stated, "Brando has no guts. If he had any class, he would have come down there and said it himself."

The members were a good deal more exasperated with Brando than they had been with George C. Scott, who had declined his award two years earlier. Scott had made clear from the start that he disapproved of the entire competitive nature of the awards and his stated reasons for declining to participate were largely laudatory to the fellow members of his profession. Brando's melodramatic gesture struck a lot of his colleagues as a more contemptuous dismissal. What riled most was that Brando chose not to appear in person to do what he thought he had to do.

Many who booed and hissed Brando's statement, nonetheless, thought that the evening's best performance was by Sacheen Littlefeather. Amidst the catcalls, she stood her ground with a cool grace, which made for a very theatrical and moving moment. However, even Brando's choice of an emissary was later criticized when it was discovered that Littlefeather was a sometime actress by the name of Maria Cruz. Among her roles, she had been "Miss Vampire, 1970" for a movie promotional campaign.

Through it all, there is little doubt in my mind that Brando acted from sincerity toward the cause he was publicizing. He did not, however, consider the consequences of his act. It was simply the wrong forum and the wrong method of drawing attention. The award was conferred by his peers, not the American public. He interposed an irrelevant issue, however worthy, without the courtesy of appearing himself.

There is also little doubt that he was fully aware there would be a rash of the mammoth publicity that would proclaim his humanitarianism to the world.

CHAPTER NINE

WIVES, KIDS AND LEGAL BATTLES

After three days on Tetiaroa, I returned to Tahiti to study the local economy and tourist industry, staying again at Tarita's house for the remainder of the week. News of the Brando Academy Award performance had reached Tahiti. People in Papeete were discussing it. Brando's ownership of Tetiaroa was well known throughout French Polynesia.

I was not surprised to find that Brando had still not phoned to explain to anyone why I was there. Nonetheless, everyone continued to accept my authority. In fact, some were crediting me with more authority than I wanted to assume. It quickly became apparent that my job might encompass managing much more of Brando's life than just his business investments.

Tarita was still not speaking English in my presence, continuing to communicate through Reiko Sato as interpreter. Reiko approached me on Tarita's behalf with a problem.

Tarita wanted more money from Brando to support herself and their two children. Tarita was not employed, nor did Brando want her to be. He was committed to supporting his Tahitian family and he wanted her to stay home to care for Teihotu and Cheyenne. However, he had not been sending as much money as Tarita felt she needed in order to take care of their daily needs. She had run up a bill of over one thousand dollars at the grocery across the road and had no money with which to pay it. The grocer was threatening to stop allowing her to charge her purchases.

Groceries were really the only large expense for Tarita or most Tahitian families. Her house was registered in Brando's name, but was paid for so there were no mortgage payments. Since there was no heating or air conditioning required, utility costs were small. Teihotu's schooling was free and the children's clothing needs were simple in the gentle South Seas climate. The rundown Citreon automobile, its once lemon yellow color faded to that of congealed pea soup, sitting in the yard cost little to operate and nothing was ever spent on its maintenance.

Tarita's request took me by surprise. Brando had given no indication that he wanted me involved in such personal family decisions. Being uncertain of what action to take, I told Reiko I lacked the authority to make such a decision, but promised to pass the request on to Marlon. He was, at the time, in the courts trying to eliminate the support he was paying Movita and involved in other court battles with Anna. Paying Tarita's bill or increasing her support level might well meet with his disapproval. Had he indicated that his personal and family budget was something he wanted my advice on, that would have been one thing. To pay Tarita's bill on my own was another.

However, I was not to get off so easily. A couple of days later, Yvonne Chung was there with the same request; more money for Tarita. It was already apparent that Yvonne was an intelligent and efficient woman who knew her way around Tahiti and she seemed to have a good grasp of Brando's domestic situation and of Tarita's requirements. She argued convincingly that the funds Brando had been giving to Tarita were indeed insufficient to support his family, even on Tahiti.

I arranged for payment of the past due grocery bill, thereby alleviating the immediate problem, and promised to discuss increasing the support level with Brando in Beverly Hills.

My first fact-finding trip to the South Pacific completed, I returned to Los Angeles, to complete my first round trip between Los Angeles and Tahiti. There would be many more over the next six months as I hopped back and forth across time zones, hemispheres, and cultures, handling investments and financial matters in Los Angles one week and construction and development activities on Tetiaroa the next.

Los Angeles newspapers were full of stories of the performance Brando had orchestrated at the Academy Award ceremony and reports that he was either at or on his way to Wounded Knee. However, my Sunday morning phone call from the airport was answered by an awakened Brando on the second ring.

A taxi brought me to Brando's home to report the results of my trip. Although the Academy Award controversy had been swirling around him for the past several days, he seemed unaffected by it. In his bedroom, he was well insulated from the world. He was not planning to go to Wounded Knee or anywhere else. He wanted to talk about tourists. Indians were the last thing on his mind. He had lit the fire, now it was time to let others tend the flame and for him to stay in the shadows until the situation cooled.

I reported my conclusions on the need to upgrade the tourist development by adding floors, bathrooms, and electricity to the bungalows. Without much discussion, he agreed to the changes. Although I'd had no experience in the tourism business and had just had my first exposure to the South Pacific, he accepted my comments as though they came from an expert.

I also reported paying Tarita's grocery bill and how it seemed appropriate to increase her support level, going through some of the cost information that Yvonne had supplied. This had been a matter of some contention between Tarita and Brando for a long time. Recalling how upset he had become at banker Lewis Horowitz's request for something as inconsequential as an autographed photo, I had been apprehensive about talking to Brando about a request that would cost him more money.

After listening to my reasoning, Marlon asked, "How much money are you talking about?"

I recommended increasing the amount by two-thirds and waited for questions and excuses.

Marlon's response was, "Okay, do it."

Whew, I wondered if I had missed my calling. Perhaps I should have been a therapist. I had no idea that solving family disputes was so easy.

My first ten days working for Brando had been filled with meeting people and with information gathering and analyzing. Even though we had agreed to my full-time employment, I had still privately thought of this period as one of evaluation before fully committing to taking on the job full-time. I had thought there might be substantial work to do initially to straighten out the Brando finances and enterprises, but that something less than full-time service might be required beyond that early period.

However, by now having discussed Brando's needs and past methods of operation with his accountants, lawyers, bankers, and others, and having observed the operations in Tahiti, I concluded that he really had, as he had put it, "needed someone like you all my life." If ever there was someone who should not handle his own money and who did indeed need help, he was it.

Brando was concerned about the low morale of the people on his payroll on Tahiti and listened to my description of the complaints that everyone had about Judge's direction of the tourist development project and how evidence indicated that a chaotic state did indeed exist. He had not indicated dissatisfaction with Judge previously; I hoped that he would not view me as trying to undermine the organization that he had established.

There was no need to worry. He now admitted to similar misgivings about Judge's management, but said he had not wanted to prejudice my investigation. He said, "Roger, maybe you should start thinking about taking over supervision of construction."

The job was taking on still broader dimensions.

This suggestion caused me to pause. It was one thing to take my family for what could be almost a vacation trip to Tahiti. It was another to bring them to the construction camp atmosphere of Tetiaroa, with its primitive living facilities.

It was time for a conference. My wife and I held a lengthy discussion, long distance. She had been enthusiastic about moving from the start. I now tried to describe just how difficult living conditions could be. Still, she wanted to go ahead. The boys, of course, could think of no better treat than to get out of school two months early.

While I could foresee all kinds of problems, I had always been a sucker for rescue operations - in businesses and even in personal relationships. Rescuing Brando in addition to his businesses was an offer impossible to refuse. It was a challenge, but I brazenly concluded that it was within my capabilities.

I told Brando I was signed on for the year and that my family was willing to stay in the South Pacific through the spring and summer.

I spent the evening at Brando's house. Although he listened to my report on the construction and my analysis of the prospects for the tourist operation, Brando was far more interested in my reports on all of the people on his Tahiti payroll. He questioned me in detail on my impression of their character and abilities, and particularly on why each of them wanted to work for Marlon Brando.

The next day, I flew back to Vancouver to complete my few remaining university obligations.

A couple of weeks later, I was back in Beverly Hills with my wife and three sons along, making preparations to depart for the South Pacific. We had decided to sell all of our furniture and most of our household goods. We had sent seven trunks on a ship in Vancouver bound for Tahiti, and loaded a half dozen suitcases of personal effects into the car.

Before leaving Los Angeles for Tahiti, however, I spent two weeks in the Los Angeles area working on Brando's stateside investment problems. We stayed in an Anaheim motel so that my wife and sons could enjoy a tour of Disneyland, Knott's Berry Farm, and other tourist attractions while I commuted to Beverly Hills.

I investigated ways to raise money to pay the income taxes, which were now past due, tried to straighten out his cattle investment, familiarized myself with the several legal cases pending, and generally immersed myself in the confusing labyrinth of the Brando finances.

Toward the end of each day, I would return to Brando's house to discuss my day's work. He was always at home. Day or night, he never seemed to go anywhere. It strangely seemed like he had suspended his life, waiting for me to decide what had to be done to straighten everything out so he could go on living. Normally I had some suggestion to make as a result of my investigation. He would usually accept my recommendation and I would begin to implement our decision.

One day, I met with Norman Garey, Brando's personal attorney from the eminent Beverly Hills law firm of Rosenfeld Meyer and Susman. Brando's legal bills the previous year had been over one hundred thousand dollars. There were several currently active legal cases. As financial manager, I was interested in their prospective effect on Brando's cash flow and in determining if those huge legal bills could be reduced.

Garey was a slim, good looking man in his mid-thirties, impeccably dressed in the style of three-piece pin-striped suit that the studio costume department would put on a fashion conscious Beverly Hills lawyer. His professionalism was impressive as he gave me a concise, yet thorough rundown of the several Brando legal files. Of the numerous legal matters pending, he was most concerned with two, one in which Brando was the defendant and the other in which he was the plaintiff.

The former case arose from Brando's involvement with the militant Black Panthers organization, whose activities made headlines in the 1960s. As always, Brando's sympathies lay not with the establishment, but with those who represented the forces of revolt. He had been horrified to hear of the death of a sixteen year old Black Panther by the name of Bobby Hutton, who had been shot by police in Oakland during a gun battle in which another Black Panther and two police officers were also wounded.

Brando had appeared at a rally of two thousand mourners held near the County Courthouse Jail where Huey Newton was being held on charges of murdering a policeman. He spoke through a public address system to the crowd, in the process allegedly accusing the Oakland police of murdering Hutton. He later appeared on the Joey Bishop Show, saying that the police had shot Hutton while he was surrendering with his arms raised. Subsequently, three of the police officers involved in the shoot-out had filed suit against Brando, seeking six million dollars of compensation for damage suffered as a consequence of his statements.

The other case was Brando's continuing battle to escape his alimony payments to Movita Castenada and child support payments for their children, who were being raised by Movita. Brando had married Movita in 1960. Although they lived together for only a few days, Movita gave birth to a son, Miko, several months later. Five years after their separation, Movita contended that she had another baby by Brando, a girl named Rebecca. After the birth of the second child, Movita sought support from Brando, asking $5,000 per month for herself and $3,000 per month for the two children. Brando's attorneys Allen Susman and Norman Garey had presented evidence that Movita had still been married to her previous husband at the time she wed Brando and managed to get the amount reduced to $1,400 alimony plus $600 child support per month. In July 1972, Movita's attorney charged that Brando had ignored the court order to make the monthly payments since September 1971. The judge ordered him to resume the payments.

Now, he was trying to get the alimony payment eliminated, contending that Movita was living with another man as husband and wife, a condition which would call for the termination of alimony. Since there were still thirteen years to go on the payments, over two hundred thousand dollars was involved.

After Garey had presented his summaries of the Brando legal activities, I tried to reconcile the hundred thousand dollar plus attorney fees for the prior year to the amount of activity that he had described. This was high priced legal talent, but the expenditure seemed too high. I questioned Garey about it. He said that he also performed many other activities at Brando's request, much of which was routine correspondence or other work that did not require an attorney's expertise. Some of his work was on matters that seemed trivial to me, but had been done at Brando's insistence.

For example, Garey was currently involved in a skirmish in the above alimony/child support battle. One of the provisions in the court order was that Brando was to pay for Miko's medical expenditures. Movita had included a bill for bottled water in a previous month's accounting. Bottled water was commonly used in Los Angeles households. Brando objected to paying this bill, contending that bottled water was not a medical expense. He had directed Garey to write to Movita's attorney explaining his refusal to pay the eleven dollar bill. That letter had been written, the other attorney had replied insisting that it be paid, and they were about to embark on another round of letters.

Later that day, I spoke to Brando about the bottled water battle, suggesting that he might be on strong legal grounds, but the effect of the squabble might be more important than legal considerations. First, he was genuinely concerned about Miko's nutrition and wanted his health needs to be reasonably provided for. Brando had bottled water in his own home for his son Christian to drink. He agreed that he thought Miko should also drink bottled water; he just did not want anyone else in the household drinking it if he was paying for it.

If he did not pay for it, Movita might quit buying it and Miko would not have it. So, even if Brando won the legal case, Miko might well lose his bottled water. Secondly, there was the cost involved. Each time Garey would write a letter, Brando would get billed. Each time they held a phone conversation to discuss the problem, Brando would get billed. Since most of Movita's legal bills were eventually passed on to Brando, each time they got a reply, Brando would again get billed. Such a matter could easily end up costing a couple of thousand dollars and would still accomplish absolutely nothing except enrich a couple of law firms. That same amount of money could pay for twenty years worth of bottled water.

Brando seemed astonished at the amount that this dispute - and his legal bills in total - was costing him.

He decided to pay for the water.

As a result of my meeting with Garey, I decided to monitor the legal activities as any other expenditure, with an objective of slashing the legal bill, while still making sure that Brando's legal needs were covered. I told Garey of my desire to see the future legal costs reduced. He described their billing as reasonable for the work his firm had done, but readily concurred that it could easily be reduced. We decided that I would take over much of the routine correspondence and other activities that did not require an attorney and that some of the legal work was of a routine nature and could be handled as well by another law firm at half the hourly billing rate.

As a result of reducing the amount of work done and moving some of it to lower priced legal talent, over the next year the legal bill was reduced to less than a third of the level it had been. The saving in legal fees alone paid my annual salary twice over. And, these savings occurred during a period when Brando managed to get into a couple of costly new legal battles.

During that period of investigating Brando's finances in Los Angeles, Alice Marchak confronted me one afternoon when I arrived at his home. It was obvious that something was bothering her.

Without any pleasantries or preliminaries, she said, "Marlon has told everyone that you are in charge of all his finances and everything. I really don't know what goes on in his mind sometimes. Does that mean that I have to get your approval on all the household expenses, too?"

The question took me aback. I had not expected that the household budget should be within my purview; Brando had not mentioned it. Nor, in truth, did I want it to be. It was already apparent that I would be up to my ears in other problems. Also, I had gone over the Brown Kraft records of Brando's past expenditures with a fine tooth comb by then and had concluded that household spending was not the source of his financial problems, but rather, it was bad investments, ex-wives, and legal expenses. The household expenses were actually fairly modest for someone with his level of income.

It was clear that Brando had not discussed the scope of my authority with Alice. It appeared that he had at least implied to her that she would essentially be under my command.

After a few brief seconds of thought, I responded, "No, that's not necessary. You've been managing the household for a long time and I can't imagine that I could just walk in and show you how to do it better than you have been."

If ever I were to draw up a list of words to take back, those would be at the top! My answer was based on practical financial information and represented what would normally be regarded as prudent management. Alice had a familiarity with running the house that I did not possess, she had not spent excessively or wastefully in her management in the past, and I would not even be in the United States to oversee the household for weeks at a time.

To my regret, I was completely unprepared for the maneuvering, manipulating, scheming, and intrigue that so often goes on amongst the inner guard that surrounds a person of high power, wealth, or prominence. One of my former university colleagues would routinely assign his students to read Machiavelli as part of his management courses. I had naively thought that such an assignment inappropriate for a management course. I no longer do.

Wallace Heath had earlier warned me that there would be continual, subtle attempts to undermine my position with Brando - not particularly because of anything I might do, but simply because of personalities and insecurities of many in Brando's inner circle. My position of authority and closeness to Brando would be viewed as a threat to their own positions, he intimated.

Alice Marchak had been the number one name on Heath's list of whom to watch out for. Alice had, as she was fond of repeatedly telling everyone within earshot, "been Marlon's secretary for eighteen years." Eighteen years earlier, she had been a secretary at MCA, the entertainment industry corporation, where she had met Brando, Sr. After a falling out with him, Brando, Jr. had hired her as his own personal secretary.

Alice had remained unmarried. Her social life seemed to revolve around her siblings' families. She drove a long gold Cadillac which looked rather incongruous parked alongside the disheveled Ford of her employer. While few secretaries drove Cadillacs, the automobile seemed to match her theatrical manner rather well.

Despite her long tenure, Alice did not seem to feel completely secure in her job. Although her title was secretary, she lacked many of the normal secretarial skills. Almost daily, she would say that she did not even know how to type. (In actuality, she did type an occasional letter, though not with secretarial proficiency.) Along with that comment always went a statement that her other duties were so much more important than anything so trivial as typing. She did not like to be thought of as a secretary, although that is how everyone, including Alice herself, referred to her.

In reality, her job was not completely secure. While it was true that she had started with Brando eighteen years earlier, she had not held the job over that entire period. At least twice, she had been dismissed from the position for some real or imagined aggravation and replaced by someone else. Reiko Sato had acted as Brando's secretary for a couple of years. Compared to Reiko, who was a sweet person, but very short on work skills, Alice would have seemed a model of organization. After becoming sufficiently discontented with her replacements, Brando would eventually hire Alice back.

In some respects, Alice was one of the most important women in Brando's adult life. Neither of his first two wives ever spent much time with him. Nor did any of his girlfriends. Only with Tarita had he maintained a relationship over a long period and that at a distance of five thousand miles and infrequent contact. Alice had been with him most of eighteen years and not only ran the household, but also helped raise Christian and acted as Brando's main buffer to the outside world.

In 1975, Alice and Linda Hunter, a secretary for Julie Andrews, wrote together a paperback book entitled THE SUPER SECS. It dealt with their experiences as secretaries for the two actors. The book gave the impression that Alice found her job filled with incomparable glamour and excitement, and that each day it was a pure delight to be able to come to work. It was filled with Alice's tales of romantic encounters with "a famous director, a man of great talent in many areas of creativity," or a "Spanish matador with flashing eyes," or an "Arabian Prince," all of whom seemed to own only a first name, or none at all.

In reality, she seemed to find her job filled with disturbing problems and constant frustration. The family of the house consisted of a single father and a child just into the teenage years. However, it was hardly a typical household. Brando's chaotic and unpredictable business and personal involvements were further complicated by the fact that it was Brando, who was less than constant or dependable in his behavior, in the center of everything. This provided Alice's biggest headache of all.

If, for example, Brando was planning to fly to Tahiti, he might change his departure date two or three times. Each change would require that Alice re-book the flight. If a friend or associate telephoned to speak to him, Alice might have to converse with the caller several times because Brando was not "in the mood" to talk to him, each time trying to cover for her recalcitrant employer. She might similarly make and have to cancel appointments several times.

She would also find her work life filled with such joys as coping with neighbors upset with the nighttime barking and marauding of the family dogs, or midwifing a litter of pups, or even caring for, cleaning up after, and repairing the destruction left in the wake of a pet raccoon. Christian had inherited his father's affection for exotic animals.

Her employment had once required Alice to rush actress Rita Moreno to the hospital when she had slashed her wrists during a lover's quarrel with Brando, and then having to lie that it had occurred in her own apartment in order to try to keep Brando's name clear of unfavorable publicity. She had even been physically attacked by Anna Kashfi.

The memories of the latter confrontation still remained. One day, when I was on the phone, the operator broke in to ask if I would terminate my conversation to accept an incoming emergency call from Anna Kashfi. I hung up and went to tell Alice about the impending call. Alice panicked at the very mention of Kashfi's name, misunderstood my message and yelled at me, "Why did you talk to her? Don't ever talk to her. Don't you ever let her know if Marlon's here or Christian's here or who you are or anything!"

She handled the call herself. Her voice was all sweetness and concern to Anna, but she came away from the call shaking.

Through it all, Alice found the day to day job far removed from the glamour and excitement she wrote about in her book. Her favorite expression seemed to be, "If only Marlon would...," rivaled only by, "If only Marlon wouldn't..."

There were, however, compensations. Her rather leisurely work day began at mid-morning and often ended by mid-afternoon. During the extended periods when Brando traveled, taking Christian with him, there was little work to do. Her 1973 salary of $2,000 per month was probably twice as much as she could have earned on any other job at that time. She would occasionally travel with Brando when he was shooting a movie in a foreign locale and had managed to see a large share of the world. So, despite her often expressed frustrations, she was not about to give up being Brando's secretary.

Alice also reveled in the perceived glamour of working for Marlon Brando and liked to tell stories about the reactions of people when she told them of her job. She would tell the stories with a transparent air of being bored by it all; it was clear that she loved the attention.

Unfortunately, Alice lacked the one absolutely essential ingredient for coping with the frustrations of handling the Brando household - she had no sense of humor.

One afternoon she told me about visiting the dentist the previous day. As she described her alleged discomfort at the attention, with an artifice of implied exasperation and in a theatrical manner, she said, "His assistant was going around the office telling *everybody* that I was Marlon's secretary. It was so embarrassing. Here I am sitting in the dentist's chair with my mouth wide open and *everybody* was coming in and looking at me."

Trying to inject a little humor into the situation - and maybe wanting to puncture her balloon of pomposity - I said, "It could have been worse. Just think if you had been at your gynecologist."

My attempt was completely wasted. Her response was spoken as though I had simply misunderstood her the first time. She said, "No, I wasn't. I was at the dentist having my tooth filled."

Alice clearly viewed keeping Brando out of trouble as her major role. When I came on board and began to solve some of his problems, she must have been afraid that her role with him would diminish. Throughout my time with Brando, I always had the feeling that Alice was busy giving subtle little hints to him that would cast my contributions in a less than flattering light. I do not believe this was paranoia, for I had no such feeling about my relationships with the people at Brown Kraft, at Price Waterhouse, or at Rosenfeld Meyer and Susman, where there was never any insecurity displayed and where everyone seemed as straight shooting as they could be.

Indeed, through all my interactions with those professionals, they were diligent in their representation of Brando's interests and served him well.

CHAPTER TEN

TWO GUYS JUST SITTING AROUND THE HOUSE TALKING

As a result of my first trip to Hawaii and other investigations, I had recommended that Brando cease his financial support of Mona Mona Inc., the lobster project. There was nothing in Pryor's earlier work history or in the progress to date to indicate that he was capable of effectively directing it to a profitable end. Brando did not have the resources to finance scientific research just to advance the state of knowledge. He had completely cooled to the project and would have likely quit supporting it anyway, no matter what my recommendation.

During that early period when I was sorting out Brando's finances in Los Angeles, Pryor came to the house twice, wanting to meet with Brando, still trying to get further funding. Brando refused to see him and stayed in his bedroom while I met with Pryor.

Pryor was also pursuing other sources of venture capital. He tried to sell me on the idea that Brando should provide funding at a reduced level in return for a share of future profits. Notwithstanding Brando's earlier $200,000 capital contribution, while Pryor had provided no funds, he now proposed a split of 45% for Pryor, 5% for Brando, and 50% for the new investors - only if Brando would immediately inject an additional $25,000.

In the manner of a promoter, Pryor was full of enthusiasm, projecting tens of millions of dollars in profits. Before our meetings would start, he would phone someone and leave Brando's phone number with that unseen person on the other end of the call, saying that his funding from New York was so imminent that he expected a confirming phone call "certainly within the next week, probably within the next day, and maybe even before our meeting is over."

No such call came.

Months later, he was still calling to get money from Brando even though he was still "expecting confirmation on a major infusion of capital in the next two or three days."

In addition to the ill-fated lobster adventure, Pryor had also gotten Brando involved in a cattle investment. Pryor had introduced Brando to his friend, James Bishop, who was a New York stock broker. The two had convinced Brando to give Bishop a check for $100,000 as a down payment on the cattle investment. Though several months had passed, Bishop had failed to provide any documents or record of sale. I was trying to straighten out the investment. Bishop was evasive and the cattle mess was taking on the smell of a stockyard.

As Pryor would suggest one investment scheme after another to try to get additional funds from Brando for the lobster project, I learned that the cattle investment served at least one good purpose. It became an effective way to close off conversation with Pryor. Only by insisting that he get his friend Bishop to straighten out the cattle investment before further consideration of the lobster project, could I manage to get Pryor to quit asking for money. He did not want to get back into discussion of that. Brando had spent $100,000 based on his recommendation and now he did not want to talk about it. Bishop had gone from being "a friend who is a genius at saving income taxes and making money" to "someone I don't really know. Somebody else just recommended him to me."

Christian Marquand was still staying at the house. Other writers have referred to Marquand as being one of Brando's closest, longest lasting friends, perhaps second only to Wally Cox. Yet, the two never seemed to converse with each other when I was around and pointedly ignored each other's presence. Indeed, in my conversations with Marquand, he displayed a sense of mystification about Brando, as though he expected some insight from me about his friend, even though I was the newcomer here. It was an unusual friendship - Marquand was paying rent to Brando for staying at his house.

Often, there were strangers popping in and out of Brando's house, but there was one young man in his mid-twenties, who just seemed to hang around aimlessly. Periodically, he would wander into the house during the day, take something out of the refrigerator to eat, and go back outside without uttering a word or even having eye contact with anyone. People in the kitchen would go on with their conversations as though he were not present.

After a few days, I discovered that when he left the house, he would go to a small ramshackle tree house precariously perched in a pine tree just outside Marlon's bedroom. He even slept there at night.

Finally, I asked about him. Brando explained that he had recently hired him to help Christian, who was then fifteen, with his school work and to watch over him when Brando was traveling. Shortly thereafter, he introduced him to me as, "Marty, who just moved down from Oregon." He gave no last name.

Over the next two weeks, Marty continued to spend most of his time in the tree house. Never once did I see him help Christian with his studies or even display the slightest interest in him. When Marty would come into the house when either Christian or Brando was present, he would pass by one or the other with neither party even acknowledging the other's presence.

As time went on, Brando said that he intended to take Christian with him whenever he went to Tetiaroa or traveled elsewhere over the next year, so I began to wonder what Marty was going to do.

It was not surprising that Brando wanted to keep Christian with him at all times. This was only a year after Christian had been subjected to a harrowing experience as a result of the unending war over his custody and upbringing that had raged between Marlon and Christian's mother, Anna Kashfi, since his birth. This fight had been filled with physical violence, accusations and arrests, and had been in and out of court several times.

In 1972, the turmoil had reached a peak when Christian had been forcibly removed from Marlon's home by Anna while Brando was in France filming LAST TANGO. Anna took Christian to Mexico and left him in care of her friend James Wooster. When Brando was informed, he hired private detective Jay Armes of El Paso to search for Christian. He was joined in the search by the Mexican federal police.

Anna returned to Mexico to find Wooster and Christian gone from the motel where she had left them. She reported to the Mexican police that Christian had been kidnapped. She returned to Los Angeles, where she was arrested for being drunk and disorderly on a bus, and spent the night in jail. Meanwhile, the world press was daily covering the story.

Armes, with the aid of the Mexican federal police, traced the fleeing Wooster and pursued him in his helicopter to a beach near the village of Puertecitos. After an armed confrontation, they found a frightened and confused Christian huddled in a tent under some clothing, without shirt or shoes, and coughing with bronchitis. Wooster reported that Anna had promised him ten thousand dollars to hide Christian.

Christian was returned to his father's custody. Kashfi filed an assault and battery suit against Brando, accusing him of having her beaten and injured by his attorney Norman Garey and ten unidentified men.

As a consequence of the kidnapping and other events, Brando had been awarded sole custody of Christian for a year, with Anna forbidden any contact with her son. Now, Anna was again petitioning the court to secure custody of Christian, contending that Marlon was emotionally and physically abusing him. So, Brando's fatherly concern to keep Christian at his side at that time was quite understandable.

One day, Alice was hiring a messenger service to pick up a book for Brando and bring it to the house. I suggested that she ask Marty to drive the ten minutes to the bookstore to pick it up, thereby saving a twenty dollar charge. It seemed a reasonable request, since Brando was anxious to receive it and Marty was being paid $2,000 per month by Brando and was just sitting around, manifestly bored.

Alice said that she had once asked Marty to pick something up for Brando and that he had done it and then submitted a bill to her for forty dollars. This rankled me. Marty had about the easiest job imaginable, was being paid most generously, and seemed to be unwilling to provide any help at all. Even though he was under the household expense budget which Alice was managing, it seemed time to take action.

Brando was in his bedroom. Without going into the story Alice had just told, I merely mentioned that there did not seem to be any real work for Marty to do since Marlon was planning on having Christian travel with him. I suggested that Marty's job be terminated, thereby saving $2,000 per month.

Without any further discussion, Marlon said, "It seemed to make sense at the time I hired him; I was concerned about Christian. But, I guess you're right. I don't really need him. Okay, I'll tell him."

Brando must have acted right away. The next day Marty was gone and I never saw him again.

Several weeks later, Alice mentioned Marlon's nephew in a context that I could not understand. Upon questioning, she revealed that Marty was actually Brando's nephew, from his sister Jocelyn's earlier marriage to Eliot Asinof.

This incident illustrates the weight that Brando gave to my advice when it came to anything involving financial matters. For the first few months, he would accept my every suggestion, even on such personal matters as changing the financial support he was providing for his family or firing his nephew.

The ease with which Brando was following my advice was in sharp contrast to the information I was getting from Brando's accountants at Brown Kraft and his attorneys at Rosenfeld Meyer and Susman. They universally described his financial behavior as erratic and uncontrolled, and talked about him as though he were an artistic problem child who had to be protected from himself.

The consistency of the pattern of their comments and the anecdotes that supported them led me to conclude that what I was experiencing was a new Brando. He was behaving rationally and even conservatively in financial matters, not erratically and out of control.

I wondered, however, if this behavior represented a real, permanent behavioral change or was just a short-term aberration. He had been shocked that all the money from THE GODFATHER had disappeared so quickly without his even fully comprehending where it had all gone. Perhaps that shock was what had prompted him to hire me. I recognized that hiring me and putting so much responsibility into my hands had been an impulsive act - he had barely met me and knew almost nothing about me.

So, despite my early success in cutting down Brando's expenses and his almost complete concurrence with my recommendations, I still had a disquieting feeling, a feeling that things could easily change. So, one evening as we were sitting in the kitchen chatting over a couple of bacon and cheese sandwiches that Brando had grilled, I questioned him about his financial motivations and the effect of money and financial security on his behavior.

"You know, Marlon, I've been wondering about something. You've talked about all this money you've made and how someone else has always pissed it away on bad investments - your father, business managers, and so on. You don't suppose that the real reason it has always been lost is you, do you?"

He put his half eaten sandwich down. "What do you mean?" he asked.

"Well, it doesn't seem like the money could've always been lost without your involvement. Didn't those others need to get your approval to make the investments? You could've at least reviewed them yourself before they spent any money. All these people couldn't have been losing your money without your knowledge. If you knew about it, you could've done something about it. Couldn't you have stopped them from throwing your money away?"

"No, no, no. I trusted them. You should've seen some of the things my father got into. He was so damn ignorant that somebody actually salted a gold mine and he bought it. He bought swamp land in Florida. He bought cattle that were just a figment of some con man's imagination. If somebody'd tried to sell him the Brooklyn Bridge, he would've bought that too, as long as he was using my money."

"C'mon now, was he really that bad?"

Brando looked away from me, out the kitchen window, saying nothing.

"Well, what about your other business managers?" I asked. "It seems to me that the guys at Brown Kraft know what they're doing. They manage money for a lot of entertainment people and, from what I've seen, they're successful at it. They tend to pick fairly conservative investments like stocks and real estate - some of them may not make millions, but they'll provide some return and at least aren't likely to go belly-up."

Brando did not respond, so I continued on.

"George and Norton keep telling me that you never go along with their investment recommendations, that you're the one who always keeps coming up with those schemes that end up losing your money. Like Mona Mona (the lobster raising project), they didn't even know anything about it until you told them to send Tap a check."

More Brando silence; his sandwich was getting cold.

"And that cattle investment, they told me that they argued and argued with you about it and tried to get Bishop to send the papers before they sent the check. They said they kept refusing until they could at least firm up the deal. But, one day you just called and said it was your money and insisted they express a $100,000 check to Bishop that day. They ended up sending it even though they still didn't know what you were getting. Those are the kind of things that you have lost money on recently and they're things that you've gotten yourself into, no one else has."

Brando paused a while, and seemed lost in thought as though pondering those investments. He wandered over to the refrigerator, poked around but came out empty handed.

"You know," he said, "those guys just want to charge fees for selling those investments. The only thing I've got them for is to pay my bills and figure out my taxes. They're just accountants, they don't have any feeling at all for what I want to do with my money. If they had their way, all my money would be in some god damn oil company's hands."

He clearly did not want to talk about lobster or cattle investments, but I was not quite ready to give up.

"Well, from what I've seen and heard, I have to wonder what your attitude toward money really is," I said. "Maybe when you have a lot of cash in the bank, you get a little bored or somehow don't feel like you deserve it. Maybe you somehow enjoy the uncertainty that comes when you don't quite know where your next dollar is coming from?"

"No, no, no," Brando said. "I hate that feeling. I want to be free of money problems. That's why I've got you. With you taking care of things, I don't think I should ever have to worry about money again."

"I know I've made some bad judgments in the past. That's why you're in charge in my financial affairs. I'm convinced you know what you're doing. I want you to handle it. You're going to keep me out of the kind of trouble I've been in before."

At the time, Brando's comments were flattering, but not as reassuring as they might have seemed. Though hardly a psychologist, I had learned something about how people handle money, having seen several business people make small fortunes and then lose their wealth in ways that seemed almost purposeful - by spending at an exorbitant rate, by expanding unto obviously unprofitable areas, or going off into entirely different risky businesses or investments totally unfamiliar to them. I had learned that there were people who just could not stand success, and had read enough psychology to realize that many people find ways of losing their wealth because of complex feelings of inferiority. They subconsciously do not believe that they are worthy of success; they therefore find ways to fail.

Actors and entertainment people are among those most susceptible to such emotions and insecurities. In the entertainment industry, success, fame, and enormous financial rewards can come with a breathtaking suddenness to people who have previously experienced little recognition or success. Also, it has often been demonstrated that many who go into show business do so as one way of covering feelings of shyness, insecurity, and low self-esteem.

Brando had begun going to psychiatrists in the 1940s and had continued for almost two decades. Among the reasons he gave was that he lacked self-confidence and had feelings of inadequacy, which is typical of someone having been reared in a family with an alcoholic parent.

So, my early suspicion that there would be more to managing Brando's money than *"debits on the left, credits on the right"* was based on a real foundation.

Still, despite my apprehension, this was a time of accomplishment and satisfaction. My financial advice was being accepted and the groundwork was being laid to improve Brando's financial position. Beyond that, he was rapidly increasing my responsibilities. While his hiring me may have been a rashly impulsive act, he had now had opportunity to observe and evaluate my performance. The extra responsibilities told me that he was pleased.

Brando was enthusiastic about my entrance into his life and delighted with my performance. He began planning trips for us to take together - to Hong Kong and the Philippines for business; to buy rattan furniture for the tourism operation and for his home on Tetiaroa. He was even talking about a trip to Paris simply because he thought it the most exciting city in the world and wanted me to experience it.

These were exciting times for me. I was learning about new businesses, technology, cultures, and investments and experiencing an entirely new way of life. Like H. F. Hutton's slogan, I was discovering that when Marlon Brando's business manager talked, people listened.

We were developing a mutual respect and enjoying each other's company. I was filled with admiration for his plans for Tetiaroa and his insight into and concern for the underprivileged. He respected my judgment and my efforts to manage his business interests and thereby make his life better.

My job was beginning with a sense of glamour and excitement. There was a certain intoxication to having Brando absorbed with my welfare and hanging on to my every word. I held high expectations of accomplishment on his behalf and viewed the job as a once in a lifetime opportunity for me.

I knew it was possible that things could change. But, it all started off so much better than I could have dreamed.

CHAPTER ELEVEN

GETTING CONSTRUCTION MOVING ON TETIAROA

While I had initially expected to be engaged in such environmentally enlightened projects as growing vegetables with hydroponic technology and developing alternative energy sources on Tetiaroa, it soon became apparent that Brando's number one objective was to complete his resort so that tourists would begin bringing dollars to the island.

First, however, cash was needed in order to get construction back on track. Brown Kraft accountant George Pakkala continued negotiating with United Artists concerning its prospective guarantee of a Brando loan from the Beverly Hills National Bank. In the interim, he found a way to obtain a short-term bridge loan from Brando's pension fund. It was not sufficient to pay his income taxes, but it was large enough so that construction could resume on Tetiaroa on a moderate scale.

Those funds on hand, I prepared to return to Tahiti, this time with my wife, Toni, and our three sons, twelve-year-old Gregory, ten-year-old Eric, and five-year-old David. Brando's travel agent Rosette Valente came to the L A airport to see us off. Her husband Bob took our photographs to send to the Tahiti newspaper to announce the arrival of Brando's new "man in Tahiti." While we waited for the plane, he took me aside and filled me with stories of the many people that Brando had sent to Tetiaroa to work for him on developing Tetiaroa and how, other than Bernard Judge, none had accomplished anything.

Rosette had been arranging Brando's travel for well over a decade. She was excited about the prospect of someone grabbing hold of construction and the thought of a family moving to Tetiaroa. She had been a creative travel agent for Brando over the years, providing services seldom required by the normal traveling public. In his younger years, Brando would frequently call Rosette from some movie location with instructions for her to find some actress, dancer, or waitress he had previously dated and have them in his remotely located hotel room by five o'clock p.m. Friday. He often had not informed the object of his interest that he wanted her to come and often had only the remotest idea of where she lived. Still, when Rosette could locate them, they usually came. Brando was accustomed to making offers that women could not refuse long before he played the Godfather.

As he now approached fifty years of age, such requests to Rosette had long since ceased.

Brando had suggested that my family and I stay at Tarita's house, saying we would feel more at home there than in a hotel. I tried to refuse, saying that it would be too much of an imposition. He could not be argued out of it.

This flight went more smoothly than the first - no problems of lost passports. However, there was one similarity to the earlier trip. We discovered that Brando had not informed Tarita that we were coming to stay with her.

While his offer was made with our comfort in mind, it gave little consideration to her. It was a considerable burden to add five strangers to a household to accommodate an absentee commonlaw husband. Tarita was accustomed to Brando sending strangers in her house. Despite the surprise, she welcomed us.

So, the five of us moved into the one small bedroom. With Reiko still there, that was the only room available. All five of us, in fact, had to sleep in one bed. Five people in one regular size bed make a crowd, even if three of them are small children. No matter at what angles everybody lay, elbows and knees were flying into faces all night long. After a week of discomfort in the crowded bed, we moved to a small bungalow at the Tahiti Village Hotel.

The money from Brando's pension fund provided money to pay the contractor, Tapituri, his back bill. However, he could not be persuaded to return to Tetiaroa. Like the worldly banker in Beverly Hills, the unsophisticated Tahitian also did not trust Brando's money management.

Architect Bernard Judge had expressed his desire to return soon to his business in Los Angeles; he had been away from it for nearly a year.

With the revision of the bungalow design to include bathrooms and electricity and the need to eventually get a building permit, however, it was necessary for him to produce drawings to satisfy the Tahiti building inspector before he could leave. Therefore, Brando and I decided to have him temporarily remain in charge of construction, while completing the drawings. I stayed in Papeete to rent an office and organize the staff to handle the tourist operation support activities which would need to take place on Tahiti. Tarita was looking forward to getting her bedroom back after a year's use as the Tetiaroa office.

With Tapituri gone, Judge and I decided to hire our own construction workers. He began hiring and soon had almost fifty workers on site. The average pay rate was just under one dollar an hour.

The Tahitians did not find Tetiaroa a particularly desirable place to work. Most preferred working on Tahiti where they could return to their homes at the end of the day, rather than staying in the construction camp on Tetiaroa, separated from friends and family. Working for Marlon Brando was not the attraction in French Polynesia that it might have been in the United States. Thus, Judge was not able to hire the best of the Tahitian workers, but rather ended up with the less skilled and less industrious, those who found it difficult to obtain or hold a job on Tahiti.

In Papeete, Judge gave me periodic reports of energetic action on Tetiaroa. Yet, when I returned to Tetiaroa in a month, following a business trip to Los Angeles, there was little visible progress on construction. Judge had not started working on his drawings.

It was apparent that it was going to take considerably longer than his two week time estimate to complete construction and have the facility ready to open for tourists. However, I could not foresee how much more time would eventually be required. Although it is not unusual for construction projects to drag out perhaps fifty percent longer or even double the time originally scheduled, Judge's estimate could have been increased by a factor of ten and still would have grossly underestimated the time eventually required.

Work on Tetiaroa had a languorous pace quite unlike anything in my previous experience. While that may have been the bane of progress, it was also part of the charm of Polynesia. Neither Paul Gauguin nor Fletcher Christian sojourned in Tahiti because of the work ethic there.

Since my arrival, I had seen almost absurd inefficiencies in operation that were contributing to the vast outflow of money. Passenger and supply planes flying between Tahiti and Tetiaroa were numerous enough to rival the Washington - New York air shuttle - almost as frequent as the expensive and interminable long distance conversations on the radio phone between the island and the Papeete office. The undisciplined conversations were known throughout the islands for the entertainment they provided to more frugal radio phone owners.

Special single engine planes had been chartered to fly sacks of cement to Tetiaroa at the same time that the regular passenger/ supply planes were being flown only partially loaded. The special flights could hold only nine 50 kilogram (110 pound) sacks. The purchase price of the cement was about forty dollars per plane load. Built into that price was the transportation cost of shipping it halfway around the world from France. The transportation cost of moving it the last twenty-six miles to Tetiaroa had been running four times the cost of manufacturing it in France and shipping it ten thousand miles to Tahiti. The extra cost of bringing a few sacks on the under-loaded supply planes or bringing the cement over the water on the landing craft, Meherio, would have been only a small fraction of what was being spent.

Laborers on the island worked with little supervision. To a Tahitian, working without supervision usually meant not working at all. Planning and organization were lacking. Workers wandered from one job to another without ever finishing anything. Unplanned purchasing meant ordering after the supplies had run out and buying whatever was available without consideration of price.

Workers were brought in without the rudimentary hand tools they needed in order to work.

Once again, it would not take a genius to make big improvements here. Before too long, I was to conclude that was just what I was not a genius at getting work done on Tetiaroa.

So, it seemed time for me to move to Tetiaroa and take over supervision of construction. Having spent a few weeks working on organizational matters in Papeete, my family and I now moved to Tetiaroa. On our moving day, Brando was in Beverly Hills. Yet when we arrived on Tetiaroa, waiting there were three sets of snorkels and swimming fins for my sons, a dozen roses for my wife, and a silver bucket with a bottle of French champagne for our first evening on Tetiaroa. Marlon had asked Yvonne Chung to have the presents there as his way of saying, "Welcome to my island of Tetiaroa."

Over the previous weeks, I had discussed the social and cultural patterns of working with the Tahitians with a few bankers, attorneys, and businessmen in Papeete and now approached the job with a firm ambition to "get things organized" better than they had been. My investigation did not provide a wealth of useful information. Despite diligent probing, I received only a few general suggestions such as: "The Tahitians like to work together. If you give anyone a solitary assignment, he will brood and do little work;" or, "Don't just give instructions. They pretend to understand even if they don't and they won't ask questions. You have to work with them and show them by example." My inability to speak either French or Tahitian made communication and supervision difficult; that was a major concern.

Still, a little information was better than none at all. I decided to mix my management knowledge with this small body of cultural knowledge. Some of my attempts worked, others didn't.

The first step was to organize the work force. The Tahitians used the word "chief" to designate a supervisor. From among the best workers, I appointed chiefs and had each chief pick his own crew of to six workers. The chiefs were given a wage ten percent higher than the other crew members. Chiefs were respected by their workers, but the jobs never really became sought after. A man might act as chief one week and then decide he preferred to simply be a worker on someone else's crew the next.

The responsibility of a chief was taken seriously, but not in quite the anticipated manner. I expected a chief to organize and schedule the crew's work, to be responsible for the crew's tools and materials, to direct and motivate crew members to work steadily and efficiently, and to assure that quality construction was attained.

The Tahitians' concept seemed to be that the chief should work harder than the other members of his crew. The chiefs always did work hard; they did not, however, take to the concept of supervision very well. Whenever someone was appointed as a chief, his motivation and effort would improve. If that same person should later become a regular crew member for some reason, he would simply not work with the same diligence he had exhibited as a chief. But, the chiefs would not supervise their crews well. They would concentrate on their own physical labor, often ignoring the other members of their crew even if they were just standing around watching.

My lack of success in teaching the concept of supervision to the chiefs was probably, at least in part, because it was not deemed particularly good manners in the Tahitian culture for one man to tell another what to do. The boss-worker relationship was just not as ingrained there as in industrial countries.

In the United States, we are accustomed to demands for work to be done, "immediately, if not sooner." Polynesia, on the other hand, is the eternal mañana land. Nothing gets done today; tomorrow is fine and some indefinite time in the future is even better. Among the Polynesians, the Tahitians have earned the reputation as the least industrious. There were three young men on Tetiaroa who had emigrated from the Tuamotu Archipelago, a group of small islands a few hundred miles east of Tahiti. They were excellent workers. When given an assignment, they would diligently work, without supervision, until it was completed. The Toamotuan workers were socially fully integrated with the Tahitians, but would frequently shake their heads and lament that the Tahitians just did not know how to work. Because of their diligence, it would have been preferable to make each of the three chief over a work crew, but they resisted the responsibility. They insisted on working together.

With organization of the work with Tahitian chiefs proving to be less than a rousing success, my search for more responsible supervision continued. It eventually led to another immigrant to Tahiti by the name of Jean Mercier (mare cee a). He was an experienced supervisor, who had just finished managing a large construction project at the Faaa Airport. Mercier had been raised in the Marquesas Islands, a group of small islands about a thousand miles northeast of Tahiti, and another part of French Polynesia. His father was a Marquesan and his mother a Tahitian.

Mercier had been highly recommended, so I invited him to come to Tetiaroa to discuss a job. His first appearance, when he climbed off the airplane, was impressive. Darkly handsome, with thick black wavy hair and the body of a weight lifter, he looked like a Polynesian Victor Mature. As we walked through the island, discussing the construction project, Mercier demonstrated a broad knowledge of construction technology. More importantly, he spoke with an understanding of the problems of organizing and motivating the workers. Despite his own Tahitian heritage, he spoke of the lackadaisical work attitude on Tetiaroa as though the Tahitians were of a different race. He seemed to almost conspiratorially suggest that the Tahitians would not work very hard for a rich white man like Marlon Brando, but between the two of us, we would get them into shape. He spoke understandable, if not fluent, English as well as Tahitian and French and that facility alone promised an enormous improvement in communication. He had a sparkling warm smile as he spoke which made it appear that he would approach the challenge of Tetiaroa with real enthusiasm.

As we walked through the tourist village construction area, Mercier stopped, looked out over the lagoon at length, and said, "Marlon Brando is crazy to build on this part of the island."

"What do you mean?" I asked.

"Too close to the sea. The winds will come here. The tides will wash everything away. He should be building on the other side, where the workers live."

"But, this isn't the ocean, it's a lagoon. You don't get big waves here, do you? I mean, doesn't the reef always break up the big waves? The architect who laid out the village said he studied all the tide tables and we're safe here."

"Forget architects. The waves will come. Any Tahitian can tell you. Just wait and see."

Mercier had arrived on Tetiaroa, clad in the usual work uniform of shorts, light shirt, and thongs and carrying a small athletic bag and an attache' case. An attache' case was a rare sight on Tahiti and was about the last object one would ever expect to find in the hands of a native. When Mercier opened the attache' case, there was a hand lettered card taped to the inside cover, where it would be a reminder whenever he opened it, which said, *"Is what I am now doing or about to do bringing me closer to my goals?"* Since it was written in English rather than his native tongue, I suspected that he meant it to be noticed by others. Nonetheless, the fact that he even thought in terms of goals seemed a good omen and quite a contrast to the typical Tahitian mañana mentality.

Moreover, although Mercier had arrived almost empty handed, he was ready to stay on Tetiaroa and go to work immediately. Mercier seemed a godsend and I hired him as chief of construction on Tetiaroa, at his customary salary, which was three times what we had been paying the crew chiefs. That massive difference in pay helps demonstrate that the typical construction worker on Tetiaroa was not highly skilled or experienced.

Mercier quickly got the workers organized in a manner I been unable to achieve. On the weekend he returned to Tahiti and brought back several workers who had previously worked for him and who were more skilled than our previous contingent.

There was immediate improvement and the work progressed better thereafter. Brando arrived on the island shortly after I hired Mercier. He seemed to enjoy watching Mercier in action. In contrast to most of the workers who were small, young, and inexperienced, the muscular and talented Mercier seemed like Gulliver among the Lilliputians. Observing him and seeing the newfound burst of energy throughout the island, Brando was full of praise for my first attempts at organizing construction.

Still, however, Mercier did not prove to be quite the supervisor I had hoped. Like the other crew chiefs, he also did too much work and not enough supervision. He was very strong, unquestionably highly motivated, and enjoyed physical work, which was how he expended most of his energy. He was effective at giving the work assignments and getting things started at the beginning of each day. But then, he would go off on some job of his own, sometimes with a small crew and other times just by himself, and pay little attention to the work force the rest of the day. While he accomplished as much physical work as any three other workers, he did not capture the full benefit of the others' capabilities. I still found it necessary to spend most of my day on Tetiaroa going throughout the island, working with one crew after another in order to keep them focused on the job at hand.

In the United States, I had often seen big increases in production result when pay was tied to the amount of work accomplished. Production management books called it "incentive wage payment systems," a fancy term meaning higher pay for more work.

With the difficulty we were having keeping workers motivated, the construction project seemed like a good place to apply incentive wages. I decided to experiment with keeping the basic hourly pay system and adding a bonus for increased production.

There was a crew of five workers assigned to the concrete floors on the low bungalows. Their job was to construct and assemble wood forms, level the ground and prepare the base, gather sand and water, mix the concrete in a small portable mixer, pour the concrete and work the poured concrete with trowels and other hand tools to finish the floor. They had taken about seven working days on the first bungalow. (By contrast, in the United States, with readymix concrete and power equipment, it would have been a one day job with a two-man crew.) Experience gained on the first bungalow would help subsequent floors take less time. The crew chief estimated that his crew could finish the second in five days.

I promised a bonus of a day's pay for each crew member if they finished a floor, while maintaining quality, within his estimated five days and also let it be known that the bonus system would be expanded to take in more jobs if this trial proved successful.

For the first three days, the crew worked with an industry heretofore alien to Tetiaroa. Everyone put forth an earnest steady effort. In fact, the crew started to gather an audience as other workers would leave their jobs and stop by to see how the work was progressing.

Unfortunately, it did not go quite as fast as the crew chief had expected and it appeared they might not make the deadline. I hoped they would and decided to pay the bonus even if they only came close to finishing, since they had worked with true diligence. During the fourth day, the crew grew by two people; there were now seven working on the floor job. By the end of the day, it had grown to eight.

It appeared to be touch and go whether they would be able to finish by the end of Friday - their target day and the end of our work week. The morning of the deadline day began with a crew now grown in size to ten and as the day progressed, the crew continued to expand until there were a dozen workers scurrying around the cement mixer and the target bungalow like a colony of worker bees supplying a demanding queen.

Still the sun kept moving unrelentingly toward the horizon faster than the concrete was filling the void within the forms. Throughout the afternoon, more and more workers came to watch and urge on the supplemented crew. Work on the other projects drew to a halt. Newcomers would have also joined in, but there was just not enough room for more bodies; the members of the floor crew were already getting in each other's way. I feared that when the floor was finished, a few slow moving Tahitian feet would be planted solidly in the hardened concrete.

Quitting time came, the floor was all poured, but the concrete still needed more hand finishing to set up properly. By now, all fifty workers on the island were at the site. Dinner would wait. As the sun settled like a large luminous orange disk into the rolling Pacific, the final touch of inscribing the initials of the original five crew members into the curing concrete at an obscure spot behind one of the pillars was made to the accompaniment of a rousing cheer from the assembled crowd.

Brando watched the whole proceedings with detached amusement.

The following day was Saturday, a day of rest. Bonuses were paid to the original five crew members. The experiment had not been entirely successful since the crew had only met their goal with the help of others, but the work had captured the workers' interest as it never had before and a general air of optimism seemed to permeate the island. Over the weekend, Mercier and I worked out targets for other crews and most of the workers were under the bonus system by the start of the work week on Monday.

It seemed to help. The work went better. However, since almost everyone was on the bonus system, there was no longer the pool of manpower available to shift to help a straggling crew. As a consequence, as the end of the week approached, it appeared that several crews would fall short of their targets.

Still, there had been substantial improvement over the past two weeks. Bonuses would not be paid unless fully earned, since to do otherwise might undermine future motivation. Some would receive bonuses, others wouldn't. In order to keep enthusiasm up for those who were falling short and in celebration of the zeal with which the work had been done, I decided a special treat for the whole work force was in order.

Tetiaroa offered little entertainment over the weekend for the workers. It was customary to bring over five gallons of wine and a few cases of beer on the Saturday supply plane for the workers' evening diversion. It was now time for a bigger party.

I contacted Yvonne Chung on the radiophone and ordered a pig for roasting and a barrel of wine - forty-two gallons - it was time for a good celebration. Brando endorsed the idea.

However, such a simple order also required planning for transportation. That was a less simple problem.

About every six weeks, a small boat came to deliver several barrels of diesel fuel for burning in the electrical generator. A delivery was due Friday. Yvonne was to put the pig and wine on the boat.

When small boats brought supplies to the island, off-loading was not a simple operation. The reef provided a barrier that prevented the boats from reaching the lagoon. The boat would have to pull up to the reef and cargo would be off-loaded by hand to workers standing on the reef amidst the breaking ocean waves. From there, it was put on small boats inside the reef and taken to the camp. It was such a perilous job that we rarely brought normal supplies to Tetiaroa that way.

It was a little simpler with the diesel fuel, however. Since diesel fuel is lighter than water, the barrels could simply be dumped into the ocean at the reef on the upwind side of the camp island and the wave action would bring them toward shore. One worker in a small boat could herd them in like a cowpoke bringing cattle to the corral.

On the phone, I told Yvonne to make very sure to instruct the captain to carefully unload the barrel of wine by hand and not just throw it into the ocean. I knew that wine had about the same density as water and suspected that this was one barrel that might not float. Near the scheduled time of arrival, I sent two workers out in a boat to get the pig and the wine, having earlier informed Mercier of our special liquid cargo. Word had passed through the island as quickly as if jungle tomtoms had been beating.

The thought of a big party filled everyone with anticipation, providing a visible distraction from the afternoon's output. Suddenly the possible bonuses seemed less important than a copiously lubricated island luau and forty-two gallons of wine for some fifty people would assure that everyone's cup would be overflowing for the whole weekend. They knew that also on board was their favorite delicacy for a celebration, a nice tender pig which would be roasted Sunday for the *piece de resistance.* Together with abundant fresh fish from the lagoon and a fresh supply of ripe tropical fruit from Tahiti, a true Tahitian feast was on everyone's mind.

Knowing that there are some things about which one cannot be too careful, I picked two of the most trustworthy workers and painstakingly instructed them before they set out in a boat to meet the supply boat at the reef. Under no circumstances were they to allow the barrel of wine to be thrown into the ocean!

A couple of hours later, the two Tahitians approached the camp. One hung back in the palm trees, the other silently stood waiting at the edge of the camp clearing. One look at his gloomy face revealed as clearly as if it were written in neon what he was so visibly afraid to tell me - the barrel of wine had been thrown into the ocean along with the barrels of diesel fuel and had gone to its eternal rest in Davey Jones' locker.

The jungle tomtoms must have been beating again or perhaps when the arrival of the boat on Onetahi had failed to fill the trade winds with the ambrosial fragrance of the fermented grape, the primed olfactory nerves had to respond. For, as I looked around, at least half of the work force begin to gather quietly around the worker in the palms. The fetid odor of the diesel fuel was no recompense for a hard week's work.

It was time for decisive action - I had a real case of South Seas crisis management on my hands. Although it seemed a futile action, we quickly mounted a massive sea rescue operation. No capsized sailor or downed pilot ever had a more dedicated party of rescuers than those who searched for our sunken treasure. Captain Ahab would have envied such a zealous crew.

Unimportant things like construction of the resort were shunted aside and every boat on Tetiaroa was soon filled with Tahitians bound for the reef. I broke out the scuba diving equipment from behind lock and key and had my choice from among the most courageous, or perhaps most thirsty divers to brave the depths beyond the reef, for unfortunately that is where the barrel of wine had sunk. Had it been within the reef, they might well found it. But, beyond the reef, the ocean bottom immediately fell off to hundreds of fathoms. Our only hope was that somehow the wave action had pinned it to the outer edge of the reef.

Throughout the remainder of the afternoon, the search continued, one exhausted diver giving way to another. They were indeed a courageous lot, for there was danger in their task. Since we had only one working aqua-lung, a diver had to go down by himself where he risked being dashed against the concrete-hard abrasive coral. Moray eels hid in dark crevices, ready to sink their sharp pointed teeth into passing limbs. More fearsome and more dangerous were the sharks that lurked around the reef, voraciously preying on brightly colored fish which darted in and out of the coral.

Inside the reef, one would often see a dorsal fin ominously cutting through the water. It usually belonged to a small sand shark or some relatively innocuous brother shark of three or four foot length, and swimming was regarded as quite safe. However, as each diver searched in turn outside the reef, an occasional six to ten foot mako or thresher shark could be seen stealthily circling, a cold unblinking eye hypnotically sizing up the lone diver. Every hour, a boat returned from the reef, bringing the dreadful news to the silent crowd on shore that the cask with its precious contents remained unseen.

Finally as darkness enveloped the reef, the search came to a reluctant end. The luau could still take place, but the epicurean delights of pit roasted pig would not be as pleasurable without the much awaited nectar of the gods. The morose workers were faced with a desultory weekend ahead. Looking at the grim faces, which provided such a contrast to the normally carefree happy temperament of the Tahitians, I tried to salvage the weekend.

I provided several bottles of rum from the meager camp liquor supply for the luau and also promised to bring out another barrel of wine for the following weekend. We really would not need another boat that soon, but we could always put the extra diesel fuel into inventory for later use.

This action was my mistake. Looking back, I should have charted a airplane for the next day with one barrel of wine for cargo. In fact, I actually checked into that, but found that the barrel was too big to fit into the single engine plane. Being a budget watcher, I did not want to spend the extra three hundred and fifty dollars for a large plane and it seemed to me that the wine would taste just as good the following weekend.

Well, maybe it would to me, but a week was too long to ask a Tahitian to wait for a party. My action met no protest, but then, it is not in the Tahitian character to protest, so the lack of complaint should not have been taken as agreement. Their acquiescence masked their disappointment.

The Sunday luau went off on schedule. The roast pig was delicious. Band music lent a festive, if not completely joyous, air as the ukuleles and guitars played a mix of the latest rock tunes from America and traditional Tahitian songs. Even though few Tahitians had much English language competency, they all seemed to know the words to the popular American songs.

...my, my, my beautiful Sunday,

This is my, my, my beautiful day.

...the words echoed through the palms.

My kids loved the singing and laughing, and the break from routine was as much fun for my family as for the Tahitians. I frequently got away from Tetiaroa and Tahiti to go to the states. However, other than an occasional trip to Papeete, they had to continually cope with the boredom of daily life on a little island, so a little Sunday picnic was a major social event.

All in all, it appeared to have been an enjoyable weekend on Tetiaroa. On Monday, work was back on schedule. On Tuesday morning, I left Tetiaroa to return to Los Angeles to work on some of Brando's stateside business. But, after lunch that day, a half dozen Tahitians went "out on strike" in protest over the lost barrel of wine. By the end of the day, about half the crew was out. After a tough tongue lashing by Mercier that evening, the recalcitrant workers were all back on the job the next morning.

However, the positive momentum of the previous week was disrupted. Bonuses for the week looked out of sight for most of the crews. Besides, the absence of the boss always seemed to provide a natural time for slackening the already tenuous work ethic. The magic of the bonuses disappeared and progress deteriorated to its previous level, despite the barrel of wine promised for the coming weekend.

I did not find out about the strike until returning about ten days later. There was another surprise as well, upon my return to paradise. Mercier had gone on a recruiting drive. There were about fifty workers on Tetiaroa when I left; I returned to find a hundred and twenty. If the workers were going to slow down, progress did not have to diminish. Just hire more.

Moreover, if there were not competent skilled workers available, then warm bodies would do. There was now a mixture of people not unlike one would expect in the population as a whole including an ample supply of young boys and girls. Everyone was on the payroll, no matter how completely unskilled or physically unsuitable to construction work. Where Mercier was busting with pride that he had filled Tetiaroa with construction workers, I saw scampering children, many of whom did not know a carpenter's hammer from a hammerhead shark.

For the next two weeks, I made sure that every regular supply plane that came to Tetiaroa carried a full load of "workers" back to their mothers on Tahiti.

Special flights also had to be chartered. It seems that a few of the workers got so lonesome that they could not wait for the regular planes. However, they never admitted to homesickness. Rather, they had to return because "my grandmother is dying." There was an absolute epidemic of dying grandmothers. With no method of communicating with Tahiti in the workers' camp, the young Tahitians displayed extraordinary extrasensory perception.

CHAPTER TWELVE

LAND OF SWINDLERS
AND CON MEN

Before long, my work schedule settled into a pattern of spending three or four weeks in the South Pacific overseeing construction and then flying to Los Angeles to handle stateside business for the tourist operation and to continue to sort out the rest of Brando's financial affairs.

Before one such early return trip to Beverly Hills, I spoke to Brando on a transoceanic phone call. At the end of our business conversation, he asked for my flight number and time of arrival in Los Angeles. He wanted to have Alice arrange a limousine to bring me to his house, all the while apologizing for not picking me up himself. I told him the limo was an unnecessary expense; a taxi would be fine. He acquiesced to my request on the phone. Yet, when my plane did arrive at LAX a few days later, a liveried chauffeur was standing outside of customs holding a card with the name Roger Vergin on it. The stretched black Cadillac limousine brought me to Brando's house. He was still drastically short of money. It took considerable effort to convince him that, while I enjoyed the comfort, it would be an unnecessary expense to send limousines in the future.

(Not having seen an American newspaper in weeks, I read a LOS ANGELES TIMES in the limo. THE GODFATHER was still playing at more than fifty theaters in the greater Los Angeles area. Brando's contract called for him to receive five percent of the distributor's gross revenue from the movie. But for one short sentence in the contract, that would have brought him over ten million dollars. That sentence limited his total payment to one and a half million dollars. There would have been a dramatic difference in his financial status and in his life without those few words.)

I spent part of my time in Los Angeles trying to raise construction funds and my search followed many diverse paths.

As the person in charge of Marlon Brando's money in the Southern California land of swindlers and con men, I heard from my share of them. Somehow, word had circulated that Brando needed money. So, in the course of my efforts to secure funding, I encountered a few of these swift talking flimflam artists.

One day at Brando's house, a phone call came from a man by the name of John H. Meier. He introduced himself as a representative of the billionaire industrialist Howard Hughes. He had heard that Brando was short of money to put into the development of Tetiaroa. He said that he was in the process of making major investments in the Polynesian kingdom of Tonga and stated that he would be interested in providing money to develop Tetiaroa, either as a direct investment from Hughes or as a loan from his own funds.

Based on his phone call, it seemed worth a meeting at least to see if Meier was for real. One thing that Brando was most interested in was obtaining funds so that he would not have to use his own money - an application of the OPM formula - Other People's Money.

If ever there was someone to whom an exotic investment like Tetiaroa would appeal, it was Howard Hughes. And, if ever there was someone who could afford it, that was Hughes too.

Think of the possibilities - Marlon Brando and Howard Hughes in business together! To put those two together into developing Tetiaroa would have been a feat worthy of nomination in the FORTUNE *Business Hall of Fame.*

Hughes was already well into his reclusive behavior pattern. Still, the thought of somehow bringing Hughes and Brando, two of the most talented and eccentric figures of the twentieth century together was compelling. Imagine listening to the two of them discussing their many common interests - movies, women, business, and life itself. Well, they had shared a house in common, though at different times. Why couldn't they share a business together, at the same time?

I lay in bed that night unable to sleep, my mind filled with visions of Brando and Hughes business enterprises. The visions did not stop with Tetiaroa; the possibility of bringing Hughes back into the movie business with Brando was a far more captivating thought. That combination would make the industry take notice.

Actually, what kept me awake was only partly business visions. For part of my wakeful hours, I reflected on other visions, visions of all the famous women who had romped through this house during the prime times of Hughes and Brando, two of Hollywood's most avid pursuers - and catchers - of the fair sex.

The next day, I told Brando about the call and my intention to follow up on it. Surprisingly, Brando seemed to have some acquaintance with Meier. He described Meier as nothing more than a gofer, court jester, and procurer for Hughes. While the smell of the Hughes fortune intrigued Brando, he said it would be a complete waste of time to meet with Meier, since Meier would have absolutely no capacity to influence Hughes' investment decisions.

Because of Brando's statement, I did not pursue it. Months later, I discovered that Brando had confused Meier with an entirely different person with an almost identical name, an earlier Hughes employee named Johnny Meyer. Several Hughes biographies describe this Meyer in the same terms as had Brando.

Because of Brando's confusion and resulting admonition, I did not set up a meeting with Meier or return subsequent phone calls from him. Many, many years later, I read a newspaper report that led me to regard Brando's misguided warning as having had a providential quality.

In 1981, Meier was accused in a Los Angeles Grand Jury indictment of having arranged the November 29, 1974 fatal stabbing of Alfred Wayne Netter, a businessman to whom he had lent money, in a room at the Beverly Hilton Hotel.

Meier had been Howard Hughes' "scientific adviser" in Las Vegas, an unsuccessful candidate for the U.S. Senate from New Mexico, and a diplomatic representative for the king of Tonga. Police came to regard him as an extraordinarily gifted con artist who had arranged Netter's death to cash in on a $400,000 insurance policy on Netter's life.

Meier working for a Hughes subsidiary when he was brought to the attention of the billionaire who had hidden himself away in the penthouse of the Las Vegas Desert Inn. Known as "Dr. Meier" despite his apparent lack of a college degree, he was told to try to persuade the government to stop underground nuclear tests in Nevada, a practice that Hughes reportedly feared would topple his hotel.

Meier was also placed in charge of a Hughes plan to acquire and eventually reopen Nevada's abandoned gold and silver mines. While acquiring the mines, he was also paid kickbacks by a company that was selling the mines to Hughes. Many of the mines proved worthless and a court ultimately held that Meier owed eight million dollars to the Hughes organization.

Meier was also indicted on charges of income tax evasion. He forfeited $100,000 bail and skipped to Vancouver rather than stand trial. He could not be compelled to face the charge because income tax evasion is not an extraditable offense.

Shortly after my telephone conversation with him, Meier met Netter. Meier allegedly loaned Netter $100,000 for his company, Transcontinental Video, and Netter agreed to repay $400,000 in six months. Meier required that Netter obtain a life insurance policy for $400,000 made payable to a dummy corporation over which Meier had hidden control.

When the loan came due, Netter could not repay it. He was slain in his hotel room, suffering fifteen stab wounds. Police contended that the killing was carried out by a purported "hit man" named William McCrory at Meier's behest.

After an indictment, Meier successfully delayed extradition from Canada for years. In 1986, twelve years after the murder, a plea bargaining agreement was reached. Meier pleaded guilty to a reduced charge of being an accessory and was sentenced to two years.

I'm glad I did not arrange to borrow any money from Meier. THE GODFATHER was interesting entertainment. This was real life. Sometimes the best deals you make are the ones you don't make.

Through our discussions about finding money for Tetiaroa, Brando would often repeat his story that most of his money had been lost because his father used it to buy swampland, worthless gold mines and cattle.

There was at least a grain of truth to his contention about bad cattle investments. Brando, Sr. had purchased Penny Poke Ranch, a farm in Broken Bow, Nebraska, in 1948, mostly with his son's money. He was not successful in operating the cattle feeding operation. It constantly lost money and was eventually sold, at a substantial loss to Brando, Jr.

That history did not completely sour Brando, Jr. on such investments, however. He had made that substantial cattle investment on his very own just before I began working for him. Unfortunately, these cattle turned out to be about as illusory as those of his father.

The case history of this investment demonstrates Brando's investment decision process and illustrates the wheeling and dealing in the often unscrupulous world of tax shelter investments.

In late 1972, Brando received his check for one and a quarter million dollars as royalties from GODFATHER, having earlier received a quarter million dollars during shooting of the film. This was substantially more than his annual income for several previous years combined. Substantial income taxes would be due in 1973 on that income.

By this time, the lobster aquaculture project with Tap Pryor had begun. In addition to managing this project, Pryor was giving financial advice to Brando. He suggested that Brando try to shelter some of the GODFATHER income in order to reduce his income taxes. Pryor introduced Brando to an acquaintance James D. Bishop of the investment firm of Stevenson Bishop McCreadie Inc. of New York.

The three met in Brando's Beverly Hills home in December with Bishop proposing a cattle investment. The nature of the proposal is not entirely clear (for reasons that will be explained), but apparently it was a proposal for the type of investment known as a rollover. One purpose of such an investment is to postpone taxable income from one year to a following year. This is done by buying something that can be depreciated in the first year, thus creating a taxable loss in that year, and then selling it in the second (or later) year, creating taxable income in that subsequent year. Thus, income is "rolled over" to the subsequent year and the payment of income tax is postponed until that year. In many cases, that income can be converted to a long term capital gain, which was at that time taxed at a much lower rate, providing further tax relief.

The investment world is filled with schemes to reduce income taxes. If the basic investment is solid in its own right, then it makes sense to take advantage of the income tax code to reduce taxes. However, in many of these schemes, the underlying investments have no real chance of turning a profit due to high commissions to the salesmen, high fees charged by the managers of the investment, and simply inept management of the investment itself. Nonetheless, billions of dollars of such investments are sold to the public every year. The appeal is to reduce taxes. Unfortunately, the money lost on the underlying investment often outweighs the tax savings.

Bishop's proposal to Brando must have been convincing, because Brando phoned Brown Kraft and asked George Pakkala to send Bishop a check for $100,000. Pakkala asked Bishop to produce written documentation for the investment. Over the phone, Bishop described the investment to Pakkala as one of buying cattle, feeding them for about eight months, and then selling them for slaughter - in other words, a typical rollover investment. Depreciation can be taken against the cattle in the year of purchase, thus producing a reduction in income taxes, and often a profit can be made from the feed operation itself. Bishop promised to provide the written investment agreement for Brown Kraft to evaluate.

The agreement did not arrive and the end of December drew near. It was necessary to make the investment by December thirty-first in order to qualify for the depreciation in that year. Brando called Brown Kraft again, now demanding that the check be sent immediately. Pakkala tried to talk him out of making the investment without all the terms nailed down. Brando again demanded and Brown Kraft sent a check to Bishop for $100,000, made payable to North American South Devon.

While Brown Kraft served as financial managers for many of its clients, Brando limited their authority to routine things like paying bills and accounting. Although they often gave him financial advice, he clearly made his investment decisions himself. Frequently, his decisions were contrary to their advice. Thus, when he insisted they send a check, they had no alternative. They had learned to delay him when they felt he was making a particularly bad decision and sometimes it worked. Brando would change his mind or just forget about it. But in the end, it was Brando's money and they had to follow his mandate.

A common result of Brando's independent investment decision-making was that Brown Kraft had to straighten out later. They were by now accustomed to that. The cattle investment proved to be another such case. Only this time, I got to help.

When I came to work months later, there were still no papers on the cattle investment. Bishop now, however, described it as an investment in breeding cattle, not feeders. Moreover, he now said that there was an additional payment of $157,000 required, and it was due soon.

It might seem that $257,000 would buy a lot of beef on the hoof. Not this time. These were expensive cattle. In fact, the $257,000 was buying only sixteen head of South Devon cattle, a breed almost unknown in the United States. Expensive indeed. While the cost of a fully grown steer ready for market was running well under a thousand dollars, Brando's herd was costing just over $16,000 a head.

Over the next several months, accountant Richard Keesling of Brown Kraft and I both tried to get the purchase clarified. We had little success. Our phone calls to Bishop went unreturned. Our correspondence was largely ignored. When we did get a return letter, it was not responsive to the questions we raised. The return letters from Bishop would refer to Schedules and Exhibits purporting to show the value of the cattle, their location, depreciation rate, and so on. Then, the Schedules and Exhibits would not be included.

Slowly, we began to piece the puzzle together. The cattle were purchased from a company called Big Beef Hybrids Inc. (BBHI). The South Devon breed had not been previously raised in the United States. BBHI had imported a small herd from Britain and was attempting to establish the breed in the U.S. BBHI was to manage the herd and produce income for Brando by selling the semen from the bulls and the offspring from the cows.

The cattle ranged in age from yearlings to nine years old. Values assigned to individual animals ranged from $8,000 to $35,000.

There were breeds of cattle - for example, Simmental - where it was not uncommon for a prime, prize winning bull to bring up to thirty five thousand dollars at auction in 1973. However, it would have been most unusual for a whole herd to consist of premium priced prize winners. None of the North American cattle industry magazines in the libraries had any information on the South Devon breed which would allow me to establish values for them. Nor were the people I contacted in the industry any help. They were unfamiliar with the breed. My continued efforts to obtain documentary information from Bishop and BBHI on how they had assigned values went for naught.

Certainly, the cattle had been overpriced for this sale. I just did not know if the prices charged were double or ten times the market value. One eight year old cow had been assigned a price of $25,000. Since the normal longevity of a cow was nine to twelve years, one had to doubt that Brando was going to get his value out of that Bossy. Her biological clock was not only ticking, the springs were just about worn out. You just can not teach an old cow to get pregnant.

Even finding the cattle proved vexing. Our demands for their location were first rebuffed, then we were given state locations, next town locations. I was beginning to wonder if we were dealing with phantom animals. Finally we found the specific farm locations. The fact that the cows were reported to be in Minnesota and the bulls were reported to be in South Dakota and Oregon led me to wonder if the distant geography might make breeding a little difficult, but then, I was just a city boy.

From this run around, we realized that Brando's cattle investment was going to be no better than his father's. To pay the $157,000 still due would be throwing good money after bad.

Throughout the process of trying to get information, I made several attempts to talk with Brando about the investment, trying to determine what he had agreed to buy the feeder cattle that Bishop had described to Pakkala or the breeding cattle which they were now trying to foist on him. My attempts could not be called conversations, for Brando would simply refuse to answer my questions. He either would complain about Pryor's having gotten him involved in the investment or simply say nothing and look out the window in response to a direct question. Clearly, he just did not know what he had agreed to buy.

In the end, it really did not matter because he got neither the feeder cattle nor the breeding cattle and breeding program.

Years later, Brando's attorneys filed a $200,000 Superior Court civil suit against Big Beef Hybrids, Inc., James D. Bishop, and North American South Devon Co. Brando accused the companies of fraud, breach of contract, violation of the Federal Securities and Exchange Act for misrepresentations and violation of the state Securities Act for failing to have a permit to sell securities.

CHAPTER THIRTEEN

BRANDO AT HOME

People strive for fame, fortune, and power for various and complex reasons, many of which lie buried deep in the psyche. Certainly, achieving these elusive goals should give the achievers the opportunity to enjoy life in special ways that are beyond the reach of the average person. Yet many who do realize substantial success continue to live quite ordinary lives.

Outside of a few indulgences such as Tetiaroa, Brando's daily life was quite unremarkable. In fact, despite occasional headlines written about him for some public spat or activist appearance, his was a rather mundane existence. While he had achieved fame, fortune, and power at a level that all but a few can only dream about, his normal daily life seemed exceedingly dull.

When staying in Beverly Hills, in a typical day, he might spend most of his time secluded in his bedroom just whiling away the time. He would have his meals brought in to him by the cook. Once in a great while, he would phone a friend from earlier days, such as character actor Sam Gilman or makeup man Philip Rhodes, and invite him to stop by and visit. Brando seemed to like to see Gilman or Rhodes for relaxing, rather than issue oriented, conversations. Their chatting was filled with discussion of what their various acquaintances from earlier times in the movie industry were now doing. When around the house, I would often come into Brando's bedroom to join in. Once in a while, Marlon would slip into character from one of his movies, speaking for a while with the raspy voice of the Godfather or perhaps the Japanese accent of

Sakini, from TEAHOUSE OF THE AUGUST MOON. It was marvelous fun to sit in the darkened room listening to show business talk with the master actor. The conversations were usually over coffee, occasionally over a sandwich and a beer, and only infrequently with stronger alcohol.

This was at a time before the VCR made movies easily available to the public for home viewing. Brando did have a movie projector and screen in Alice's office and he had access to movies from the studios, but the dusty projector never left its cabinet.

On infrequent occasions, he would have a business meeting at home with his attorneys or sit in on a meeting with someone I brought over in regard to the Tetiaroa development. Sometimes, he would meet with a producer or writer in regard to his plans to produce one of the Indian movies that he has talked about making for the past twenty years. His then current project idea was to make a movie based on the book, BURY MY HEART AT WOUNDED KNEE.

At one time, producer John Foreman called to postpone such a meeting because he could not find a copy of the book anywhere in town and therefore had not been able to read it. It turned out that Brando had previously had Alice phone all the local bookstores and buy the few copies they had in stock. A copy was sent by messenger to Foreman and the meeting held the next week.

Such meetings might be the only thing to bring him out of his bedroom in a day, other than evening forays into the kitchen for food, after the daytime help had gone home.

Occasionally Jill Banner, his companion in Tucson, would interrupt these periods of solitude and spend a day or two at the house with him. Jill was a small town Iowa woman with long brown hair and a shy smile who, in her late twenties but seeming younger, was half Brando's age. She had appeared in seven forgettable movies from 1966 through 1968, the only slightly familiar one being THE PRESIDENT'S ANALYST, which starred James Coburn. She'd had a featured role in a low budget film titled SPIDER BABY.

When Jill was at the house, she and Brando would seldom emerge from his bedroom/den, spending the day clad in kimonos, he with the bulk approaching that of a sumo wrestler and she, reed thin and girlish, looking more like a playmate for fourteen-year-old Christian than a companion to his father.

On occasion, when Brando would become involved in a phone call, Jill would come out for a cup of tea and conversation. Her movie career seemed to have ended abruptly when she became involved with Brando and she never expressed any interest in rekindling it. She seemed to have little ambition and was dependent on Brando for financial support.

Jill was sweet and pleasant, but did not provide intellectual stimulation for Brando for her conversation range was limited to the events of daily living, such as picking up laundry, having lunch, and so on. She seemed content with her position in his life. She would appear when he called and leave the next day. On occasion, they would travel together, but only for trips of short duration. She expressed a desire to see Tetiaroa, but said that Marlon had told her he would never take her there because, "Tarita would be jealous." She did not seem to realize that he often brought other women there without Tarita raising any objection.

Some other biographers and profile writers have depicted Brando as a voracious reader with a broad range of interests encompassing history, philosophy, politics, sociology, and science. Often, he has been heard to profess his deep and abiding passion for reading and study. He is indeed a man of wide and varied interests. Yet he brings little discipline to those interests. His reading was at best sporadic. There were many shelves of books in the den. But they represented some twenty years of accumulation and the collection had not grown much recently.

Although he claimed to never read fiction, the shelves were liberally sprinkled with novels. A few books bore inscriptions indicating they had been gifts. Since he never set foot in a library or even went into a bookstore to my knowledge, he followed little pattern of study, but seemed to find his reading matter haphazardly. He would on occasion have Alice order a book that he had read about in the newspaper. The one topic which was a continuing interest was the treatment of the native American.

At one point, Brando expressed an interest in the books I had written, college texts on production management. I gave him a copy of one of them. It is unlikely he looked at it; if he did, he never mentioned it.

While there were frequent phone calls from producers and directors wanting him for movie roles, Brando never would speak to them and asked me to tell them not to send scripts.

Although he recently claimed on a television interview to have spent much of his last twenty years writing, he did no writing then and nothing of his has ever been published.

On his solitary days in his bedroom, he would often seem to just putter the day away. When in Beverly Hills, much of my time would be spent in meetings or running around dealing with bankers, accountants, or others involving Tetiaroa development problems. Typically several hours a day would find me working on the phone at the Brando home. I had no other office. When entering Marlon's bedroom to discuss something with him, I was likely to find him watching television, tinkering with some little project such as figuring out how to rearrange his bedroom, reading, or just lying on the bed staring contemplatively at the ceiling, a reclining Buddha-like figure in his Japanese kimono. He would stay up late into the evening and sleep late into the day.

My travel schedule usually found me either on an airplane or in the South Pacific on weekends. However, one weekend I was staying in Brando's Beverly Hills home. On Saturday afternoon, Marlon and I were chatting in his bedroom. He was in a particularly advanced state of passivity. Christian was staying overnight with a friend. Jill had been with him earlier that week and he was not in a mood to see her again so soon. Brando could find nothing to occupy him.

"How would you like to go out for dinner tonight?" I asked.

"No, I hate to go out to restaurants." Brando had a meat and potatoes appetite, with few strong food preferences. Occasionally, he would have Alice order oriental food to be delivered from Trader Vic's Restaurant.

"Well, the Dodgers are playing in town," I said. "Why don't we take in the game? We can grab a hot dog out there."

"You mean to a baseball game? No, I'd never go to a baseball game. I don't have any interest in sports."

"How about taking a ride down to the LA Art Museum? I've always wanted to see it."

"What for?"

"Well, I thought maybe to look at the art. Okay, if you don't want to do that, let's at least go to a movie or a play or just do something."

"No, there isn't anything worth seeing." Brando never went to the movies or plays.

"Well, I've got an idea. Let's drive over to Vegas. We can see a show, enjoy a good meal, and do a little drinking and gambling."

"No, I don't know anything about gambling. It's boring."

"Well, maybe I can teach you, Marlon. I like to think I'm kind of an expert on blackjack. When you learn the proper strategy and keep track of the cards that have been played, you can actually win most of the time. When you approach the game that way, it's not boring at all, it's very challenging. And, it's not that hard to learn. We could practice with a deck of cards here for a couple of hours and then run over to Vegas."

I told a few stories about my small-time gambling excursions. When Brando seemed interested, I again proposed going to Las Vegas.

"No, I hate that town."

"Well, let's at least go out for a walk or a swim in the pool and get some fresh air."

All that suggestion got was a long sigh as Marlon settled in to spend the remainder of the weekend studying the cracks in his bedroom ceiling and I retreated to the living room to bang on the piano.

After twenty minutes of my loud discordant hammering failed to drive him from his bed, I telephoned a college professor friend from UCLA, who invited me over to visit with himself and his wife for the evening.

The next day Brando asked, "Where did you go last night, Roger? I looked for you."

"I just went over to visit an old friend."

Marlon had only one question. It was brief and to the point, "With tits or without?"

He was disappointed to hear it had been a male friend.

Brando was the master couch potato, before the term was even coined. He displayed one of the classic symptoms of ACOAs, which is the inability to play or to just have fun.

Brando was getting no exercise at all and his physical condition showed it. At about two hundred and thirty pounds on his 5'9" frame, he was at least 60 pounds overweight. A set of barbells lay on his bedroom floor, an unused artifact from his youth.

Although a service kept his pool glistening with a sparkling clarity, Brando never used it. Neither did Christian. It might have been a refreshing pickup for me at the end of a long day of meetings and LA traffic. However, whenever I swam, Brando's German shepherd would run outside and dash excitedly from one side of the pool to the other - yelping, salivating, and running toward the edge of the pool threatening to dive on top of me at any moment. The dog would soon drive me from the pool more harried than relaxed.

When staying at the house, I would often go for a run. Brando was in no shape to begin jogging, but I would try to convince him of the benefit of long walks and volunteered to go along. While he enjoyed discussing the benefits of walking and running and admitted that he should be exercising, he could not be convinced to actually do it.

The narrow and winding Mulholland Drive was a hazardous place to run. Early one evening, I had returned from a run on Mulholland and was walking up the driveway to cool down. A woman puttering in the yard of the house next to Brando's stopped me and began a conversation about running. She had been at Brando's several times visiting with Alice and Blanche, the cook. She seemed to look familiar from somewhere else, too. She said her name was Helena and asked where I had been running. When I told her, she said it would be much safer on nearby Franklin Canyon Road where she said, "Jack always runs."

She described it as a scenic winding dirt road less than a mile away. Helena said, "There is almost no traffic and no one ever bothers Jack when he runs."

Our conversation led me to believe that Helena was a housewife with a husband named Jack.

After chatting a while, I continued back to Brando's house. Upon thinking about our talk, it appeared that Helena had spoken as though she had assumed that I already knew Jack. After showering and dressing, I went back to the house next door, to get the directions to the canyon road and to meet Jack. Helena invited me in, but said "Jack's not home."

We visited for a while and, in the course of the conversation, she mentioned Jack again. "Do you expect Jack home soon?" I asked.

"No, Jack's in Egypt - with Anjelica. You know Jack, he's always going somewhere," she replied.

"Well, actually, no, I don't know Jack. That's why I came over, to meet him and see if we might go running together sometime. You talk as though I should know Jack. Jack isn't your husband, is he? Who is Jack, anyway?"

"Jack Nicholson," she replied.

Although having lived next door on and off for three months, I'd had no idea that there was another actor living immediately adjacent. Brando, who displayed little interest in anything happening in the movie industry, never mentioned it.

Helena showed me around the house. It had hardwood floors with area rugs. A black grand piano was the central feature of the living room and the one concession to luxury in the home. It was an even more modest home than Brando's, indeed, smaller and less plush than the homes of most of my former university colleagues. Now, all my illusions about the glamorous homes of the movie stars were destroyed. Even more convincing that this was not the "lifestyles of the rich and famous" was Helena pointing out Jack's only automobile, a several year old, dust-covered Volkswagen bug.

Helena described herself as a performing belly dancer and dance instructor. She had been living in Nicholson's home for several years. She said that she was not romantically involved with Nicholson, but rather managed the household. It was strange to hear that, although Nicholson and Brando had been next door neighbors for years, neither had ever set foot in the other's home.

Later, I discovered the reason she had looked familiar. Though she did not mention it, Helena Kallioniotes was also an actress and had been acclaimed for her role with Nicholson in FIVE EASY PIECES and as second lead and Raquel Welch's chief antagonist in KANSAS CITY BOMBER. (Subsequently, Nicholson bought the third home on the driveway and Kallioniotes resides in it and continues to manage Nicholson's household.)

A couple of weeks later, Marlon talked Helena into taking Christian's pet raccoon to Nicholson's house to care for it. It tore up everything in her room that night and she brought it back the next morning. Brando found it all rather amusing, which upset Helena.

I used the information that Nicholson ran regularly to supplement my efforts to coax Brando into exercising. He did not respond to the name Nicholson, seeming almost to deny his existence next door. My new information did not help. Brando still preferred talking about exercise to doing it.

One of Brando's most frequent pastimes on his days at home was to talk on the telephone. I would always check the light on the phone system before going into his bedroom to talk to him. There were many days when it would be a couple of hours before the light would be off for more than a few minutes.

The house telephone system had two lines. One was normally answered by Alice when she was there and would be put on an answering machine when she was not. This was regarded as the "business" phone. The second line was regarded as Brando's private line and he would usually answer it himself. If he was not in the mood to talk, Alice or I would answer it, depending on who was home.

He frequently had the number on his private line changed. This was not because it would get out to the public. No stranger ever seemed to ring on this line. Rather, it was because he would tire of talking to some of the people to whom he had given his private number. He could be as fickle as a pubescent teenager in his friendships. Brando would meet someone, either male or female, and strike up an almost immediate friendship. It might be someone with expertise in a particular field or it could be a lost soul type who was just sort of struggling to find a place in life and evoked a sympathetic reaction in Brando. Brando would befriend them and pursue them. Then, just as quickly his interest could vanish.

Typically, the other person's ardor for the friendship would continue. The intoxication to the typical noncelebrity to find someone of Brando's celebrated status taking an almost passionate interest in him or her can be very strong. I know; I felt that mesmerizing charm. The sudden termination of that interest can leave feelings of rejection akin to being spurned by a lover.

Although Brando's interest would cease, his way of handling the situation was to avoid the person, not to ask him or her to stop calling. His preferred solution was to change his telephone number. If the party then phoned on the business line, Alice would always indicate Brando was busy or out, and the calls would never be returned.

One such lost soul became a nuisance that could not be cured by merely changing a telephone number. There was a young man in his early twenties, whom I shall call Billy, who would drop by the house at any time, day or night. One day he talked to Alice for hours. Overheard portions of their conversation seemed to be of a very disjointed nature.

Next, he arrived at the house early one evening when Brando and Christian were in their rooms. I came from the guest room/den and answered the door. Billy came in without being invited as though he were used to being there.

He then began to engage me in conversation. His behavior was quiet but his discourse was startling in its rambling, unconnected range and in the degree of paranoia that it exhibited. There was a misplaced word here, a jumbled thought there, and the pairing of topics that bore no logical relation to one another. From the beginning of a sentence to its end would cross such a variety of topics that I could not intelligently respond to his remarks. His behavior seemed that of a deeply disconnected person in need of medical treatment. Next door neighbor Jack Nicholson's institutionalized companions in ONE FLEW OVER THE CUCKOO'S NEST were, by comparison, more coherent. After going on for a while, he finally asked me to tell Brando that he was there.

I went into Brando's room and told him that Billy was there to see him. He asked if Billy knew that he was home. When I told him that he did, Brando came out to the living room. Billy came from the den and the two spent some time conversing in the living room, out of my hearing.

After Billy had left, Brando came into the den and said to tell Billy that he was not in if he ever came around again. I promised to turn him away next time and told Brando my impression of Billy's strangeness. Brando explained that Billy's scrambled mind was a tragic result of his drug use as a teenager. Billy's mother had once worked for Brando, which was the reason Billy would now return to the house.

Brando then asked me to not turn Billy away if he came back; to let him in but just tell him that Brando was not home. He said that Billy would talk for a while and then leave. At the time, I thought little of it and agreed.

A few evenings later, Billy returned again. I immediately told him that Brando was not home (even though he was) and was not expected back. Uninvited, Billy simply made his way in. He followed me to the den and again embarked on a paranoiac discourse encompassing politicians, doctors, local officials, and unnamed mysterious strangers. Under the pretense of using the bathroom, I sneaked into Brando's room to warn him that Billy was there. Billy seemed to barely notice my absence. Our strange conversation dragged on for a couple of hours to my discomfort. His remarks were so far out in left field and he was so inattentive to my responses that there seemed no way to communicate with him. Finally he left.

It happened again, this time on an evening when Brando was planning to go out. I again warned Brando of Billy's presence and volunteered to just tell Billy to leave so Brando himself could leave. Brando again told me to just let him stay and talk. He talked on and on. By the time he left, it was late and Brando never did go out as he had planned.

Brando preferred to hide in his room rather confront the hapless young man and hurt his feelings, yet was unwilling to permit me to turn him away. He wanted me to sit through a thoroughly uncomfortable situation with a stranger, while he himself was unwilling to show an interest in Billy.

Billy came around frequently. He may still be coming there and Brando may still be hiding in his bedroom.

There were few entertainment programs Brando cared for on television and he did not watch it often. However, one presentation which totally absorbed his interest was the Watergate hearings. Since the hearings were held three time zones away in Washington, D.C., it was still early morning in California when the hearings began. Although Brando was often still sleeping when they began, he watched all parts of the hearings that took place during his awake hours.

One afternoon, while he was watching the Watergate hearings on television, the responses of the person being questioned by the committee were not transmitting clearly. After straining to hear the remarks for a few minutes, Brando picked up the telephone and called information to get the phone number of the network headquarters in New York. He then placed a call, identified himself as Marlon Brando, and asked for the president of the network. Within seconds, the network president was on the phone. Brando explained that he was listening to the hearings and could not hear the witness clearly; he asked if they could do something about it. The network president promised he would look into it.

In less than a minute, there was a hand on the screen reaching up from below and in front of the table, pushing the microphone closer to the witness.

Since Brando hated Nixon, he took a vindictive pleasure in watching the dirty work of layer after layer of his administration being revealed on television.

Brando's distrust of and distaste for politicians was unhindered by party lines. He liked to tell the story of an encounter at the White House when Jack Kennedy was President. Brando had been invited to a state dinner. After the dinner, an aide to the president requested that he stay because President Kennedy wished to speak to him. According to Brando's account, after a long wait, he was later ushered into the presidential living quarters where he found Kennedy in an intoxicated state. Kennedy then told Brando that he was a troublemaker who they were keeping their eye on and warned him to cease his inflammatory public remarks in support of the civil rights movement - that he was doing more harm than good. Brando said Kennedy slurred and stumbled over his words and appeared too drunk to stand up.

Brando kept anything he had said in reply to himself. Because of Kennedy's remarks to him, Brando had formed the opinion that Kennedy was really not very serious in his civil rights efforts, that all his actions and his words were typical insincere political posturing, done for personal, political gain.

Brando also said that the government was monitoring his phone calls and had been periodically for years. He would warn me to be careful of what I said on the phone. It seemed to be a statement exhibiting paranoia. Yet, years later, columnist Jack Anderson disclosed that the FBI had been tapping Brando's phone.

Another use Brando had of the telephone was to order products. He would not go anywhere to shop, so when he did want to purchase something, he would either have Alice buy it or would get on the telephone and order it himself. The electronic battery operated calculator was then still quite new. It was an expensive item and I had not yet purchased one. A simple model which might sell for $5.95 today, cost over a hundred dollars then. One day Brando asked if my work might be easier with a calculator. I admitted that it would. He said he would have Alice buy one for me.

A week or so later, he gave me a new calculator. He had two, one to keep in Beverly Hills and one to take to Tetiaroa. They cost $129.95 each. I assumed that Alice had purchased them.

Several years later, I was reading a book written by Joseph Sugarman. The book told the story of his success in building his large mail order firm, JS&A Associates, which is heavily advertised today in upscale magazines. Sugarman told how he was trying to impress a couple of business associates in his office one day and had his secretary page him with a fake phone call from Frank Sinatra. He then carried on a onesided conversation with an imaginary Sinatra on the empty line in front of his amazed audience.

The punch line of Sugarman's story was that while he had staged the phony Sinatra conversation one day, the very next day he had gotten a real phone call from Brando in which Brando ordered two calculators.

My calculator is by now quite antiquated and sitting unused in a drawer. However, since it is the subject of a chapter in an interesting book and one of the last physical mementos from my sojourn on Tetiaroa, I have decided to hang on to it.

CHAPTER FOURTEEN

BRANDO ON DRUMS
AND
IN PURSUIT OF THE PERFECT WAVE

With Brando's financial position, in his own words, "ready to receive the last rites," George Pakkala and Norton Brown of Brown Kraft kept suggesting that he take advantage of the unprecedented level of demand for his services as an actor created by the successes of GODFATHER and LAST TANGO and take another movie role in order to refill the coffer. I too pointed out the need for income if he wanted to complete development on Tetiaroa - to say nothing of paying my salary, which was now several months in arrears.

He was not interested. He simply did not want to act. Any passion he might once have had for his profession had faded to almost complete disinterest. Even though he remained in poor financial condition, offers of three to four million dollars still did not whet his appetite.

However, in response to his financial problems, Brando came up with a novel idea one day. Instead of making a movie, he would cut a record. He informed me that he had once been very good on the drums and that, with a little practice, he would regain his once formidable skills.

There was that large set of drums gathering dust on a platform at one end of his bedroom.

The first time Brando mentioned this, I was dumbfounded at this incongruous and audacious remedy for his financial woes. The idea was so bizarre that I could think of no response.

When the subject of his taking an acting job came up again a few days later, he said, "I just don't have any interest in acting. I'm not going to be forced to slave in that ridiculous posture of standing in front of a camera mouthing somebody else's idiotic words. Anyway, I'm still planning on making that drum record."

"Drum record? I can't imagine a drum record bringing in any money," I replied, "certainly not enough to pay your taxes or finish Tetiaroa. Norton tells me you can easily make three million dollars for a few weeks work on a movie."

Brando had been lying on his bed, hands behind his head. I waited for a response, but he remained silent.

"Has any drum record ever made even a hundred thousand dollars? I sure haven't seen any crowds in the Gene Krupa section lately."

"You've got to understand, Roger, it's not the record itself that will attract people," Brando explained. "It's the fact that I'm playing the drums. I think it could outsell any drum record ever made."

"Well, Marlon, there might be some interest if you were singing. Some people might buy it just for curiosity. But, if you're playing the drums, who cares? Half the people wouldn't even believe you're playing, anyway. Frankly, I've never even heard of a record that's just drum playing. Drums go with a band. Are you planning to put a band together for this record?"

"No, I'm just going to play a drum solo. There's a lot of money to be made in records today. Somebody like Elton John makes ten times the money I do. I don't see any reason why it shouldn't make a million dollars. All I have to do is practice a little and I'll be ready to do it."

"Marlon, while you are practicing on the drums, I think I'll get busy and practice tap dancing. Let me know when you're ready to record. You can play the drums and I'll dance."

He gave a half smile to show that he understood the joke, but did not think it particularly funny, and silently stared at the ceiling. I left him to his mental composition of THE BRANDO CONCERTO FOR DRUMS AND FEET.

Brando's reference to Elton John was an oblique response to a jibe from his son Christian a day earlier. There had been an item in the LOS ANGELES TIMES reporting that John had given a new Rolls Royce to his business manager. Christian, like a typical fifteen year old, would have liked an upgrading in the quality of automobiles around the house. He had asked, "Dad, why don't you buy a Rolls Royce for Roger?"

That question had demonstrated that son Christian could get the Brando silence just like anyone else.

Over the next couple of months, Brando referred again and again to his upcoming record.

I never did hear sound one from the drums in his bedroom. That's too bad, I was getting my Bojangles Robinson act down pat.

However, shortly afterward, a more practical money making idea emerged. I happened to meet author and producer Don Widener. A documentary he produced had received an Emmy Award the previous year. Widener was a close friend of Jack Lemmon and was then writing a biography which was later published under the simple title, LEMMON.

As we conversed over a cup of coffee, Widener tossed out the idea of making a travel documentary on Tetiaroa and the South Pacific with Brando narrating. We discussed the concept and I later mentioned it to Brando. He warmed to the idea and quickly came up with several intriguing ideas for scenes and concepts for narration.

I was uncertain of the potential profitability of such a film and suggested that Widener investigate the market. Within a few weeks, he put together an impressive package. He proposed a sixty minute documentary on the South Pacific to be shown on network television. General Cigar Corporation was interested in paying production costs of $500,000 for the right to sponsor the first showing and $125,000 for a second showing. Further investigation had suggested a market in theaters outside the United States for an expanded ninety minute version.

RCA was ready to start marketing their first home videotape system in December of 1973, some six months off, and had no programming to sell with it. RCA would put up $350,000 to cover production costs to produce ten to twelve half hour cassettes from the South Pacific material. RCA would also pay royalties on sale of the cassettes, which they forecast would sell for several years.

Widener proposed that he produce the multifaceted project. Brando would receive a $150,000 fee for an expected eight to twelve days on background shots and narration. He would also receive half the profits from the venture.

This was a venture worth considering. It provided some ready cash; the $150,000 was to be paid up front. It provided tremendous publicity for Tetiaroa. It allowed us to get in on the ground floor in the video tape industry, which promised to be a burgeoning market. It would also provide the basis for negotiating rebates from and promotional agreements with the airlines and travel industry - which was something I was working on.

Also, it was not the "acting" which Brando so detested. In fact, the argument that appealed the most to him was that the cassettes could be used in teaching geography and history in grade schools. Brando was enthusiastic about the project and told Widener he was committed.

Widener was familiar with Brando's reputation for delay and for failing to see projects through, so he wanted a letter formalizing his intention and approval, subject to working out a final agreement. He could then firm up the arrangements with General Cigar and RCA. Their interest was dependent on Brando's participation. Widener had not brought such a letter to the meeting, so nothing was signed that day. Brando told him to drop by anytime and he would sign it.

Widener went back to work on the project. I went back to Tetiaroa to supervise construction of the tourist facility. Upon returning to Los Angeles a few weeks later, I found that Brando had not signed the letter of intent. The day after our previous meeting, Widener had stopped by and left the letter with Alice Marchak for Brando to sign. Alice, who liked Widener and approved of the project, had given it to Brando and repeatedly asked him to sign it.

Widener and I met. He was making progress on organizing the project, but was very concerned about Brando's failure to sign. He could not get the sponsors to sign contracts without it. Time was crucial since he wanted to get film covering Bastille Day, which was the big national holiday celebration in French-governed Tahiti. July 14th was drawing near, and to miss it now would mean delaying another year. Each conversation with Widener was filled with his lamentations he could not rely on Brando's word the way he could on Lemmon's.

I brought the letter to Brando's attention and suggested he sign it immediately, so Widener would not be further delayed. He would not sign.

He made several excuses which did not hold water. After hemming and hawing on his reluctance through a long conversation, he finally said that he had viewed one of Widener's films and thought that the sound quality was poor. He did not want to be associated with a second rate production.

Widener had earlier explained the extra precautions he would be taking in handling the film because of the temperature and moisture in Tahiti. That and other details in his planning, as well as several awards he had received, led me to believe that he would do a first rate job. I suggested having Widener bring over several of his productions so Brando could evaluate them.

Brando would not respond to this idea. Instead he went into an explanation of the wave action on the reef at Tetiaroa. He said, "Each wave is unique. You can sit there in a boat all day long watching the waves and each one is different. No two break alike. You might have to have your camera shoot waves for a month before you came up with a shot of the perfect wave. Maybe this will be only a ten second sequence in the film, but it has to be just right or it will ruin the whole production. You just can't use an ordinary wave."

Throughout his explanation, his eyes were evasive, as though he was visualizing a scene in his mind. He went on, "And even if you see the perfect wave, your camera angle might not be right and you have to start all over."

"I don't believe that Widener can appreciate that feeling. He wouldn't wait a month to find the perfect wave."

(Brando absolutely loves waves. Producer Frank Rosenberg had described how, in Brando's only movie directing effort, the hugely over budget ONE-EYED JACKS, he would sit with a cameraman for hours on a rock, "waiting for the right wave." Returning sunburned and cold with useless film, he would lament that he never could find the perfect wave.)

"Well, Marlon," I said, "Don has told me again and again that he wants your participation in planning the film and welcomes all your suggestions. He's willing to shoot whatever you want. And, if you think the quality of any of it is not up to your standards, he said he'll re-shoot it until you are satisfied."

"Besides, if you think there is a perfect wave on there and Don can't find it, you can take a cameraman and sit at the reef and film waves all day long."

"No, that's about the last thing I want to do," he replied. "If I wanted to do that, why would I need Widener? If I get a dog, I'm not going to bark myself."

"Besides," he added, "Christian Marquand said he's interested in producing the documentary."

"Maybe he is interested," I said. "What out of work producer wouldn't be? Particularly after Widener has put the entire concept together and lined up all the money and with you providing the main attraction for the whole project."

"So what if he is interested? You already committed to Widener on the project and, because of that, he's spent several weeks working on it. How can you take his work and just hand it to someone else? Besides, what makes you think that Marquand can do any better? You don't want to be an another disaster like CANDY, do you? What does he know about the South Pacific?"

"Yeah," said Brando, "maybe Marquand wouldn't be such a good choice."

"Well, good. How about signing this commitment letter then, so Don can get on with it?" I asked.

"No, I'm not ready to do that. Maybe I'll produce it myself."

Oh, Oh, good-bye Widener, I thought.

Brando never did sign the letter. The project died.

CHAPTER FIFTEEN

PROMOTING TETIAROA: AIRLINES, FILMS AND TOURS

The public has long been enamored with actors; they top the celebrity list. Madison Avenue recognizes this love affair. Advertisers are willing to pay huge amounts for product endorsement and promotion from the top movie stars.

Multimillion dollar fees are not unknown. Few can resist the blandishments and emoluments. Sir Lawrence Olivier hawked Kodak cameras. George C. Scott dramatized the merits of the Renault automobile.

Brando would rather starve.

He has never endorsed a product. He never will. He regards the sycophantic fawning of the public over actors as the pinnacle of absurdity. That's mild compared to his contemptuous regard for corporate America and the advertising profession. At the merest mention of an offer for his endorsement, Brando would spew forth a vitriolic discourse on the evil and selfish intents of the leaders of the large corporations. Though spoken softly, there was a deeply felt passion in his words. Inevitably coming in for the most vehemently focused disapproval were two or three particular movie industry executives with whom he had crossed swords in the past.

Yet, somehow he wanted to sample the fruit of the corporate tree. He just did not want to have to do anything to earn it. It is as though his stardom was of such magnitude that even a remote and indirect association with his name should be sufficient to shake loose a flow of money, products, and services for his benefit.

That was one of my assignments, to obtain the corporate largess in promoting Tetiaroa tourism, but to yield only a tantalizingly ephemeral brush with Marlon Brando's shadow. It was a Herculean task, but I plunged ahead. Although I was to meet with more rejection than a life insurance salesman, there were a couple of offers that were surprising in their generosity. One, in fact, was so liberal in its terms that it was in violation of government regulations.

There were three groups that I approached - product suppliers, travel agents, and airlines. Although Brando would not sign the Widener commitment letter, neither would he cut off the project completely. So, the South Pacific travel documentary remained in a planning stage over a period of several months. At Brando's request, I made proposals to the major manufacturers of heavy construction equipment - Caterpillar, International Harvester, Case, Ford. We would show their equipment in use on Tetiaroa on the documentary in exchange for their providing the equipment without charge. This is commonplace in movies and television today. For example, Philip Morris Corporation paid $350,000 to have James Bond ostentatiously smoke LARKS in LICENSE TO KILL and twelve different products were plugged for a fee in MURPHY'S ROMANCE. However, such arrangements were infrequent in 1973.

All the manufacturers declined to participate, none even showing any interest in negotiating or investigating our plans. Brando could not believe they would be uninterested. Still, this endeavor got nowhere.

The major travel company promoting tours to French Polynesia was *Ted Cook's Islands in the Sun,* located in Newport Beach, California. Cook put together package tours to Tahiti, Moorea, Bora Bora, and the other islands, which were in turn sold by travel agencies to individuals throughout North America. Cook was a former engineer who had once taken a vacation to Tahiti and became enchanted with it. He returned frequently to travel among the islands. Eventually, he gave up his job, sold his house to provide capital for establishing a travel business, and moved into his sailboat at the Newport Beach marina for living quarters.

I met Cook in Tahiti. He immediately recognized the value of an association with Tetiaroa. He felt that the inclusion of *Marlon Brando's Tetiaroa* in his advertising would not only produce a substantial increase in tour sales, but would also enhance his reputation within the travel industry. It could provide a springboard to establishing *Islands in the Sun* as purveyor of tours on a much larger and broader scale throughout the South Pacific and Far East.

Cook and I quickly worked out prospective terms for an agreement. We established the daily charge rates that Tetiaroa would include on the package tours. They were similar to those charged by other area resorts. The unique part of our agreement was that Tetiaroa would receive a commission (pronounced *kickback*) of thirty dollars per person on all the *Islands in the Sun* tours that included Tetiaroa, in addition to the normal per diem charges. It was an arrangement that other tour operators would have envied and available only because of the magic of the Brando name.

During my next time in Los Angeles, Cook came to Brando's house and we went over the proposal with Marlon. To make an agreement with Brando often seemed to depend more on his liking someone than on the terms of the agreement. Cook was a quiet, selfeffacing person who seemed a bit bewildered at the process of dealing with Brando. He met with Brando's approval. During the meeting, Brando imposed even more restrictions on Cook than I had. He would not allow his photograph to be used in any advertising and he would not endorse *Islands in the Sun* or any of the other resorts on the tours. He made it quite clear that the extent of his participation would be that *Marlon Brando's Tetiaroa* could be used in typeface no larger than that used in advertising the other resorts. Although this was less than Cook wanted, he accepted the limitation.

Brando had given up nothing. He was getting a lot. *Islands in the Sun* would provide a steady stream of customers at normal prices. The agreement would also provide a nice supplemental income to Tetiaroa via the kickbacks. He was happy with the arrangement. It would have been preferable if Brando had allowed a broader use of his name in promotion, but given his self-imposed limitation, the benefits Tetiaroa would receive were substantial.

Cook returned to *Islands in the Sun* to revamp his tours and develop his advertising.

The third group I approached was the airlines. There were three airlines providing service to Tahiti from the United States - Pan American World Airways, Air New Zealand, and UTA French Airlines. Before my arrival on the scene, Bernard Judge had initiated discussions with UTA. At Brando's suggestion he had asked UTA for a kickback for every passenger who flew between Los Angeles and Papeete and also came to Tetiaroa. Specifically, he requested that UTA pay Brando fifteen dollars for each passenger who took UTA on one leg of the LA - Papeete flight and thirty dollars for each one who flew round trip.

All Brando offered to do was provide some vague undefined promotion of Tahiti and Tetiaroa, not specifically of UTA. The whole transaction was unusual since first, it was in violation of the rules of International Airlines Transport Agency (IATA), the regulating body governing international airlines, and second, UTA would receive no direct benefit. Yet, UTA was interested.

However, Brando was not satisfied with the above proposal for UTA. He had a long time acquaintance with Walter Elsaesser, a vice-president of Pan American World Airways, and suggested that I meet with him to try to get a better deal. When we met, Elsaesser was cordial, but stated that Pan Am would have no interest in any arrangement with Brando or Tetiaroa other than mutual promotion on package tours such as they would undertake with any other resort.

Brando found this difficult to accept. He repeatedly urged me to pursue Pan Am further. I discussed it with others in marketing at Pan Am, always with the same results. Eventually Brando suggested he would be willing to promote the South Pacific through the aforementioned Widener travel documentary which he would allow Pan Am to show without charge on their transPacific flights. Pan Am still showed no interest.

Air New Zealand similarly was not interested in any special connection with Brando or Tetiaroa.

Brando continued in his dissatisfaction with the UTA offer and urged me to demand more. I met occasionally with Didier Fornier, the UTA marketing representative in Los Angeles. Despite Brando's exhortations, I was trying to finalize an agreement on the previous proposal, not to increase the already generous terms. Because of its transgression of the IATA rules, Fornier was reluctant to put even that arrangement down on paper. He also wanted a more specific commitment from Brando on promotion before he would agree to any specific dollar amounts.

Finally one day, Fornier mentioned that Mr. Massot, the President of UTA, would be in Los Angeles from Paris and would like to meet with Brando to finalize the agreement. Brando agreed to go to lunch with Massot, whom he had previously known.

I looked forward to this. I wanted to see how Brando was going to ask for more money.

The UTA office was on Airport Boulevard, near LAX. I drove, continuing my resolve never to ride with Brando behind the wheel. This was the only instance during my time with Brando that he ever left his house for a meeting, so he evidently regarded it as important.

While walking to the UTA offices after parking the car, we passed the Tishman Building, which had its title prominently displayed. Brando could not believe the "monumental arrogance and colossal ego" which would cause anyone to put his name on a building.

Brando's appearance in the UTA office brought a flurry of activity among the secretarial staff, all ignored by Marlon himself. Massot, however, did introduce Jean Marie Sauvage, the head of UTA in the United States, and both of their wives. We walked to a nearby restaurant. It soon became clear that the purpose of the meeting was not really business, but rather a chance for the wives to have lunch with Marlon Brando.

We went in a UTA limousine to a nearby French restaurant. It was after the normal lunch hour and there were only a few diners remaining.

Fornier apparently was not of sufficient rank within the company to join this august social occasion. I felt like I should have stayed home too, since ninety percent of the conversation was conducted in French. Brando had a passable facility with the language.

Brando charmed the ladies, as he always did when he was in the mood. It was a simple task. Normally, women might be entranced most by a man who paid close attention to their thoughts, words, and deeds. With Brando, women were captivated when he talked about his own thoughts, words, and deeds.

He talked about the beauty and serenity of Tetiaroa and described his intended participation in the South Pacific documentary and even mentioned that he planned to appear on occasional television talk shows during which he would spend a portion of the time promoting the Tahiti - South Pacific area. The UTA contribution to the business discussion was Massot's comment that we should develop a "mutually beneficial promotional arrangement" and Fornier and I could work out the details.

Brando made no mention of wanting more money.

As we lingered over a glass of wine after lunch, a man about Brando's age, another diner, approached the table with a menu which he asked Brando to sign "for my wife." Brando took it from him and signed it without making eye contact. In all of the times I was out with him in public, this was the only instance of anyone ever asking him for an autograph. This is a dramatic contrast to the way so many celebrities are besieged when out in the public. There seemed to be an intimidating quality to the Brando persona that kept the world at bay.

As our after lunch conversation dragged on, Massot, perhaps in compensation for somewhat deceptively having drawn Brando into a social occasion under the pretense of business, suggested that, "Perhaps, Marlon, you would like to have some of your friends or associates view what you are doing on Tetiaroa. I would be pleased to offer you ten complimentary round trip tickets on our airline to use as you see fit."

Brando muttered something about knowing several people who would like to see Tetiaroa.

This was a generous gift, since round trip tickets cost over five hundred dollars each, at that time. It was fortunate that Massot chose to use English for this portion of the conversation, or else we would have never received the tickets. A few minutes later, the luncheon ended and we bade adieu to our generous host. As we were returning to our automobile, I told Brando that I would follow up the next day with Fornier to make arrangements for the free tickets.

His response was, "What tickets?"

Even though his conversation with Massot had taken place only ten minutes before, Massot's offer had somehow completely escaped his comprehension. It took me several minutes to convince him that I had not been hallucinating. The following ten minutes were spent with Brando puzzling over Massot's surreptitious motivation, displaying the typical problem that ACOAs have in trusting and their tendency to constantly question the motives and behavior of everyone.

The free tickets helped the Brando travel budget over the next few weeks. Whatever Massot's motivation might have been, the gift did serve to make my job easier. After that meeting, Brando stopped telling me to demand more money from UTA.

After further negotiations with Fornier, we came to an agreement which provided that Brando would promote the South Pacific area through the production of the documentary, which would be shown on network television, and through occasional appearances on television talk shows. In turn, UTA would provide to Brando a fee of twenty dollars for each passenger who would fly between Tahiti and Los Angeles on UTA (either oneway or roundtrip) and also visit Tetiaroa. That was actually less than the amount that Brando was earlier requesting since most tourists who flew oneway on UTA would also take UTA for the return trip. However, that earlier figure had never been accepted by UTA.

Brando was happy with the agreement and fully recognized that he had agreed to promote the South Pacific.

UTA would not provide a signature on the agreement or allow it to be written on UTA stationery because of its violation of IATA regulations. It was to be a gentlemen's agreement, the precise terms of which were recorded on a letter from me to UTA.

With the *Islands in the Sun* and the UTA agreements, the prospect for success of the Tetiaroa operation seemed high.

Operators of most resorts might be happy with a net profit margin of ten to fifteen percent of sales revenue. Tetiaroa would be getting about thirty percent extra revenue from most of the customers, which would translate directly to thirty percent extra net profit. And if Brando actively promoted Tahiti and the South Pacific, the stream of customers promised to be large and continuous. The stage was set for a profitable business.

Chapter Sixteen

He Coulda Bin A Contenduh

Early in June, after Brando had been on Tetiaroa for two weeks, he told me that he was leaving for New York to appear on the Dick Cavett Show on ABC Television.

We talked about why he was appearing and what he would be discussing on the program. Brando's motivation for doing anything was seldom simple. There was an interplay of many forces, goals, and feelings that guided his behavior. This appearance was totally uncharacteristic. He had never before agreed to such an exposure, ninety minutes of concentrated questioning as the sole guest in front of a national television audience. There was something on his mind.

His stated motivation was simple. He said this would be a wonderful opportunity to bring his Indian cause before the public; the Academy Award ceremony message had not been sufficient. Reading between the lines, one could see that the residue of the negative response reported in the press and his subsequent failure to go to Wounded Knee weighed heavily on his mind.

This would provide him an opportunity to say to the critics, "See, Brando really is a humanitarian, vitally concerned with improving the lot of the Indian." He did, after all, have a monumental confidence that, put before a camera, he could portray any role convincingly.

Along with the positive motivations influencing any Brando action, one could often find an ulterior motive. In particular, a bit of revenge often lay hidden not far beneath the surface, kind of an "I'll show you" attitude. Anna Kashfi, in her book, revealed that he would flauntingly bring his girlfriends to their home during their short lived marriage.

In this case, Brando displayed a vindictive pleasure in relating how his appearance on Cavett would give him the opportunity to repay Johnny Carson for an alleged transgression that Carson had committed five years earlier.

During the urban black uprisings of the mid-sixties, Brando had been one of many show business personalities to voice support for the black community. In 1968, shortly after the assassination of Martin Luther King, Brando had appeared on the Carson show to talk about the racial crisis in the country. During the program, both Carson and Brando had made a financial commitment to the late Dr. King's Southern Christian Leadership Conference (SCLC).

A newspaper account of this appearance reported that Brando said he was pledging one percent of his income to the SCLC and that King's murder had shocked him into "trying to rectify the situation we are in. Nothing is really going to change unless I do it, unless the trombone player, the guy watching TV with a can of beer all do it."

Carson then said that he too would pledge one percent of his income.

Brando's memory of it was strangely different. He said that Carson had been the first to pledge the one percent and that he had been almost forced to follow with a pledge of his own. Brando said, "It was just a publicity stunt. If I didn't agree to kick in my one percent, Carson could just act so God damn morally superior. Besides that, the only reason he did it in the first place was find out how much money I was making."

Since Brando's money would certainly not pass through Carson's hands, his last statement seemed totally illogical.

Regardless of who got those particular pledges started, Brando certainly got into the pledging spirit. Two weeks later, he appeared in Albuquerque, New Mexico with Joan Baez and said he would dedicate the rest of his life to the civil rights movement. He increased his pledge from one percent to twelve percent. If Carson's one percent pledge had allowed him feelings of moral superiority, Brando's twelve percent pledge must have put him on the absolute top of the morality heap.

Such appearances and pledges present a dramatic picture of Brando, the humanitarian. As far as the SCLC was concerned, however, it made little difference whether Brando pledged one percent, twelve percent, or even fifty percent of his income. The SCLC could only hope that "the trombone player and the guy watching TV with a can of beer" would do as Brando said, not as he did. For, his actual financial support to SCLC, and to all other human rights and charitable organizations combined, was not twelve percent. It did not even approach one percent. In most years, such organizations failed to pry loose a tenth of one percent of the Brando income.

In 1973, Carson's TONIGHT SHOW and THE DICK CAVETT SHOW were frequently compared in the press and they competed for guests. Brando knew that his appearance would be regarded as a blockbuster attraction for Cavett. Oscar Wilde suggested, *"Revenge is a dish best served cold."* Five years after the original alleged transgression, Brando was striking a blow to Carson by appearing on the Cavett show and extracting his own sweet revenge.

Construction was still proceeding toward the opening of the Tetiaroa tourist operation. I was in the midst of trying to firm up the deal with UTA French Airlines, and so suggested that this would be a magnificent opportunity to generate interest in Tetiaroa and that he should plug the South Pacific vacation attractions, thereby demonstrating to UTA an example of his future promotional efforts.

Once again his ambiguous stance toward the use of the Brando persona for publicity emerged. He now demurred, suggesting that to publicize Tetiaroa would detract from his message about the rights of the American Indians.

I suggested that it need not be a blatant commercial, but certainly Cavett would inquire about what he had been doing and it would be entirely appropriate for him to mention that he had just returned from Tetiaroa and casually describe the serenity and natural beauty of his island, without necessarily even alluding to the development for tourism. He agreed that it would be appropriate to casually talk about the island, but I left our conversation feeling uneasy.

The New York trip proved eventful for Brando, not so much for the Cavett show as for a hassle he got into afterward.

Snaring the elusive Brando for a lengthy interview was in itself regarded as a significant coup for Cavett. This was demonstrated by the way that the press reviewed the program as they might the opening of a Broadway show or the premiere of a movie.

Cavett introduced Brando as "probably the best actor in America, maybe in the world." Brando appeared in a dark sweater, red ascot, casual slacks, and western denim jacket. The magic of his presence seemed as potent as ever. As he strode across the stage, the audience went into the kind of shrieks and squeals usually reserved for rock stars.

Brando's entrance was perhaps the high point of the otherwise listless ninety minute program. Cavett persistently needled Brando with gossipy questions about his movie roles and the acting profession. Brando, however, rebuffed such questions or at best provided terse answers and finally ruled out any discussion of his films. He preferred to grill Cavett for two segments of the program on the limitations of his show. When Cavett asked if he ever went to the movies, Brando replied, "Once in a while," and dropped the subject into the first of many awkward pauses filled with a lot of hollow smiles.

Despite Cavett's strategic advantage as emcee, Brando eventually gained the upper hand and doggedly kept returning to the topic on which he had come to speak words of wisdom, the American Indian. But the sparring rather soured the whole program, leading host and guest into increasing discomfiture and embarrassment. Speaking on the Academy Award incident, Brando said that although he was embarrassed for Sacheen Littlefeather because of the discourtesy of the audience which was actually directed toward him, he did not wish that he had done otherwise.

Yes, he had tried to go to Wounded Knee, but had abandoned his plans in Denver when a contact had been unable to meet him.

Upon hearing that, I wondered how he had managed to sneak out of the house, travel eight hundred miles, and return without any of the household staff having known that he had ever left. It was too bad that such a dedicated person could not have found his way to Wounded Knee without a guide.

Brando made no mention whatsoever of Tetiaroa or the South Pacific on the show.

Given the rather lackluster program, Brando may have been in a surly mood as the show ended. He and Cavett immediately left the studio and walked to Chinatown for dinner. They were followed by free-lance photographer, Ron Galella. The forty-two year old Galella made his living selling photographs of celebrities and had made the news when Jacqueline Kennedy Onassis had sued to obtain an injunction prohibiting him from taking photographs of her and her family.

Galella took pictures of Cavett and Brando, both wearing dark glasses, as they walked the two blocks to the restaurant.

According to Galella, he had taken eight pictures and then the following conversation took place. Galella said to Brando, "I'd like to have a couple with your glasses off."

Brando said, "Don't you have enough pictures?"

Galella said, "That's the type of variety I'd like."

Thereupon, without warning, Brando took a powerful right handed swing. The punch landed solidly in Galella's face.

Brando's version to me upon returning to Tetiaroa a week later was only slightly different. He claimed that, after Galella had walked in front of them for two blocks taking photographs, he stopped and told Galella, "I'll pose for one more shot. After that, I expect you to leave us alone because you've taken enough shots."

He said he posed and Galella snapped the shot and then made ready to take another. Brando added, "Since he didn't listen to my warning, I hit him."

This was not a little slap in the face. It was an absolutely vicious punch, one worthy of Terry Malone's best effort from ON THE WATERFRONT when he claimed, "Chahlie, I coulda bin a contenduh."

With a punch like that, Terry would have been the champion.

The only question was, who was injured worse, the assailant or the victim? Galella immediately went to Bellevue hospital where doctors used nine stitches to close a cut in his lower lip and braced a fractured lower jaw. He was treated and released.

Brando's right hand was also damaged. He managed to get through the evening without treatment. After the incident, he and Cavett left Chinatown and went instead to the Russian Tea Room for dinner. However, the following day Brando was admitted to the hospital for an "acute infection" of his right hand. He remained hospitalized for several days.

When he returned to Tetiaroa a week or so after the punch, his hand was still badly swollen. The teeth marks of his victim were still in evidence, having pierced the skin and made deep cuts into the knuckles of his first two fingers. To cause such a deep indentation, the punch had to have been impelled by a deep sense of anger and outrage and backed by the full force of his 230 pounds.

When Brando showed his hand to me, with an apparent sense of pride and amusement, it gave me such a cold chill to imagine the impact of that blow exploding in someone's face that I had to stop our conversation dead and walk away.

I later read the LOS ANGELES TIMES of the day following the Cavett program. The irony of two juxtaposing headlines must not have been noticed by the editor. The first said "Actor-Humanitarian Brando Visits Cavett." The story below was headed, "Brando Hits, Breaks Jaw of Photog."

A month later, Galella sued Brando for $250,000, alleging that Brando broke his jaw and damaged his face. The suit asked for $100,000 for medical expenses and personal suffering plus $150,000 in punitive damages.

Although he showed absolutely no remorse whatsoever for his action, Brando realized he could not go around hitting people, even if they were taking his photograph, because he asked attorney Steven Kroft to talk settlement to Galella's attorney.

Galella's attorney immediately proposed $75,000, which Kroft declined. The case was eventually settled out of court for $40,000, according to Alice Marchak.

CHAPTER SEVENTEEN

CON MEN IN CORPORATE CLOTHING

B y midsummer, although several outflows of cash had been cut off or reduced, Brando was still in bad shape financially. In Los Angeles, cars lined up at gas stations for blocks to fill their tanks in a suddenly oil scarce world. Cash was as scarce to Brando as gas to the last car in line.

George Pakkala had run out of reasonable cause for additional time extension and filed Brando's 1972 income taxes on June 13 without payment. Brando had previously left the United States for a one day trip just across the border to Mexico on April 15th so the IRS penalty for late filing could be avoided. We estimated that $250,000 was needed to pay taxes, Brando's living expenses, and complete construction of the tourist facility.

I had been working for three months and had not yet received a single day's salary.

Although by now the box office figures reported in the trade papers for LAST TANGO made it certain that Brando would be getting substantial royalties, Lewis Horowitz of the Beverly Hills National Bank (BHNB) remained unwilling to approve a loan, even with an assignment of those funds. He continued to insist that United Artists guarantee repayment.

Pakkala was negotiating on an agreement with William Bernstein, vice president in charge of business affairs at United Artists. The proposed terms were: (1) UA would guarantee repayment of $250,000 to the bank; (2) UA would hold all money up to $250,000 that Brando had coming from UA for LAST TANGO until June 30, 1974; (3) any amount in excess of $250,000 would be paid to Brando as accrued.

The interest rate quoted by Horowitz was twelve percent per annum. The result of the agreement was that UA would be getting free use of Brando's money and he would be paying twelve percent interest to BHNB until June 30, 1974 or longer. Thus, the interest bill would be at least thirty thousand dollars. If the guarantee had not been necessary, Brando could have paid back BHNB as he received the funds, thus reducing the interest cost. The precise amount of the reduction would depend on the rate at which the LAST TANGO royalties accrued, but the announced box office figures suggested that substantial Brando royalties were accruing already.

This agreement was very beneficial to UA. Since it was handling the distribution of LAST TANGO, the executives knew with certainty by this time that Brando's royalties would run well in excess of a million dollars. Thus, the guarantee was completely risk free for UA, and UA received the benefit of hanging on to Brando's funds for a year.

Pakkala got written approval of the agreement from Bernstein and Horowitz. From his Beverly Hills office, Pakkala dictated a letter to me on the afternoon of Friday, July 13, 1973. The letter gave the details of the loan and informed me that they would be closing it Monday morning, July 16.

It was not uncommon for mail to take two weeks to reach me, five thousand miles away on Tetiaroa. This letter turned out to be a little different. It was typed that afternoon and posted in a Wilshire Boulevard mailbox. The letter must have then been picked up by a postal truck, deposited in a main Los Angeles post office, immediately sorted and taken to Los Angeles International Airport where it was placed on the evening UTA flight to Papeete. The letter made the nine hour transPacific flight and reached Faaa Airport Saturday morning.

The previous steps brought the letter five thousand miles by circumstances that were fortuitous, but not unduly bizarre. The next steps which brought it the last twenty-six miles to reach my hands on Tetiaroa, however, stretched the limits of rational probability. While this series of coincidences was merely amazing at the time, the letter's speed of delivery was to assume immense importance some eight days later.

The pace of wo~~rk in~~ Tahiti was such that it was not uncommon for a letter mailed in Papeete to take three days to be sorted and put into a post office box. Yet this one went right into the box on Saturday morning, a normal Tahitian non-working day.

Since we received so little important mail, Yvonne Chung normally checked the box only about once a week. Though she did not work Saturdays, Yvonne mailed some personal letters at the post office that morning and therefore saw the letter in our box.

It usually took several days to a week to get to Tetiaroa, since we had only one or two plane flights a week from Papeete. However, there was a flight scheduled for that morning. Realizing that the letter was from Brown Kraft and might be important, Yvonne drove to Faaa Airport on her day off and put the letter on the Tetiaroa charter.

The Air Tahiti plane landed on Tetiaroa by late morning, bringing the letter into my hands less than eighteen hours after it had been dictated.

I read the letter while the supplies were being off-loaded from the plane. It said that Pakkala would be taking the loan papers to Brando for signature and the transaction would be closed Monday, two days hence.

The loan terms were disturbing. By that time, even from my remote location point in the middle of the South Pacific, it appeared that the first royalties from LAST TANGO were imminent. The loan, with its thirty thousand dollar interest charge, might not be needed at all.

It was surprising to hear that the loan was ready to close. I had already made reservations to fly to Los Angeles the following weekend, on the PanAm morning flight Sunday, July 22, to work out a much smaller short-term bridge loan. Now, it would be too late and the thirty thousand dollar interest charge would be inevitable.

Once the guarantee agreement was signed by Brando, the $250,000 of his money was irrevocably in UA's corporate till for a full year.

I immediately wrote a note to Yvonne Chung and handed it to the pilot with instructions for him to telephone Yvonne at home and read it to her. The note requested Yvonne make a reservation for me to fly to Los Angeles the next day, Sunday, July fifteenth and cancel my previous reservation. It was necessary to have the pilot phone because no one would be in our office in Papeete on Saturday or Sunday, so we were out of radio contact.

A couple of hours later Yvonne radioed Tetiaroa, informing me that all flights were full. However, she had waitlisted me.

Later she called again. There had been a cancellation and I could get on the flight. She promised to send a plane to Tetiaroa early Sunday morning to pick me up.

I packed my clothes, loaded my paperwork in a briefcase, and was on my way to Los Angeles the next morning. A nine-hour flight and a taxi ride brought me to Brando's home. He was surprised to see me, but welcomed the company. I told him why the loan should not be executed. We spent the evening discussing business and I settled into the guest room/den for the week.

The next morning I was at the Brown Kraft offices at opening to meet Pakkala to tell him about my concerns. We both believed that some royalties were already due and wondered if United Artist was stalling until the loan agreement was signed.

Pakkala phoned Bernstein of UA in New York. His secretary said he was in a meeting and took the message to return the call. A couple of hours later Pakkala called again and left another message. That call was also ignored. This strengthened our suspicions.

As it approached five o'clock eastern time, Pakkala made ready to call again. I suggested we try some other approach to get the desired information, perhaps circumventing Bernstein. Pakkala proposed phoning the accounting department. We decided to wait until five-thirty. By then any manager with instructions to not release information might have left. We could perhaps reach some late working accountant who might have no awareness of the pending loan.

Pakkala phoned UA, asking this time for the accounting department. The department receptionist had left; an accountant answered. Pakkala introduced himself as Marlon Brando's accountant and said, "Maybe you have heard about Marlon's island near Tahiti. He's having some construction done there now and I'm trying to do some cash flow planning. Can you tell me how much his next check will be from the LAST TANGO IN PARIS royalties?"

The accountant replied, "Hold on a minute. I'll look it up."

A few minutes later, he came back on the line. "It's $411,256."

"Thank you", Pakkala replied. "How soon can we expect to receive the check?"

"I don't understand it. It should have been sent out two weeks ago. I'll see that it gets in the mail tomorrow."

Pakkala had been holding the phone away from his ear so that I could hear the incoming conversation. I whispered to him, "Because of the delay, ask him to send it express mail."

He did.

That was the end of the loan. From that point, the UA checks came in monthly and the cash shortage problem was ended for the rest of my time on the job.

My actions had just saved Brando thirty thousand dollars. That was enough to pay my salary for a year or almost enough for him to go out and punch another photographer.

Seldom have I saved thirty thousand dollars in a day. Using Ben Franklin's sage wisdom, it equated to thirty thousand dollars earned. I was curious to see Brando's response to the news of the incoming check.

When I got home that night, he was in one of his quiet moods. The news that the $411,256 which would relieve his money problem was on its way failed to bring a smile to his face. His attention focused, instead, on United Artists and he went into a monologue, expressing his disdain for the business people who ran the movie studios. At the time, he was refusing to act in THE GODFATHER, PART II, despite promise of an enormous salary and profit share for a small part and despite pleas from director Francis

Ford Coppola. He refused primarily because he was carrying a grudge against Frank Yablans of Paramount. Even though Brando was broke, he would rather forego the large expected income if his acting meant the Paramount would also profit. I could now see United Artists being added to the Brando blacklist.

After his anger at UA passed and Brando reflected on the results, he began to appreciate my efforts. He said, "Roger, you've put in a pretty good day's work. Yesterday, you had that long flight and I know you've been working your ass off over there. You ought to relax a little this evening. Maybe you'd enjoy a nice massage and a soothing evening of pleasure. I can make a phone call and get a girl over here to take care of you. It'll be on me."

The suggestion was so sudden and out of the blue that I could not think of any kind of a response. I finally mumbled something to the effect that I'd better take a rain check.

Sam Gilman, a longtime Brando friend, was with us in Brando's bedroom at the time, listening in. Sam was a character actor who did not often find work. Brando's offer seemed to take Sam too by surprise. "Christ, Marlon," he said a little enviously, "how come you've never done anything like that for me? I've been coming over here for twenty years and all you've ever offered me is a sandwich."

"Go ahead and make that call. Roger can go sleep at my house tonight and I'll stay here!"

Brando's generosity did not extend that far.

In reality, Brando had given Sam a lot more than a ham and rye, including obtaining parts for him in several Brando movies. Maybe, however, Sam's comment reached home because a couple of weeks later Sam arrived on Tetiaroa, compliments of Brando.

On the plane from Tahiti I had put together a list of the things to do that week in Los Angeles. It totaled twenty-two items, a couple of which required a day by themselves. I worked day and night to get through the list.

My exhaustion by the end of the week had me wondering if it was too late to cash in my rain check. I rushed to take care of the last items on Saturday and caught the late night Pan Am flight back to Tahiti.

When the plane landed in Papeete Sunday morning, Yvonne Chung had an Air Tahiti charter waiting to return me to Tetiaroa. It had been a productive trip, but it was good to have it behind me. Due to the unbelievably fortuitous timing and circumstances that led to my receiving Pakkala's letter the previous Saturday, I was back to my little Polynesian bungalow at almost the exact minute that the plane of my original reservation was taking off for Los Angeles.

Jean Mercier gave me an update on the construction progress of the previous week and I spent the afternoon boating on the lagoon with my family and picnicking on one of the outlying islets. The next morning, I was up with the sun as usual to get to work. About eight o'clock, I stopped at the camp for breakfast. While enjoying my first cup of coffee, one of the Tahitian workers came to the camp and asked me, "Did you hear what happened to the plane to Los Angeles yesterday?"

"No, what happened?"

"It crashed into the ocean. They've found only one survivor."

The Pan American World Airways Boeing 707 jetliner had plunged into the ocean ninety seconds after departure from Papeete on its way to Los Angeles. Seventy-eight passengers and crew were killed as the plane sank sixteen hundred feet to the ocean floor

There was one survivor; James Campbell of Wadawasta, Ontario suffered only two broken ribs.

One's first thought on hearing such shocking news is grief for the passengers. Coming so fast that the impression of the first thought is still in the brain, comes the second thought, "Thank God, I wasn't on that plane."

After the initial shock of the crash had a moment to wear down, a third thought came into my mind, "Thank God for delivering the mail."

Had that letter from Brown Kraft not reached me the previous Saturday, it would have been too late to influence the guarantee and the loan so that I would have taken the ill fated crash flight on which I was originally ticketed in order to handle the other stateside Brando business.

The United States Postal Service, Tahiti Post, and the Tetiaroa crew would not get a letter from Beverly Hills to Tetiaroa in less than a day one time in ten thousand.

Someone else must have been helping.

CHAPTER EIGHTEEN

CONSTRUCTION CREEPS
AT A SNAIL'S PACE

Working with the Tahitians was not at all like working with American workers in the United States. Not necessarily worse, not necessarily better but certainly different. It would be a patronizing arrogance for us to evaluate Tahitians by how we live in our society. Tahiti belongs to the Tahitians. If we should want to work, live, or vacation on Tahiti, it should be up to us to adapt to the Tahitian society, it is hardly their obligation to act like Americans.

It was not surprising that their motivation to work was different than ours. If five minutes with a net will yield delicious and healthful fish for sustenance, a few months work will produce a livable dwelling without a thirty year mortgage to follow, two square yards of cotton and a pair of thongs will provide a comfortable wardrobe, and everything important is within walking distance, then why is it necessary to work unremittingly, striving for every material possession that money can buy?

Working in the South Pacific and living with the Tahitians reminded me of a story I had once heard in a college course about third world economic development.

It happened in a South American country where an American company had established a large mining operation. Native laborers worked the mine. The labor turnover rate was so high that reasonable productivity could never be attained. Immediately after each payday, many workers would quit. Although they worked hard when on the job, none would work for more than a few weeks.

After months of investigation and discussion, the American management concluded that the workers had very short time horizons. They had no interest in saving for the future and were quitting as soon as they had a little money in their pockets because their immediate needs were satisfied.

The company management decided to provide the wives of the workers with Sears mail order catalogs. The change in labor turnover was dramatic. The wives found many things to purchase and the men kept working and bringing home the money to acquire these new "necessities." The mine reached the desired productivity level. Sears did all right too.

That move seemed very clever, but also somewhat reprehensible. It was one thing to exploit the mineral riches of the earth in a foreign land, it was quite another to manipulate the culture in order to do so. Eventually, the mine would close, but the created material desires would remain, now without the income to satisfy them.

Brando had a true love for the Tahitians. He enjoyed coming to Tahiti and Tetiaroa because he could relax and unwind there in a way he was unable to do anywhere else. His movie star status meant almost nothing to the Tahitians. If any were impressed, they were too quiet and timid to reveal it. They seemed to pay no attention to him. He could move among them virtually unnoticed and certainly without encountering any of the fawning behavior and obsequious unsolicited praise that he would encounter in other societies and which he so detested.

Yet, his behavior resembled that of a remote benevolent plantation owner. While on Tetiaroa, he would rarely even speak to any of the Tahitians; his time was spent with the few Americans who were on the island, and, even among those, typically only with his long time friends. If there were scientific researchers or other strangers on the island, he would usually dine alone and decline to participate in the evening conversations, remaining in his bungalow by himself.

Brando's concern for the Tahitians was genuine, just as it is for the American Indian. In his "best of all possible worlds," he would have the American Indian still roaming plains covered with waist high grass, feeding on abundant herds of roving buffalo, and Tahiti would remain the pristine paradise it was when Fletcher Christian and the crew of the BOUNTY first landed there.

He would rather have seen construction edge along at a snail's pace than use anything as manipulative as the Sears catalog ploy. He watched my attempts to spur motivation by use of the goal and bonus system with detached amusement, appearing somewhat amazed at the temporary increase in production, but not altogether disappointed when it eventually failed. The intruding white man had not been successful in subverting the native.

I eventually concluded that the best way to stimulate progress was to work alongside the Tahitians as much as possible and to apply an ample dose of praise for work well done. (As a matter of fact, that recipe works well in any society.) In several instances, even the mildest criticism had resulted in extended periods of workers sulking or even quitting. So, when on Tetiaroa, most of my day was spent roving from one crew to another, working an hour here and an hour there. Whenever anyone displayed progressively innovative behavior, particularly dedicated effort, or unusual concern for quality, I made sure he knew how much this was appreciated.

This meant planning and paper work had to be done in the evenings and on weekends. Most of my travel was scheduled for Sundays, thereby allowing an extra day's planning and paperwork to be fit in on the long nine hour flights between Papeete and Los Angeles.

When I had been only supervisor, there were constant problems of broken equipment, misunderstood directions, supply shortages, and so on which took fully half of my workday. With Mercier added, this eased a bit, but he remained a better worker than supervisor.

Through it all, I worked harder and put in longer workdays on this job than ever before. I have never been able to work as devotedly in my own businesses as I did for Brando, but somehow it seemed more important to succeed there than it ever had before.

The differing level of motivation of the Tahitians from American workers was only one impediment to production. Another problem was the lower skill level. They simply had not received much training in construction. So, as I made the rounds from one crew to another, it was not just to attempt to increase motivation, but also to enhance production skills.

My background in construction was limited, but simple observation had taught me some things that few Tahitians seemed to know. Some were easy to convey, such as driving a nail by taking a long, even swing rather than tap, tap, tapping at it.

However, other simple construction concepts seemed to remain almost beyond their comprehension. For example, there was one plumbing problem that never was solved. There is an old construction joke that, to be a plumber, you need to know only three things: (1) shit won't flow uphill; (2) payday is on Friday; and (3) never chew your fingernails. Well, a variant of the first rule never did take hold on Tetiaroa. No matter how often it was demonstrated that water will not flow uphill, the Tahitians could not seem to believe it.

The bungalows had been redesigned to contain a bathroom with a shower. In the low bungalows, the bathrooms had concrete floors. The plumbing drains for the showers, which had to be installed before the concrete was poured, were run in directly under the shower head, near the edge of the circular shower basin. In pouring the concrete shower basin, then, the surface should have been sloped so that everything ran to the drain. Invariably, the Tahitians would pour and finish the concrete so the low spot was in the middle, rather than at the drain. This would, of course, leave a puddle of dirty water whenever a shower would be taken.

Despite my demonstration of the problem, each new pour was the same. If I was not standing there emphasizing the proper placement of the drain, the low spot would end up in the wrong place. Telling them before each pour was not sufficient; they would still attempt to slope everything to the middle.

One of the buildings being constructed was a small cocktail bar, octagonal shaped with a twenty foot diameter, located near the restaurant. The bar top and the cabinet works were being constructed from a hardwood which had been obtained from a small grove on one of the islets across the lagoon and rough cut on our improvised chain saw sawmill. Finishing of the wood surface was done by a small electric sanders and a lot of hand work. The tight brown grain provided a very attractive surface, similar to walnut.

Two of the most highly skilled carpenters were assigned to the cabinetwork, along with one less skilled worker to do the drudge work. They were motivated men and had worked with a constant dedication on this job, clearly taking pride in the attractive cabinetwork they were producing.

Brando's friend, the aforementioned Sam Gilman, came to the island for a week's vacation. In addition to being an actor, Sam was a skilled amateur handyman and carpenter who frequently worked on projects in his workshop.

I took him on a tour of the construction and showed him some cabinetwork behind the bar, which was by then looking quite impressive. We were discussing the languid work pace on Tetiaroa and I asked Sam to guess how long it had taken to bring the cabinetwork to its current stage.

After sizing up the job, and running his fingers over the wood surface in a gentle tactile examination, Sam replied that if it were an American carpenter, it would have taken one day, but it probably took five man days there on Tetiaroa.

He was more than mildly surprised when I informed him that it had already taken twenty-one days for the three man crew - a total of sixty-three man days.

When Marlon Brando's own unique concept for the design of a Tahitian village is added, the construction schedule expands exponentially. He wanted to build a village without acquiring building material. Only improvised resources native to the island should be used.

Brando would have been content transporting the tourists from Papeete in outrigger canoes or on the three masted schooner BOUNTY, feeding them with food cooked over an open fire, having them bathe in the lagoon, and taking care of their elimination problems behind a coconut palm. If that was good enough for the Tahitians of bygone times, it was good enough for contemporary tourists.

Well, even the Tahitians were changing. They were not content with the life of their forefathers. Blame it on the invasion of French rulers and American tourists, the influence of television, or simple "progress" of the twentieth century. Whatever the cause, the pristine Tahitian life of a bygone era was becoming more history than reality. Many of the modern young Tahitians spent their evenings in the discotheque, dancing to American rock and roll, with a cigarette in one hand and a rum and coke in the other. Their ambitions were to have an interesting job, own a sleek automobile, and settle down in a modern comfortable home along the ocean. Their desires had increased; the work ethic had not quite kept pace.

Brando would have liked to turn back the clock, to drag Tahiti back to the nineteenth century. It was a solo pursuit. Even within his own Tahitian family, he was fighting a losing battle. Tarita had a home in a beautiful setting on the ocean that had all the modern conveniences, but it was a little old, perhaps thirty years or so. She wanted a home like those she saw in Los Angeles. So, Brando built one for her, hidden from the ocean by her old home. It had less charm than the older home and none of the magnificent view, but it was the "modern" home that she wanted. Brando lamented Tarita's choice, but he valued her happiness, so he built it.

Perhaps he had little influence on Tahiti, but on Tetiaroa, he was sole ruler of all he surveyed. His desire was to build a nineteenth century village for twentieth century tourists. Thus, the buildings were to be constructed from all native material, primarily from the coconut palm.

It had been easy to convince him that such minimal comforts as electrical lights and bathrooms were necessities. This meant that some material would have to be imported, but he was still bound to use as much native material as possible. While importing had its own unique problems, producing material on the island was far more difficult.

Tetiaroa was a former coconut plantation and was still covered with the coconut palm. There were very few coconuts, however.

Rats were as numerous as the palms and kept the trees barren of the delectable coconuts. On Tahiti, many of the palms were encompassed by a strip of sheet metal about one foot wide circling the trunk ten to twelve feet above the ground. The rats could not climb over the sheet metal and the coconuts remained to ripen in the trees. On Tetiaroa, however, the palms remained in their pristine state and the rats feasted on the white meat and milk of the coconut, allowing almost none to reach maturity.

The coconut palm had its value, however. It provided construction material from both the leaves and the trunk. The leaves or fronds grew six to eight feet long and up to two feet wide. The coconut palm periodically sheds its leaves. Unlike the deciduous maple or oak, however, this is not a seasonal occurrence. It is a year around pushing out of the old growth by newer young green leaves. Thus, each morning, workers could walk through the island and find fresh fronds that had fallen since the previous day. The fronds were then woven by female workers into a product called niau (nee ow). The niau has a braided appearance and, when stacked in overlapping layers, provides a virtually water tight matlike surface that was used for both the walls and the roof coverings of the buildings.

The trunks of the mature palm grew to eight to fifteen inches in diameter. They were used for the posts that held up the roofs and formed the support points for the walls. Also, they were cut into planks for the floors of the high bungalows. Finally, they were cut into boards for building the furniture beds, chests, chairs, and so on.

On one of the other islets grew slim hardwood trees which produced trunks of three to four inch diameter. These were used to form the superstructure above the coconut palm posts that supported the niau roofs, the native version of the roof truss.

On a typical day there were three workers gathering up fronds and four to six women weaving them. Three workers were gathering the hardwood supports for the roofs and peeling the bark, three workers were cutting and hauling the coconut palm posts, and three workers were operating the sawmill. Almost half the work crew was gathering or preparing material.

The sawmill was makeshift and primitive. The production machine was a chain saw mounted horizontally on a handmade frame. The coconut trunks were pushed along a table and fed into the saw. The rough cut produced would not have been suitable for a polished hardwood floor, but it did produce the rough hewn look that Brando desired for the floors of the high bungalows. I would not recommend, however, walking on the floor barefoot but then, who would ever think of going barefoot on a South Seas Island?

Unfortunately, the coconut wood seemed to devour chains. They had to be sharpened after every four or five passes, and they frequently broke. While a liberal supply of spares was kept on hand, this constant sharpening and changing kept productivity low. There were days when the crew failed to produce ten planks.

To the best of my knowledge, no one else was using the coconut palm for lumber. Other builders claimed it was a worthless tree because of its rather soft grain. Credit Brando's imagination for the productive use of this plentiful resource, though the durability of the resulting floors, furniture and other products remained in question.

There was also a by-product from the coconut tree that everyone at the camp enjoyed. The very top of the trunk where the leaves emerge has a soft white texture that is not only edible but quite tender and flavorful. It is the heart of palm. A heart of palm salad might cost $7.50 at your better French restaurants. With perhaps two or three pounds of heart of palm from each tree, we had a plentiful supply and the price was right. Fortunately, no one had told the rats how delectable it was.

One problem of using the native material was its impermanent quality, particularly the coconut frond niau material. It was expected to have a life of only two years, meaning the walls and roofs would need replacing with an expensive regularity. Throughout the rest of the South Pacific area, the frond from the pandanus tree was used for niau for the roofs in the native type dwellings. The pandanus did not grow on Tetiaroa, but was plentiful on nearby islands. The pandanus roofs would not only last three times as long as the coconut roofs, but also the pattern of the weave produced a more pleasing design. Entreaties to

Brando to acquire the pandanus from Tahiti always fell on deaf ears. It was not "native to Tetiaroa," although there wouldn't have been one tourist in ten thousand who would have ever known the difference.

A second problem of using native material was its lack of dimensional integrity. Each post, each beam, and each plank was of a different size. The rough hewn doors and windows had frames made from the bent and gnarly hardwood trees and never produced a close fit. The rampant rats could roam through the bungalows unhindered by barriers.

In order to speed up construction and to provide more habitable and longer lasting buildings, I and many others would urge Brando to purchase some ready made material. He would never agree.

On one of his absences from Tetiaroa, I tried an experiment. We purchased a few sheets of plywood which the carpenters used to construct a portion of one bungalow. We then covered the plywood with niau. On his return, Brando inspected it. The frame was not visible to the eye. He liked the appearance. I then explained that there was some plywood in the building, and asked for his approval to use the same method on the remaining bungalows. He walked over, lifted the niau to make a closer inspection and ordered it torn down.

The Tetiaroa primitive lumber manufacturing operation continued.

CHAPTER NINETEEN

CROSSING THE REEF

L iving in a typical American community, when we want food for a meal, a nail to repair a broken door, or gasoline for our automobile, we just go to a store and buy it.

Not so on Tetiaroa. Commonplace foodstuffs and material might require a radiophone order and a charter plane from Papeete. For other items, the nearest supply might be several thousand miles away in the United States. Acquiring very large objects would require planning for transportation as much as six months in advance. Logistical planning was, by necessity, a major and vital activity.

Supplying Tetiaroa with large shipments by sea was an exciting and dangerous adventure. It carried some of the same problems as the military planners of the invasions on Guadalcanal or Kwajalein had faced during World War II. Indeed, the supply ship was the Meherio, a landing craft from World War II that was still circling the South Pacific some thirty years later, serving the outlying islands. And, we had snafus and just plain bad luck to rival anything experienced by those military planners.

The cost of chartering the Meherio was about $800 a day. If scheduled when it was already at Tahiti, the charge was only for the direct days of loading in Papeete, off-loading at Tetiaroa, and travel in between. Billing for a large shipment would be about $2400. However, the Meherio operated on a flexible schedule serving a large geographic area and would be absent from Tahiti for up to six months at a time.

We had to wait for other users to bring it to Tahiti, the cost of bringing it to Tetiaroa solely for our own use being prohibitive. There was substantial demand for its services and it was necessary to make reservations several months ahead, but even then you were never quite certain when it would arrive or how long it would be available.

Charter planes cost about $150 per round trip for a small single engine, two-passenger Cessna to $350 for a twin engine, nine-passenger Dehavilland and $600 for a nineteen-passenger Twin Otter. There were no cargo planes in the area and carrying cargo on the passenger planes was not very efficient.

A small fishing boat could sometimes be chartered for about $150, but there was then the problem of off-loading over the coral reef.

The most efficient policy was to bring in a six month supply of material periodically on the Meherio and fill in between with chartered passenger planes. Since we had significant passenger traffic between Tetiaroa and Papeete, moderate amounts of cargo could regularly be carried at no incremental cost. However, most of the available cargo space was taken up by the large food supply required to feed sixty or so people.

Upon taking responsibility for construction, I determined to cut down on the indiscriminate chartering of planes for cargo, such as the $150 flights to carry $40 worth of cement, in order to reduce the excessively high transportation costs.

So, I began planning for the next Meherio shipment. Eight hundred fifty-kilogram sacks of cement were included in the planned cargo. This was enough to complete the planned construction plus a hundred sack safety factor and inventory for future use. I had also purchased a used Case front-end loader/backhoe in Los Angeles and it was sitting on the wharf in Papeete. Plumbing and electrical supplies, restaurant appliances, furniture, and even a beginning liquor supply were among the other material assembled. It made sense to take full advantage of the large hold of the Meherio.

The expense of shipping to Tetiaroa was not limited to the Papeete - Tetiaroa leg of the journey. Many supplies were acquired in Los Angeles, with transPacific shipping and high Tahiti tariffs added to their cost. Any work done on the Papeete wharf made the U. S. longshoremen seem like charity volunteers by comparison. After many weeks, the seven trunks of personal belongings we had shipped from Vancouver arrived in Papeete. A local trucking firm picked them up from the docks and delivered them to our downtown Papeete office. It was agonizing to find that the bill for this local delivery over a distance of one mile was more than the bill for shipping the trunks more than 6,000 miles from Vancouver.

Since Brando had done an award winning job on the New York docks some twenty years earlier, I suggested it was time for him to go back down on the waterfront to straighten things out again.

Once everything was ready for the Meherio, one had to hope that the weather would cooperate or the voyage might be canceled and it would be six months before the ship could be scheduled again. As the time drew near for our shipment, we ran into one supply snag. Because of the shortage of fresh water on Tetiaroa, we used a special kind of cement that was suitable for mixing with the salt water from the lagoon. There were not 800 sacks available on all of Tahiti. By depleting the inventory in all the building supply stores on the island, we had to be content with 500.

The scheduled day for loading broke cloudy and windy on Tahiti. The Meherio captain in Papeete refused to load the boat. Brando, on Tetiaroa, was fretting about the weather. The second day was the same. Our three day envelope was closing. The captain announced that he was moving on to his next port of call. To wait another six months for the next shipping opportunity would be a major setback. Yvonne Chung intervened with the captain and managed to charm him into waiting until the next morning.

As the day went on, the sun broke free of the clouds, the wind faded, and the seas calmed. In Papeete, the Meherio was loaded with our cargo and made ready for early departure to Tetiaroa the next morning. One of the staff members I had inherited supervised the assembly and loading of the cargo in Papeete.

Early the next morning our work force made ready for an arduous day. There were thirty workers assigned to the off-loading crew. We had constructed a large raft using rough hewn planks for a deck and empty barrels for buoyancy. The raft and three small motorized boats were available for transporting the cargo across the lagoon. As the Meherio appeared on the horizon, it was a somber crew that crossed the lagoon to begin off-loading. Working amidst the crashing waves on the reef was not taken lightly.

I had heard many tales about the reef and was apprehensive about the work ahead. The first time that Brando had crossed the reef, he had met with near disaster. He had hired a boat manned by Tahitians experienced in reef crossing for his first time on Tetiaroa. They sat outside the reef waiting for just the right wave. When the chief yelled, everyone dug in and paddled but the boat made no progress and an even larger wave slammed the boat down on the reef, throwing Brando and half the crew over the side. Brando landed on the reef, the cart-wheeling boat slamming down inches away. He emerged bruised and bloody from the jagged coral. The boat somehow escaped serious damage and most of the supplies were recovered.

The pickup boat, which arrived several days later, was less fortunate. A government boat showed up to pluck the South Pacific's most illustrious new denizen from his island. This was a sturdy twenty-four foot whaleboat, manned by a crew of fourteen hardy paddlers, who were long accustomed to shooting a reef. After waiting outside the reef for the right wave, they made their attempt. Brando said this boat was also smashed on the reef and the crew suffered scratched and banged up heads and knees and elbows and broken ankles.

To be sure, few crossings were like that, but there was good reason to respect the power of the ocean when it met the barrier provided by the reef. Indeed, during the filming of MUTINY ON THE BOUNTY, one Tahitian had been killed and several injured when a boat smashed against the reef.

There was no good place on the reef to off-load the Meherio, but some spots were better than others. Our chosen location was near the islet of Rimatuu, because it was closest to the reef, thereby reducing the time required to bring the cargo to dry land.

The off-loading process called for the Meherio to run up against the reef. The Captain would then lower its ramp and keep power running so that it would maintain its position amidst the waves while the workers carried the cargo from the Meherio onto the reef, then walked, ankle to knee deep in water, atop the irregular, jagged coral to a spot where they could climb down the reef to the waist deep water near Rimatuu and wade ashore with their load.

After everything was unloaded, the process of ferrying the cargo on the raft and small boats about two miles across the lagoon to Onetahi would begin. The last step was time consuming, but not dangerous in the comparative calm of the lagoon.

It was a fairly calm day, the swells of the Pacific only three to four feet. Had the seas been like those of the day Brando first crossed the reef, off-loading would have been impossible; the Meherio would have been unable to maintain a position on the reef. Even if that had been possible, the workers would have been knocked off the reef by the waves.

The workers laboriously made their way across the reef to the shore, 110 pound sacks of cement slung over their shoulders. They might not have been the most skilled construction workers, but when there was a tough job to be done, they could work until exhausted.

There were several workers among the crew who never wore shoes. Years of walking barefoot had given them thick tough soles. However, I expected everyone would protect their feet from the jagged coral. Though some did wear borrowed shoes, three or four workers still worked barefoot, gingerly carrying the heavy loads of cement on their backs.

I too struggled back and forth from the Meherio to shore, under the strain of the 110 pound loads. As my rest periods grew more frequent and of longer duration, I began to appreciate anew how the Tahitians could work doggedly under difficult conditions when they were motivated to do so.

With some of the 500 sacks of cement out of the way, it was time to start the most difficult job while everyone was still fairly fresh - moving the Case front end loader. It must have weighed 4,000 pounds and could not simply be carried off, even with thirty strong bodies. It would have to be driven, first off the Meherio onto planks on the reef and from there onto the raft. One error and the Pacific could claim it, a $15,000 investment lost. The reef would not provide a smooth level platform, so some workers would have to support the loader on the twenty foot journey over the reef and others would have to stabilize the raft so that it would not turn turtle as the loader was run onto it. It was a strenuous yet delicate job, but it had been done before. Tapituri, the contractor, had already brought three vehicles onto the island.

As we went to warm up the loader, the first snafu was revealed. The vehicle was in two pieces, the loading arm and bucket lying apart from the tractor. Our supply officer in Papeete had neglected to have it assembled into a working vehicle. It could not be operated. Hydraulic hoses were disconnected and it could not be started. On my earlier inquiry about its condition over the radio phone, the supply officer had informed me that everything had been fine on its arrival from Los Angeles. Now, another radio phone call revealed that he had only visually inspected it; he had not operationally tested it. In Papeete, it had been loaded on the Meherio by a dockside crane, not driven onto the landing craft. Well, we did not have any dockside crane here; we did not have any dockside.

This turned out to be the final foul up for that less than industrious staff member. This mistake resulted more from laziness than lack of knowledge. He received his walking papers the next day.

The only way it could be unloaded would be to get it operational. Klaus Rober, the mechanic, feverishly went to work trying to assemble it. Without the operating manual, which the supply officer had also neglected to send, he was unable to get it running in the several hours it took to complete off-loading. We would have to send it back on the Meherio. It would be six months before there would be another chance to bring it over.

The loader had been acquired as a backup for one already on Tetiaroa which had a lot of downtime, so its absence was not the problem it might have been.

An even more serious problem had occurred with a large heavy object the previous time the Meherio had brought cargo to Tetiaroa. That time an electrical generator was being delivered. The workers managed to get it onto the reef late in the day. Darkness fell before they were able to wrestle it onto the raft, so it was left there overnight. The sea was calm and, since the generator weighed over a thousand pounds, they did not expect it would be going anywhere.

They were wrong. They awoke the next morning to a still calm sea, but the generator was nowhere in sight. Divers searched, but were unable to find a trace of it. There was not even an oil slick from the brand new $4,000 machine. Since there were not any shoplifters out in the middle of the Pacific with the capacity to pick up this thousand pound bauble, the only thing that could have happened was that a wave swept it off the reef during the night.

Before our current off-loading venture was complete, I would fall witness to the ocean whose rapacious nature contrasted so sharply with its tranquil name, Pacific.

There was a large pier made of steel I-beams set in concrete on Rimatuu, a remnant of the copra plantation days. The pier was perhaps thirty feet inside the reef and rose five feet above the water level of the lagoon. The planking and deck had long ago disappeared, but the denuded steel skeleton of the pier had withstood the pounding of sea and weather for decades and was still rock solid. As we off-loaded, several of the workers handed their sacks of cement up to another worker who piled them onto the crossbeams of the pier rather than make the longer walk to shore, thereby hastening the unloading process.

Toward late afternoon, off-loading was complete, and the Meherio left, taking the front end loader back to Papeete. The crew then began transferring cargo across the lagoon to Onetahi. Past dinner time, we called a halt to the work and everyone returned to Onetahi. Everything had been moved off the beach, but about 150 sacks of cement remained stacked on the pier. Except for the problem with the front end loader, it had been a successful day. We were thankful that the weather had cleared, for another day of bad weather would have cost us the whole shipment.

Alice Marchak happened to be on Tetiaroa for a two week vacation at the time. In the afternoon, Brando had taken her over to observe the off-loading. At dinner time, she walked into the camp area muttering about Marlon. He had gotten into a conversation with the captain of the Meherio and had promised to give him a new color television and a video cassette recorder.

Ever the practical penny pincher, I started trying to figure out how to minimize the cost of shipping and tariffs. Alice told me not to bother, saying that Marlon was always promising to give away things like that, but he forgot his promises as soon as made him.

She was right about this one. He never mentioned it to me. The captain is still waiting.

The adage, "Red sky at night, sailor's delight," foretold a pleasant evening. There was no sign of rain in the sky or on the weather forecast from Tahiti, so we were unconcerned about leaving the sacks of cement out overnight. During the night, a stiff wind began to blow, waking me. I listened for rain, but hearing only the sound of the wind and the waves, contentedly returned to sleep.

In the morning, I left our bungalow to discover another ideal day on Tetiaroa with a high clear blue sky and a mild trade wind blowing across the lagoon. To look out over the aquamarine waters lapping at the shore always elevated the spirit. I stood on the beach stretching out the kinks from a good night's sleep, looking around across the lagoon at all the surrounding islets and then went in for my breakfast grapefruit and coffee.

Halfway through my first cup of coffee it suddenly occurred to me that something had been missing. The cement had not been on the pier across the lagoon. No, surely it had been there, I just had not noticed. After all, it was a mile away and the pile had only been a few feet high on top of the pier.

Still, it bothered me, so I picked up the binoculars and walked to the beach and looked again. The pier was bare. There was not a single sack of cement on it. There had been at least 150 sacks there the night before. Now there were none.

Jean Mercier and I took the Zodiak over to Rimatuu. We found nothing there - no sackfuls of water hardened cement in the water, no broken sacks scattered along the shore, not so much as a telltale trace of gray cement powder anywhere.

The ocean's force had reached far inside the reef and completely obliterated the cargo we had left there, high and dry. No one had even guessed that water might splash up and wet the sacks and now the sea had completely devoured them. For that is surely what happened, there was no other possible explanation for its disappearance and as Sherlock Holmes was wont to say, "Eliminate the impossible and what remains, no matter how improbable, must be the explanation."

CHAPTER TWENTY

BRANDO ON TETIAROA
FINALLY, WE GET TO THE SEX

When Brando would grow sufficiently bored in his Beverly Hills bedroom, he would go to Tetiaroa. During this period, he spent about half of his time on his island. He made many trips there, but would stay only a short time. Although he was fond of talking about the beauty and serenity of the island and the contentment that he found there, he preferred to take that contentment in small doses. He would get "island fever." After two or three weeks, at the most, he would fly back to the Los Angeles smog and his Beverly Hills edroom.

While Tetiaroa did indeed have its charm, creature comforts were still quite primitive. In his earlier days of island ownership, Brando had stayed either in a small canvas tent or in one of the partially constructed bungalows with a sand floor, kerosene lamp, and complete lack of plumbing. After several months of construction under my supervision, his accommodations were still far from luxurious. A concrete floor had been put in place and electrical lighting had been installed. A large bathroom had been added and the pipes put in, but it sat unused because the sinks and toilets had not arrived.

Bernard Judge had selected real shells from giant clams to be used for the wash basins. They were to be drilled for water supply and drainage pipes. Although Judge had ordered them some eight months earlier from a supplier in Hawaii, they still had not been delivered. Considering such South Seas supply problems, it looked as if Judge's early projection of two weeks until opening could be changed to two years.

The toilets had not arrived because of design uncertainties. It had been Brando's early decision to have a waste system in which the human waste would be drained into barrels and then collected from every toilet weekly. His amorphous plans one day would be to use the waste to generate methane gas. The next day it might be to use the waste as fertilizer for growing vegetables on the island vegetables to be fed to the tourists. Judge had tried to design a system but had been stymied by Brando's vacillations. Since either system involved considerable complexity, it was not surprising that the design had not been fixed. Without a design, the toilets could not be acquired.

In actuality, neither plan was practical. The amount of methane that could have been produced was almost inconsequential, considering the relatively small potential population of Tetiaroa. Wind energy or solar energy were far more economical.

The fertilizer idea was even more bizarre. Brando was unaware that it was unlawful to use human fecal matter as fertilizer for growing food which was to be consumed by humans. When I told him, he abandoned that idea, but he still clung to the methane concept.

It seemed as if he felt committed to generating methane simply because he had told so many people of his intent. The economic impracticality did not deter him. What finally convinced him to abandon the idea was the argument that the collection process was degrading to the Tahitian workers. Construction supervisor Jean Mercier reported that the workers were complaining that they dreaded doing anything that involved collecting the toilet waste.

Finally, reason won out and it was decided to install a standard toilet system. Well, almost standard. Even after abandoning the exotic design concepts, there was still an environmental problem to deal with - there was a limited water supply on the island. Because of that, it was prudent to select a toilet that had low water usage. Naturally, such toilets were not available in the South Pacific. Toilets were ordered from Monogram Industries in Los Angeles that used only one gallon of water, in contrast to the five gallons commonly required, but of course they had not yet arrived.

Because of all the delays, we eventually made one accommodation for Brando's comfort. We built him his very own outhouse. Now he would have only a twenty foot walk from his front door instead of a five minute hike to the communal facility.

So, with the lack of everyday comforts, it was hardly surprising that he was always ready to leave his island paradise after a couple of weeks, particularly when one adds to that the boredom factor. For his life on Tetiaroa was undeniably quiet, varying between tedium and lethargy, at times almost comatose.

Each trip to Tetiaroa would find him fresh and happy to be back. The pattern of his visits remained constant. First would be the announcement that he was coming, via a phone call from Alice Marchak in Beverly Hills to Yvonne Chung at our Papeete office. Usually one of his sons, either Christian or Miko, would be coming with him. Sometimes he would return to the island alone because he had left Christian on Tetiaroa with my family while he was in Los Angeles for a couple of weeks. An arrival date and time would be given. That date would arrive but Brando would not. Another phone call, another arrival date, another no show. Finally, on about the third announced date, he would manage to make his flight. A couple of times, he had planned his arrival in order to be in Tahiti for one of his children's birthdays. On those occasions, he would miss only one flight, rather than two, and arrive only a day late for the birthday.

He would first spend a couple of days on Tahiti with Tarita and the children. Then he would come to Tetiaroa, often bringing Teihotu to spend a couple of days there with his father and half-brothers. He never once brought Tarita or three-year-old Cheyenne to the island.

Although the period of cohabitation of his first two marriages was measured in weeks, Brando maintained a relationship with Tarita that had lasted almost two decades. Although they had the two children together, it was from the start a casual affiliation. Brando came and went when he pleased and stayed as long as he chose. If he did not show up when he had promised, Tarita went on with her own life. While she did not always welcome him with open arms, she at least tolerated his presence for the sake of the children.

Still, Brando expressed consternation about his relationship with Tarita and her intermittent refusal to allow him the sexual relations to which he felt his financial support entitled him. Yes, even for Marlon Brando, women would get a headache.

He continued to become involved with other women in both sexual and platonic relationships. It was Tarita's equanimity and undemanding nature that allowed their own relationship to last. Although Brando had a strong respect for Tarita, spoke of his love for her, and treated her well, he would remain with her only a day or two at a time and then be off to his own interests.

On arriving on Tetiaroa, Brando would sometimes want to tour the island to see the progress in construction since his last departure. Other times, he did not want to bother with a construction tour. Although construction always proceeded slowly, he seldom expressed disappointment at the lack of progress. It was as though he did not care if the resort ever opened.

The next day, he might wander around observing construction for an hour or two, driving the camp jeep if it was running. He would usually eat and socialize with the group in camp. Since he often had at least one of his sons on the island, he might spend some time with the boy, on rare occasions taking him for a sail in the lagoon, but more often seeing him in his bungalow. He would always make one trip down to the workers camp and observe the growth of the turtles that were being raised there. Within a day or two, however, he would lose interest in construction, camp guests, and children, and spend more and more time in his bungalow alone.

With its warm and inviting waters and smooth sandy beaches, the lagoon had a natural beauty to match any vacation spot in the world. However, there were sharks around. The cook would catch them, in fact, within feet of the shore. They were small, however, and regarded as harmless, so the children and the rest of us would often swim. Brando, however, never was seen to set a single toe in the water.

There was one project which briefly captured his interest. It involved a coconut palm located just outside his bungalow, near the shoreline of the lagoon. The shoreline was subject to the vagaries of nature and the water had been eating away at it. On days when a heavy wind was blowing in, the waves would lap away at the tree, further exposing its roots. Although the tree had been there for decades, the sea was now relentlessly wearing away its underpinnings.

This tree had no distinguishing characteristics. There were thousands and thousands of other coconut palms of equal distinction and majesty on the island. Indeed, if you closed your eyes and started walking in any direction from any point on the island except the landing strip, it is unlikely you could have taken ten steps without running your nose into a coconut palm.

Brando, however, decided that he liked this particular tree. He wanted it saved. So, he would requisition the Michigan front end loader with a driver and a couple of other workers with hand shovels. Under his supervision, they would pile a few tons of sand back around the exposed roots of the tree. The first time he did so, Jean Mercier tried to talk him out of the effort, pointing out its futility. The sea would be back to claim it. Several guests on the island told him the same thing, one making rather derogatory comments to him concerning his brainpower or lack thereof. Brando readily admitted that he too thought it was a doomed effort, but he nonetheless wanted to try.

The predicted result occurred. The next heavy incoming wind brought wave action that removed all the newly deposited sand plus a bit more and added another five degrees of list. Brando did not give up. Again the front end loader and crew were called back to duplicate their earlier effort. Again the results were the same. They returned for a third try. The next heavy seas were even more destructive. This time the waves took the tree down. The sea had its way, the three reinforcements adding only a few weeks to the life of the palm. Oh well, this was not quite like the Leaning Tower of Pisa falling, there were still about 99,999 coconut palms left.

The wave action on the solitary palm was a portent of greater troubles with the sea that lay before us.

Beyond his initial tour on arrival, Brando showed no interest in the daily progress of construction. He was unburdened by the urge to pitch in and work, and perhaps get a little exercise at the same time. However, on one isolated occasion he decided to assist in preparing the tourist facilities. Apparently growing bored after many days of idleness, he announced one evening that he and Christian were going to work the next morning. They were going out to the reef to gather coral.

Coral is actually the hard skeleton secreted by certain marine polyps. The deposits of countless organisms over centuries are joined together to form large agglomerations. In this case, the coral formed the reef which encircled the island and reached from the ocean bottom to the surface of the sea. It is mostly white with yellow highlights and has a hardness approaching concrete. Select pieces near the extremities are very attractive, the winding alabaster tendrils forming an artistic labyrinth. Brando wanted to harvest the coral in order to use it as natural sculpture to decorate the bungalows.

Morning came, the Tahitians went to work, Christian readied the Hobie catamaran, but there was no movement from Brando's bungalow. Around noon, he made his appearance in time for lunch. Finally, at about two o'clock, the voyage was launched. The trade winds caught the Hobiecat's sail and they tacked out toward the reef, Christian at the helm. A couple of hours later, they returned. The hold was not exactly overflowing. The harvest was two small pieces of coral.

Thus endeth the Brando working career on Tetiaroa.

Brando had the habit of inviting women to Tetiaroa, women of many nationalities and many descriptions. He had a well documented history of romances with glamorous, famous, and exciting women. But, those were not the women he brought to Tetiaroa. His Tetiaroa women were not famous, not exciting, and most distinctly not glamorous.

They also were not young and attractive, as one might expect someone of his stature and reputed appetite to collect. A more accurate description of his typical female guest would be middle aged, overweight, dowdy, and with a basketful of neuroses. They were usually oriental and sometimes had a husband waiting at home for their return.

The women would show up unannounced to me or anyone else on the island, always when Brando was himself there. He never brought one with him or left with one; they traveled alone. He was at the plane to greet them and direct them to a bungalow, never his own. Thereafter, he might pay them scant attention, not bother to introduce them to anyone else on the island, and leave them to develop their own acquaintances and to entertain themselves.

Most of them had been girlfriends from times long past often ten, twenty, even twenty-five years earlier. In visiting with them around the camp in the evenings, they would tell tales, not of torrid long-ago romances, but rather of how they would continue to get late night calls from Brando, spaced years apart. He would converse for a half hour, an hour, and then would be gone for another three years without ever giving much of an explanation for the call. Their invitations to Tetiaroa had come from such a phone call. Now, they were there and Brando was ignoring them. They could not understand it.

They would arrive singly, but in a pattern so that their visits overlapped. With two, three, or four there at a time, none could freely lay claim to Brando's full attention.

Whereas they might have been rivals two decades earlier, they now often became friendly, sharing the same frustrations caused by their mystic Fantasy Island host. Although they were cordial face to face, they created a whole distinct dimension of gossiping and behind-the-back maneuvering on the island.

One of the visitors departed slightly from the usual mold. True, she was middle aged, overweight, dowdy, married, and neurotic. However, she was not a former girlfriend. Rather, she was a Beverly Hills neighbor who had only recently met Brando as a consequence of the nighttime barking of his German shepherd.

This woman was tagged with the name Amazing Grace on the island. She had a fuzzy and distorted view of the world and confessed to having been recently discharged from an institution where she had been undergoing psychiatric care. She expressed astonishment that Brando had invited and paid for her to come to Tetiaroa after they had shared only a brief conversation. She spent her days in puzzlement, trying to figure out why she was there. She was perplexed that Brando never spoke to her throughout the duration of her week on Tetiaroa.

One evening after dinner, a group was visiting in the radio shack. One of the other woman visitors asked Amazing Grace what she did in Los Angeles.

"I have this corporation," Amazing Grace said.

"Oh, that's nice. What is your corporation?"

"It's called Little Tots, Incorporated."

"What does it do?"

"My husband had an attorney draw it up and I own it," Grace said.

"But what does it do?"

"I'm anxious to see how it develops. I think it is really going to be just what I need."

"But just what does it do? Do you manufacture something for kids? Or do you provide some kind of service?"

"Well, no. We don't make anything."

"How many employees do you have?"

"I don't have employees. I just own the corporation and I think it's going to be a very big corporation some day."

"Well, what do you want to do with it? What service is the corporation going to offer? What is its purpose?"

"A corporation doesn't have to do anything," said Grace. "Don't you see, it's just a corporation. General Motors was just a small corporation at one time and look at it now."

"But if you aren't going to do anything with your corporation, how is it going to grow? Do you think it's just going to grow by itself without employees or products or advertising or anything?"

"Well, it might just do that. In fact, I want to go into town tomorrow and call my husband and see if it's grown since I've been gone."

Amazing.

Brando walked into the radio shack in the midst of the conversation. He caught the chuckles from Amazing Graces' comments and could not stop laughing. In the background, foreign conversation, apparently in some middle-European language, came over the radiophone, which we usually kept on at a low volume. To try to gain his composure and stop laughing at Amazing Grace by directly his concentration elsewhere, Brando picked up the phone and made a few comments into it, interrupting the conversation taking place. He threw in a barrage of gibberish, mixing a handful of French, German, Tahitian and other phrases.

Surprisingly, he got a response. He threw back another mouthful of gibberish. Another response. Another Brando comment, another response. The upward voice inflections at the end of each response made it clear that the person on the other end did not understand what Brando was saying, but that did not stop the conversation. Brando finally tired of it, but the foreign language questions still kept coming over the radio.

It was hard to judge whose comments were more nonsensical, Amazing Grace, Brando, or the disembodied voice on the other end of the radio phone.

Eventually, I began to resent the intrusion of Brando's guests on the work and the burden that he was imposing on those who were trying to build the resort. He would leave his invited guests unattended, even boycotting the noon and evening meal gatherings and then raiding the kitchen after everyone else had retired.

One day when he was complaining about the disruption that one of his guests was causing, I asked him, "Marlon, why did you invite her to come to Tetiaroa?"

"Well, I thought she might have some insight on how we should run our tourist operations."

"Where would you ever get such an idea? She has no background in tourist operations or experience in any kind of business. Why would you think she would know anything about running a tourist operation?"

"Well, actually she's an old friend who I hadn't seen in ages and I just thought it would be nice to visit with her again", he replied. "And it would be a nice vacation for her too."

"Has it been nice to see her? I haven't even seen you talk to her since she arrived. You keep bringing all of these old girlfriends here and then you ignore them. They don't know what to do. There is nothing to entertain them all day long, so all they do is go around stirring up trouble. I spend as much time taking care of their problems as I do trying to build the resort."

"Well, Roger, look at it this way. It keeps life interesting for you anyway."

"Yeah, thanks, thanks a lot. I tell you how interesting it is. Yesterday, we had to make two radio calls to Papeete to make sure the next shipment of Cadbury bars had the right kind of nuts in them. The last ones had almonds instead of hazel nuts and you would have thought people were being tortured over here. I'm sure everyone within a hundred miles who has a radio phone was entertained by those conversations."

"Why don't you wait until we're open for business before you invite any more old girlfriends here. At least then they'll be able to visit with the tourists," I suggested.

Marlon thought a bit and then said, "That would seem to make more sense. The way it is now, the tension gets so thick around here that half the time I hate to even come out of my bungalow."

Although many of his female guests were married, what their husbands thought of their going off to see Brando I never knew, for we never heard from any of them. One of the husbands was his country's ambassador to the United Nations.

Muhammed Ali traveled with an entourage. So did Elizabeth Taylor. Marlon Brando had his own entourage. Unfortunately, it surrounded me, not him.

Ah, could the clock have been turned back to the days when he preferred the company of glamorous actresses...

CHAPTER TWENTY-ONE

ARCHITECTS, ARCHITECTS ARCHITECTS

Architects he got. Unfortunately, not Polynesian architects, not even architects with experience in designing for the tropics. He hired Los Angeles architects. Then he hired a New York architect. If construction was half completed, that was no time to stop. Let's get another New York architect.

Architects were hired. They were flown halfway around the world. They were not always told why they were being flown halfway around the world, but nonetheless, they arrived. If they had a spouse, the spouse arrived also. Children? Why not bring them along, too?

During my time on Tetiaroa, three different architects were brought there to contribute their design concepts. There had been others before that. They did not produce radically differing designs. In fact, most did not contribute any design ideas at all. In the end, the huts that were constructed had an amazing resemblance to what the average sixteen-year-old Polynesian would have sketched in the sand.

The architects did not always charge large fees, although their travel expenses were always considerable. In a couple of instances, Brando invited age-old acquaintances to come to Tetiaroa to contribute to the design. In both cases, they made no suggestions whatsoever, proving again that free advice is worth what you pay for it. Ultimately, the disruption and delays they caused were more costly than any fees they might have charged.

Design started shortly after Brando purchased Tetiaroa in 1966, before he had the vision to construct a tourist facility. Brando hired a Los Angeles architect to design a house for himself. The design he produced was simple, as was appropriate for the environment. The entire house was under a soaring conical roof sixty feet in diameter, which sat on top of coconut palm posts every twelve feet around the perimeter. The roof was constructed of panel woven by the natives from fronds of the pandanus tree. Support for the roof was a lattice of three to four inch round rafters, harvested from a native hardwood tree. The symmetrical design and the interplay of lines and curves of the fronds and rafters were pleasing to the eye. The interior had a few partitions for separating cooking, sleeping, and bathroom areas. The balance of the living area was open - extremely open, there were no exterior walls. Between the support poles were mounted rolls of canvas, which could be drawn down to provide privacy or protection against the occasional storm.

Such a design was quite feasible in that environment. Because of the remote location in the middle of the Pacific, walls were not needed to maintain privacy. In the tropical climate there is never any cold to keep out. The gently caressing trade winds are far more soothing than noisy and harsh air conditioning. No wild beasts roamed the island. Only the ever present rats were a problem, and there were ways of eradicating them.

Compared to building a home in the United States, the cost on Tetiaroa should have been reasonable. There were no windows, doors, walls, heating or air conditioning, paint, or insulation to purchase or install and no lumber or roofing to buy. Because of shipping, a few purchased items like plumbing, wiring, and appliances would cost more.

This first design sat on a shelf in Brando's Beverly Hills home. Nothing was ever done to construct the home.

The major architectural effort was Bernard Judge's comprehensive three phase Tetiaroa master plan that Brando had presented to me before my first trip to Tetiaroa. This was a broad conceptual plan for development of facilities for tourists; it did not contain any detailed floor plans, bills of material, specifications, or any other construction drawings.

In contrast to the elemental materials and simple construction methods for one simple Polynesian style house, there are formidable obstacles to overcome in establishing an entire village or high rise hotel on a remote atoll. Acquiring and transporting material, hiring, training, transporting, and housing workers, dealing with communications and with distant regulating agencies all result in costs and delays that cannot be foreseen by someone inexperienced in working in a remote location. There are special environmental problems, such as developing a fresh water supply system and a sewage system. It is necessary to put in some type of electrical system and to provide for things like emergency medical care.

One cannot estimate the cost of building a high rise in Los Angeles and then add twenty or thirty percent to allow for the extra costs due to the remote location. One could add two or three hundred percent and still overrun cost estimates. (I recently evaluated a mining project on a remote frozen Canadian island where the costs ran more than twelve times those of a comparable project in Nevada.)

Brando had been so pleased with Judge's initial design that he hired him to go to Tetiaroa and supervise construction of phase one of the plan. This turned out to be bad casting. Judge had little construction experience and Tetiaroa was no place to learn. Judge spent a year or so in Tahiti and Tetiaroa. He hired Tapituri, the Tahitian contractor, to construct the airstrip. Tapituri brought his equipment over the reef and the strip was finished after several months. The airstrip passed inspection by the French aviation regulatory authorities and construction was then begun for the tourist village.

From 1966 to 1973, Brando seldom visited his island because of the difficult and hazardous passage across the ocean and over the reef. It was only at the time that I started working for him that he began to spend significant time there.

Upon first arriving on Tetiaroa in the midst of the construction of phase one, I had asked to see Judge's construction drawings. Although he had formulated the conceptual plan which was on Brando's Beverly Hills coffee table, Judge said that he had never made any construction drawings. However, he was now going to produce them because the building inspector from Papeete was insisting on drawings before he would authorize opening. This was a rather interesting concept that I had never learned in business school. Execution first, planning second.

It was to take several more months, but Judge eventually produced drawings to submit to the building inspector. They turned out to be nothing more than rough, freehand sketches.

He did come up with one drawing, however, that was unlike anything that any Polynesian would ever dream up - the Judge Emergency Water System.

Providing water for the village was difficult in this environment. Tetiaroa is a low lying island in the middle of the vast saltwater Pacific Ocean. There are no streams, rivers, or fresh water lakes. Fresh water could be obtained only by collecting rain water or by digging wells. However, there were few hard surfaces for gathering rainwater, really just one small metal roof, and wells have very limited capacity on an atoll. There is only a narrow convex lens-like water table beneath each islet, the accumulation of centuries of rain soaking into the ground. The lens of freshwater is narrow near the perimeter of the island and wider in the center. Below the freshwater table is saltwater. So, indiscriminate pumping of a well leads to quick depletion of the fresh water around the well-head and an invasion of saltwater from below. Once saltwater has invaded a well, it could take decades of rainfall to restore the water table in the vicinity.

The water collection system that Judge designed was based on research done by the Army Corps of Engineers in the South Pacific islands during World War II. The Corps had developed a design that had fifty feet of horizontal perforated drain tile buried within the water table with a solid vertical well pipe meeting the horizontal pipe in the center of its run. Fresh water would seep through the perforations. Thus, the water would be drawn from a wide area, not just from the bottom of the well pipe. The Army Engineers discovered that by slowly drawing the water from a wide area, the life of the freshwater lens in the vicinity of the well would be substantially prolonged.

Judge had designed a system using four such wells in order to spread out even further the water taken from any single portion of the lens. This part of the system was logical. However, the next step caused concern. The water was pumped from all four wells into a small central reservoir, which was actually a small above-ground swimming pool. From there, it went through a single pump to the tourist village.

It was the combining of the output of all four wells that troubled me. If the pump beyond the reservoir broke down, the entire water system would be out. Had each of the four wells pumped their water into the distribution system independently, then a pump failure would have left seventy-five percent of the capacity of the system intact. In another locale, a pump breakdown might not be much of a problem; if a breakdown occurs, just call a plumber. However, we were in the middle of the Pacific, and the nearest supply of spare parts for the main pump was in Warren, Ohio.

I expressed my concern to Judge. He acknowledged the problem and promised to work on it. A few days later, he came up with the design for the Judge Emergency Water System. He proudly thrust his design in front of me and seemed to be waiting for congratulations on his imaginative concept. It was indeed imaginative, a fanciful creation that must have come to him in the midst of a dream, for surely no wakened brain could have produced such an incongruous masterpiece.

The drawing showed a coconut palm tree about twenty-five feet tall, its long fronds drawn freehand, with a small wooden platform attached at about the sixteen foot level and two fifty-five gallon cisterns on top of the platform and lashed to the tree with rope. If the main pump on the island water system had a failure and was down for a week waiting for spare parts to be flown in, not to worry. This hundred and ten gallons of water would take care of everything.

There is an old song with lyrics about romantic moonlight underneath the swaying palms. On Tetiaroa, the palms did indeed sway. Many days had twenty to thirty knot winds. Frequently, a tree would simply fall over in the breeze, its shallow root system pulling out of the loose soil.

Water weighs about eight pounds per gallon. The water in two cisterns would weigh 880 pounds. Add the weight of the cisterns and platform and there would be over a thousand pound weight up in that tree. I would not choose to be standing underneath. Imagine how this added burden would increase the angle of sway during winds. If the palm survived the initial filling of the cisterns, it would surely succumb to the first full sustained exhalation from the trade winds.

The Judge Emergency Water System was to be tied into the main water system by a vertical pipe running down the length of the palm, attached to the main system water line laid along the ground. I tried to picture the results of this connection if, by some revision in the laws of physics, the palm would manage to stand upright through the Tetiaroa breezes. A hefty wind would easily cause a normal palm to sway at least three feet in either direction. Suppose that the effect of the top-heavy weight were to increase that to five feet, thus generating a total arc of ten feet.

Recall the childhood game of "crack the whip" where the last ice skater in a line is sent flying as the effect of a small movement early in the line is magnified as the movement accelerates when it passes through the line. Then try to picture a little old gray haired lady sitting on the last toilet on the plumbing line when a heavy gust of wind hits the palm and the effect ripples through the pipeline. In my mind's eye, there was a vision of her bursting through a thatch covered roof, flying through the sky, arms and legs frantically wind-milling as she tries to pull up her pants before splashing down ignominiously in the lagoon.

I chose not to install the Judge Emergency Water System.

One sunny afternoon while Judge was still on the island, Brando informed me that another architect would be arriving on Tetiaroa the next day. Well, not quite an architect. Actually, she turned out to be a New York interior designer. Brando had asked her to come to assist Judge in the "architectural" design.

Out of the supply plane the next morning emerged a tall, slim woman of Chinese heritage whom I will call Sue Ming. She was another former Brando girlfriend from years long past.

Ming spent the first couple of days getting acquainted and looking around. Her response to my tour through the project included a lot of horizontal shaking of the head and audible glottal clucking. She "confidentially" told me that both Judge's design and the construction were abominable. She "confidentially" told everyone else on the island the same thing within the next day. She vowed to produce something of which Brando could justly be proud.

Ming meandered around observing and talking to the Tahitian workers. After a couple of weeks, she had produced nothing. She had, however, gone on interminably about her favorite topic, Judge's incompetence. As time dragged on, I asked to see her work, but was always put off. It eventually became apparent that she would be producing nothing.

Her presence was proving disruptive. She would wander about clad in a pareau, spending the day in conversation with whoever was around the camp, usually gossiping about everyone else on the island. Brando grew weary of her negative influence and wanted her to leave the island. However, he seemed to dread telling her and refused to allow me to do so, always putting it off with the observation that she would undoubtedly soon leave on her own. She was living in her own bungalow, and it was obvious that she and Brando had not rekindled any of their old romance.

Still, she gradually and unilaterally assumed the role of Brando's major-domo in regard to his other personal guests, even going to the extent of trying to tell them when they would be allowed to converse with him in his bungalow. She attempted to ingratiate herself with Brando's fifteen-year-old son, Christian. She took on the role of surrogate mother, minding Christian's clothes and cleaning his hut. Concurrently, she slipped him cigarettes and soda pop, two items which had Brando's disapproval.

While Brando would not ask her to leave, he did come upon his own creative revenge for her meddling, resulting in a situation that, if not suitable for the movies, was at least worthy of an episode in a sit-com.

It happened that there were two other former Brando girlfriends, one from Los Angeles and the other from Pakistan, plus Raiko Sato,

Tarita's companion and baby sitter, on the island at the time. Raiko mentioned to Brando one evening that Ming had admonished her for spending so much time talking to him and forbade her from speaking to him that evening. Thereupon, the other two women also mentioned that Ming was trying to block their access to Brando.

It more astonished than angered him that she had such audacity. He decided to teach Ming a lesson in his own inimitable way. He and the other three women collectively came up with a scheme whereby each of the three would alternate sleeping with him on sequential nights. Prior to that time, each had occupied her own bungalow every night and Brando had slept alone in his. Even though each had once been his girlfriend and had each shared his bed at an age when the sexual sap flowed faster through their veins, each one's relationship with him now appeared to be strictly platonic.

Whether Brando's revenge resulted in a rekindling of any old passions remained a secret between each night's pairing, but it all made for interesting conversation over the next week. It also soon resulted in Ming abandoning her role as major-domo.

This occurred when Alice Marchak was spending her two week vacation on Tetiaroa. Although she enjoyed chumming around and sharing complaints with Ming during the day, she collaborated in planning the revenge and delighted in its absurdity, but did not partake in sharing Brando's bed. Their relationship had never been a romantic one.

Counting Alice and Ming, Brando had five female guests on Tetiaroa at the time. Excluding the nightly musical bed partner, there were four women alone in their respective bungalows and beds at night. There were also about fifty Tahitian men on the island who were without women. The former attracted the latter. Every morning, one of the women would report having been awakened by a middle of the night visitor with romantic intentions. A simple command to "Get out of here" was sufficient to send the midnight Lothario on his way. In another country, such an intruder might have caused panic among the women. Here, with Brando's assurances that the mild mannered Tahitian men would respect the wishes of the women without protest, the intruder's efforts were met with simple amusement.

Brando encouraged the women to accept the romantic overtures. Perhaps the musical bed game was taxing his strength.

He particularly lamented that Alice would not succumb to the midnight visitor - he thought it the best cure for an advanced case of vanity and irritability. (It could have provided material for another chapter in Alice's book, THE SUPER SECS. It would have been one time when she could legitimately claim that "the bronze Tahitian god with romance on his mind" really did not have a name.)

Ming was chastened by the group discipline, but not upset enough to leave this expense paid tropical vacation paradise. When even she gave up the pretense that she was going to produce that "design that Marlon will be proud of," she decided to work for her keep. She announced that she would complete the rope windings where the tops of the structural support poles met the bottom of the horizontal connecting roof supports in the restaurant building.

The joints were connected by large spikes which provided structural strength. The rope windings were primarily decorative, providing an attractive and authentic Polynesian appearance. The design was simple, consisting of winding the rope over the horizontal member on one side of the pole, around the pole, and then over the horizontal member on the other side of the pole; with each cycle the rope was wound immediately adjacent to the previous wind. The Tahitians had completed the windings on two poles in the restaurant building to illustrate the pattern.

Ming recruited Alice to help. With self-provided fanfare appropriate to the beginning of construction of the Panama canal, they began their work in the restaurant building, which had about twenty joints to wind.

Though the pattern was elementary, it baffled them. After several abortive attempts, they pulled one of the workers off the job to demonstrate the process. Back to work they went, still unable to duplicate the pattern.

They finished one connection. Their winding more resembled the design of a dyslectic first grader in a creative basket weaving class than the desired pattern. By noon they had struggled halfway through another winding.

When lunch-time came, Ming and Alice went off to their respective bungalows and did not emerge until evening. It was the end of their work. The windings remained, the unfinished end of the rope on the second connection waving back and forth with each breeze for several weeks until removed by a worker.

After Ming went back into her vacation mode, Brando informed me one day that he was going to invite another architect to come from New York to Tetiaroa to provide even more input on design for the tourist village. I respectfully suggested that did not make much sense because construction was so far along that it simply would not be feasible to make more than minor changes. He admitted to the logic of my argument, but then revealed that the architect was already on the way and had, in fact, reached Papeete.

The next morning, I was at the plane to welcome the latest addition to the Brando International Institute of Architecture. The sequential number to assign this newest member was uncertain. On occasion, mystery people had shown up on the island to be greeted by Brando, taken on a tour of the island and had departed again the same day. There was reason to suspect that at least one of those had also been an architect. This time, at least, I knew why the deplaning passenger was here.

Stepping off the plane was architect Matsuko Garber and family. Matsuko was in her mid-thirties and of Japanese heritage. She had formerly lived in California and now resided in upstate New York. She arrived with Don, her school teacher husband, and a seven year old son and four year old daughter.

The Garbers took the bungalow next door to ours. Brando's other visitors on Tetiaroa had all arrived alone. It was nice to have a family there. My wife finally had someone to visit with who was not primarily concerned with maneuvering for Brando's attention. Their children played with ours and we quickly became friends. The Garbers swam in the lagoon, suntanned on the beach, and participated in the camp meals and evening conversations. Again, it did not appear that the latest architect was going to produce any new design ideas.

Whereas I would supervise the normal work contingent, after my experience with Ming, it seemed appropriate to steer clear of assigning work and deadlines to the people Brando brought to Tetiaroa on an informal basis. So, I did not ask for design suggestions from Matsuko. In the course of time, she became acquainted with Ming and the other visitors on the island. In fact, one day Ming spent a couple of hours with Matsuko, taking her through the tourist facilities, and describing them in elaborate detail and with considerable fervor. It struck me that Ming had certainly changed her mind about Judge's design.

My wife and I spent that evening visiting with the Garbers in their bungalow. Matsuko told a familiar tale about her relationship with Brando. She said, "I'll get these strange phone calls from him. I might not hear from him for two or three years and then the phone will ring one night and it will be Marlon. He might talk for a half hour or more. I can never figure out the purpose of the call. After he hangs up, I sit back and wonder what that was all about. I don't think I've figured one out yet."

It was not clear if Matsuko, like the other visitors, was a former Brando girlfriend. With her husband there, it was hardly an appropriate topic to raise.

"I know just what you mean," I said. "I frequently have difficulty understanding what he is saying or doing. Strange people keep showing up on the island. Half the time I can't figure out why they are here. I don't know if I am supposed to put them to work, entertain them, or ignore them. That's why it was nice when you arrived. At least I knew why you were here."

A look of incomprehension seemed to pass between Matsuko and Don. Something mysterious was going on between them, but neither spoke. Each seemed to be waiting for the other. Finally, Don said, "It's real interesting to hear you say that, Roger. This is very embarrassing but we have been trying to get up the courage to ask you something that has really been bothering us." There followed a pause and then he added, "Just why in the hell are we here?"

After we all stopped laughing, I passed on Brando's explanation that he had brought Matsuko to Tetiaroa to design the bungalows. It was news to them. Brando had just called one night and asked Matsuko to come to Tetiaroa. When asked why, he said that he would rather discuss it when she arrived. He told her to bring the whole family. Now, they had been there for a week, Brando had been spending most of his time in his bungalow (often visiting with one or more of his other female guests), and their conversations with him had not gotten beyond pleasantries.

Matsuko was relieved to hear my explanation, but not entirely pleased with the information it conveyed. She confessed to being completely unprepared to make any design contributions concerning Polynesian architecture. It was entirely outside the realm of her experience and competence. Given my previous experience with architects on Tetiaroa whose egos, though not their talent, seemed to have been developed at the Frank Lloyd Wright School, it was refreshing to hear such an honest admission.

This revelation led us into a discussion of the previous design efforts. Judge had, by this time, produced the drawings required by the building inspector. As I described his drawings, a look of amazement appeared on Matsuko's face. It seems that the enthusiastic descriptions I had seen Ming provide to Matsuko earlier did not reflect a change in mind about Judge's designs at all. Instead, she was proudly claiming to have designed everything herself. She had even, out of my earshot, showed Judge's unsigned drawings to Matsuko and claimed them as her own.

CHAPTER TWENTY-TWO

THE MARCHAK SOUP REBELLION

W hile there were many architects to design bungalows on Tetiaroa, the prime architect of the palace intrigue was Alice Marchak. With little to occupy her time during her vacation on Tetiaroa, she devoted much of her attention to stirring the pot. It was time to take the new financial manager down a peg or two. Dr. Wallace Heath, the man who had brought me to Tucson and introduced me to Brando, had earlier warned me that Alice would view me as a threat in her relationship to Brando. He had thought the potential problem sufficiently important and difficult to deal with that he wrote to me on Tetiaroa a few weeks later with a similar warning.

Part of the reason for Alice's downgrading of my efforts was her preference for having Bernard Judge run the Tetiaroa operation. Judge's skill and inclination at charming Alice were clearly greater than mine and his performance paid dividends.

When Alice arrived on Tetiaroa and stepped off the plane, Judge greeted her with an effusive and ingratiatory welcome. Alice loved it. I found it somewhat nauseating. He then took her on a guided tour of the island, with an eagerness to please that fell a hair short of embarrassing. His obsequious commentary made me think that the clock had been turned back and one of the ladies from the royal family of Tahiti had again been brought to Tetiaroa for fattening.

Despite Judge's attentions, Alice was not happy on Tetiaroa. With the comfort and luxury level being several leagues below that of a movie star's home in Beverly Hills, Alice's attitude toward Tetiaroa could at best be described as tolerance - definitely not enjoyment.

It was more than the lack of amenities, however, that made her uncomfortable. In Beverly Hills, she was the chief of the house and the other household employees followed her orders. After eighteen years, it was a role she had come to expect and enjoy. On Tetiaroa, she had no such special position. The employees there merely regarded her as just another guest. Although her time there was entirely a vacation, she could not wait to leave.

Sometimes, Alice's hints about my lack of competence were less than subtle. Throughout her stay on Tetiaroa, she found many faults, but her major complaint was that the food was grossly inadequate for her comfort. This criticism was not directed solely to Brando, but was readily shared with anyone within earshot.

The Tetiaroa camp did fall short of restaurant row on La Cienega in Los Angeles, but the nearest grocery was a chartered plane trip away, the closest supermarket three thousand miles further. Still, there was always a variety of nutritious food in ample quantity. If quality sometimes suffered from the lack of skills of the temporary Tahitian cook, the kitchen remained open to anyone who preferred to fend for herself. (By comparison, Blanche, the cook in Beverly Hills, uniformly provided excellent meals, but that was half a world away.)

In Beverly Hills, Alice often told the story of her earlier time on Tahiti when Brando was filming MUTINY ON THE BOUNTY. She had difficulty keeping his quarters in provisions, generally attributing her problems to thieving by the Tahitians. She would grumble that Brando was always mad at her because there was nothing in the house for him to eat or drink.

That house had been located on Tahiti, near grocery stores. Feeding dozens of workers and guests on Tetiaroa was a bit more of a logistics problem than Alice had experienced. Daily, she would vehemently criticize the provisioning on Tetiaroa while repeating the tale about her earlier *"completely impossible"* situation on Tahiti. The incongruity apparently did not strike her as it did the other guests.

Her discontent reached its peak one day. The natives had held their wine rebellion. This would be the day of the Marchak soup rebellion. The first was comedy; this one was farce.

Alice had arranged for her nephew to come to Tetiaroa during a portion of her stay there. He was a young man about twenty years old who, in contrast to his aunt, thoroughly enjoyed his time on the island. One morning, he decided to go sailing in the lagoon. He returned an hour or so after lunch. He was hungry, a not unusual condition for a young man who has missed a meal. Since the cook was off until evening, Alice decided to prepare something for him to eat. She searched through the supply shed and, despite an ample larder, found little to her liking.

Ultimately, she concluded that lunch would have to be either a sandwich or a bowl of Campbell's chicken noodle soup. Her nephew decided that he would prefer the soup. In fact, he made it completely clear - to everyone's comprehension except Alice's - that he was completely content with a bowl of soup. With abundant fanfare and flourish for the benefit of the several people around the camp, Alice opened the can, added the water, and heated the soup - all of the time filling the air with lamentations over the inadequate food supply and the resulting damage that such a meal might inflict on her nephew's health. He, nonetheless, consumed it with apparent satisfaction and enjoyment, amidst his efforts to quiet his agitated aunt.

From the hue and cry made during the soup rebellion, it was as though I was cast as Captain Bligh of a century earlier, as though the mutiny on the BOUNTY were to be reenacted as mutiny on Tetiaroa. It sounded like I was depriving everyone on the island of fresh fruits and vegetables with the express desire to inflict scurvy on a deprived, starving, and over-worked crew.

With the many well fed and contented bellies in the camp, there were to be - to put it mildly - no followers in this rebellion.

By the time Alice was scheduled to return to Los Angeles, Sue Ming's originally planned week on Tetiaroa had now stretched into six or seven weeks. Although Brando normally stayed on Tetiaroa for only short periods of time, the presence of his many female guests during this trip had kept him on the island for almost two months. While the "island fever" was getting to him, he did not want to leave with Ming still there. After weeks of muttering and complaining about her, finally, he had enough of her disruptive presence. However, he still did not directly tell her to leave. Instead, he had Alice make a reservation for Ming to accompany Alice back to Los Angeles. Alice did, and gave Ming her departure schedule.

When Ming was informed, she laid plans for one final dramatic appeal to remain in paradise. Hitching a ride on the jeep for the lengthy journey of a hundred yards to the dinner table the last evening, she managed to stage a pratfall while climbing out. She lay on the ground like a quarterback blind-sided by a 280 pound defensive tackle, professed acute pain, and complained that she had suffered a dislocated hip. When her groans were met with guffaws, her complaints with chuckles, and her squawking with sniggering, she quickly managed to regain her feet and meekly joined the group for dinner.

The next morning, Air Tahiti finally lifted off with the M and M twins, Marchak and Ming, on board. That was one chartered plane I would have paid for myself. I found myself merrily singing the old country western song, THANK GOD AND GREYHOUND SHE'S GONE, through the rest of the day. Somehow, one rendition was never enough, I always had to sing it twice.

Thereafter, whenever passing the restaurant building, I would pause and look at the unfinished loose end of the rope on Alice's and Ming's aborted second winding. I would watch it sway with the breeze, contentedly picturing each arc as a wave good-bye to two small, but irritable, Tetiaroa problems.

Brando had been planning to return at the same time as Alice, but instead remained on Tetiaroa.

A couple of days later, the level of intrigue having dropped dramatically, Brando said to me, "I want to get out of here, but now I can't even go home. Can you imagine, after all the havoc Ming created around here, she had the nerve to ask me if she could stay at my house for a week before returning to New York? I'll be damned if I'm going to go back there with Alice and her both in the house."

"Why in the world didn't you just say no?" I asked. "Or, you could have at least made up some excuse, like you were expecting company and there wouldn't be room for her."

"Well, I figured this would be the last I'd ever see of that woman, so I thought I'd just let it go and stay here until she gets out of there."

It was sometimes hard to believe that this was the same person who would not hesitate to chase and physically beat on a reporter or photographer disturbing his privacy.

While Brando often failed to recognize the imposition of more or less abandoning his guests to my care, in many respects, he could also be a very considerate, caring employer.

In the construction camp atmosphere on Tetiaroa, daily life obviously lacked some of the conveniences to which one is accustomed. Absent were such things as washing machines, television, newspapers, magazines. The radio broadcast only fifteen minutes of news per day in English with the balance of the transmission in French. While I was too busy to miss entertainment and other normal diversions, the days often grew long and boring for the rest of my family. Tetiaroa was an island paradise, but even an unchallenging paradise can become tedious. One can only indulge in the sun and luxuriate in the water for just so long. Brando recognized the boredom factor and repeatedly would do what he could for our comfort - things as trivial but gratifying as ordering Chinese food sent over from Papeete or as considerate as buying bicycles for my sons to ride around the island.

The most disconcerting problem of life on the island was the lack of privacy. On Tetiaroa, there was de facto segregation; the Tahitians had their camp on one side of the island, everyone else used the camp on the other side of the island, be they guest or worker. For our camp, there was one shower, shared by everyone. There was even just one community outhouse.

In the beginning, our family meals were taken together with two or three employees plus the guests who happened to be on the island. Eating with the same people meal after meal, day after day soon became uncomfortable. When Brando saw the strain this arrangement caused, he insisted that we place first priority in construction on completing a private kitchen in our bungalow. It made life much easier.

Indeed, Brando would get so concerned about my personal comfort that he would at times become frustrated at my refusal to take advantage of his kindness. For example, I purchased an inexpensive cot for our Papeete office to sleep on during the occasional night spent on Tahiti, to save the expense of a hotel room. If Brando was on Tahiti or Tetiaroa and knew that I was spending the night in Papeete, he would insist that Yvonne Chung make a reservation for me at the Hotel Tahiti, despite my expressed willingness to sleep in the office.

Yvonne would make the reservation. I would cancel it. Brando would find out and have Yvonne make it again. I would cancel it and swear Yvonne to silence.

The only way to finally prevail was to pretend to Brando that I had spent the night in the hotel. I learned to ruminate on the delights of a hot shower at the Hotel Tahiti, a luxury absent from Tetiaroa. Maybe I could not convince Brando I liked dogs, but my acting was not a complete failure.

His concern for my comfort extended beyond Tetiaroa. Whenever I returned to his home in Beverly Hills after a day at work, Brando would assure that my needs were taken care of there as well. If I had not had dinner, he would have the cook prepare something for me, and even on occasion he cooked something for me himself. He would frequently inquire if there was some particular thing I liked to eat or drink so that he could have Alice stock it.

When we would go anywhere together, he would always be grabbing my luggage and opening doors for me before I would have a chance to do it for him. In many respects, I could not have asked for a friend or employer to do more for my daily personal comfort and well-being or for those of my family.

CHAPTER TWENTY-THREE

KLAUS ROBER'S STORY

B rando decided that the mechanic, Klaus Rober, should be fired. It was not a decision that I would have made, but his reasoning was logical. Klaus was a hard worker, probably the most diligent on the island, and he had earned my respect. However, there was one major problem which Brando correctly pointed out - everything was broken down all of the time.

That may be exaggeration, but only a slight one. The motorized vehicles, for example, seemed to be inoperative most of the time. When Klaus did get them running, it was only a few days until they were down once again. However, he was operating under trying circumstances, with great difficulty getting spare parts and with heavy footed drivers using the vehicles. Brando, himself, was one of the worst offenders. It seemed that every time he came to Tetiaroa he would throw a rod in the jeep or leave it hung up on a log on the far end of the island. Still, a mechanic is hired to keep mechanical equipment running and Brando insisted that Klaus was failing in that duty.

Brando had suggested several times earlier that we replace Klaus. Although I long resisted, the breakdown problems continued, and I was finally worn down by Brando's complaints and acquiesced.

This occurred during the time when Brando had five different women guests in the camp. So, the conversations had not been restricted to Brando and me. Rather, he had made his case to the women and sounded them out before again broaching the topic with me. They - profound experts all! - agreed with Brando; Klaus should be fired.

I had mixed feelings, hating to fire someone who tried so hard and knowing that we might not be able to find another mechanic willing to live on Tetiaroa.

Klaus had a fearsome reputation. To begin with, he had served in the French Foreign Legion, which was a normal indication of a troublesome background. He stood a half head taller than anyone else on the island and carried the weight and bulk to go with his height. With the hot Tetiaroa sun and his own activity causing steady rivulets of sweat to pour down his bearded Germanic face, he had the look of a jungle mercenary.

His natural expression was more a frown than a smile and, since he did not speak English, the inability of the Americans to communicate with him added an apparent extra measure of menace to his bearing. He had recently had a couple of loud tangles with Jean Mercier, the construction boss, who himself resembled a prime condition body builder.

When Brando brought all the women in on the decision to fire Klaus, they had also discussed who should do it. There were two candidates for the messenger bearing the bad news. Each stood five foot, nine inches tall and would have to stand on a footstool to talk with Klaus on an eye to eye level. There was one skinny guy weighing in at about 140 pounds - me; and a true heavyweight, at a portly 230 pounds - Brando.

As the manager in charge of Tetiaroa, I was the logical person. However, several of the women thought Brando should perform the task since he had originally hired Klaus and he was the one promoting the firing.

Now, Brando had gotten into more than his share of physical confrontations. One could not contest his courage. On several documented occasions he had chased away or punched out people who were invading his privacy. From the damage inflicted on the other parties, one could not question his strength either. Still, the other fights had been largely the result of an exploding temper. Now, we were looking at a contemplative act that some of the women in the camp feared could lead to an exploding temper on the other side - Klaus'.

Brando nominated a third candidate to do the firing. He suggested the muscular Jean Mercier, saying that Klaus would think twice about starting any trouble with Mercier.

The conversations went on in camp and at the dinner table for a couple of days whenever Klaus was absent. Whenever he walked into the camp, an embarrassed silence would descend until someone got the conversation started on another topic. This really should not have been a very big deal, but there were a lot of people sitting around the camp all day long with little to do, so they made it a big deal.

After this had amused the camp idlers for a couple of days, I decided to get it over with. I knew that the others' imagined possibility for any real problem with Klaus was highly overblown. I had fired people before with never a physical confrontation and did not expect one now. Brando did not want to do it, and Mercier would have been the worst choice. Since he had almost come to blows with Klaus before, his telling Klaus he was fired could be the one possible trigger to Klaus's temper.

Besides, it was not Mercier's duty to fire Klaus since Klaus was not under his command; it was mine. The factor that caused me to hesitate was the language barrier. Klaus was fluent in German and conversant in French, but spoke little English. I spoke only English well, with just a touch of ages old college German. Since Klaus had worked by himself independently of the construction crew, he had required little supervision for his day to day work. I could probably say, "You're fired," in sign language and make the message understood. But, Klaus's firing was not such a clear-cut decision or the result of dereliction of duty and therefore he was entitled to a full and reasonable explanation.

So, I gathered up a bilingual worker to try to interpret and told Klaus the bad news, explaining through the interpreter the problems of needing to keep the machinery running better and our desire to find someone else to do the job.

He accepted the news with a mature degree of composure. He provided the explanation expected, blaming his problems on the lack of spare parts and improper use of the vehicles. While visibly and rightfully emotionally upsetting to Klaus, the termination was otherwise as uneventful as paint drying on the wall.

Firing Klaus on Tetiaroa was not quite like firing a mechanic at your local auto service department. He could not just be handed two weeks pay, wished good luck, and eased out the door. Klaus not only worked on Tetiaroa, he lived there. His tent was his hearth and his home. All his worldly possessions were there with him, including his recently acquired and heavily mortgaged speedboat, and he had nowhere else to go. It was a few weeks before Klaus actually left Tetiaroa.

Perhaps the most telling part of the story of firing Klaus was yet to come. The firing had taken place out of the sight of anyone other than Klaus, the interpreter and me. Two of Brando's women guests reported that, later that afternoon, Brando was in the camp, visiting with them. He said to them, "Well, I finally fired Klaus today. I should've gotten rid of him a long time ago," implying that he himself had done the deed awaited with such apprehension by everyone.

At the time, Klaus was approaching the camp - seemingly not in a confrontational mood at all - the camp was simply the pathway back to his tent.

Just as he boastfully uttered those words, Brando detected Klaus' footsteps and, in mid-sentence, made a quick pivot and headed off in a perpendicular direction toward his bungalow. There he remained through that day and the next. By the third day, he must have figured any storm had blown over, for he came back to the camp, socializing with his guests including, eventually, Klaus.

Klaus was in no hurry to leave Tetiaroa for another job. Over the next several weeks, with his work obligations removed, he spent lots of time boating, fishing, and drinking coffee in the camp. Strangely enough, with all the time on his hands, he and Brando became closer friends and companions than they had previously been.

Indeed, it was just a few days later that they went out together on an eerie midnight sail. Brando had invited another of his woman friends to Tetiaroa. This woman, with the euphonious Tahitian name of Puraya, had been an acquaintance of Brando since his MUTINY ON THE BOUNTY days in Tahiti. She was the widow of a businessman from Tahiti and the mother of our banker in Papeete. Puraya was a slim woman in her sixties. Her slow walk and stately posture gave her an aura of dignity. She filled my mind with a vision of a royal Tahitian queen coming for a vacation retreat decades earlier in an outrigger canoe.

Brando had a particular purpose in inviting Puraya to Tetiaroa. He explained, "Puraya is a very wealthy woman and well connected in the French society on Tahiti. She knows all the bankers, lawyers, and government officials there. I'm going to offer her a piece of land if she'll build a vacation home here. Having her as a part-time resident of Tetiaroa will result in all kinds of benefits from Papeete society."

Brando's natural inclination was to repel any attention that any society elected to shower upon him. In addition, he had a particularly intense dislike for the French authorities on Tahiti, believing that Tahiti should be independently governed by the Tahitians. This sounded like a reasonable, even rational, political compromise from a normally irrational guy.

Since he was trying to obtain a concession from Puraya, Brando acted the charming host when she arrived and joined everyone for Saturday evening dinner. There was a small group for dinner including Reiko Sato and Klaus, who was now enjoying a life of leisure on Tetiaroa since losing his job. My family and I also joined the party.

We enjoyed a convivial evening, the wine flowing in pace with the lively conversation. It was as enchanting as Hollywood's most romantic movie might have portrayed a South Seas Island evening. The perfect temperature warmed the body and the trade winds gently flowed through the camp. As the sun settled over the lagoon amidst a gentle pink western sky, a young Tahitian maiden, who must have stepped right out of a Gaugain painting, moved softly about filling our glasses with a warm French claret.

Puraya was flattered as Brando made his offer of land and promised to begin building a house immediately.

As the wine and the evening soaked into the body, a full moon rose like an enormous luminous disk against a clear star filled sky, producing a phosphorescence on the softly gurgling waves.

The clear South Pacific night produced a star cover totally uninhibited by ambient artificial light.

Brando suggested a moonlight sail on the lagoon. He gathered up Klaus to act as helmsman, escorted Puraya and Raiko to the Hobiecat, and they set sail, wine bottle in hand. Jauntily, Brando tossed off a good-bye, "If we're not back in a couple of hours, you better send someone out to rescue us."

The rest of us, having indulged of the juice of the grape as freely as the moonlight sailors, soon returned to our bungalows and went to sleep.

The next day, being Sunday, the camp inhabitants were a little later rising than normal. As we nursed a second cup of coffee - Marlon, Reiko, Klaus, and Puraya absent - someone casually asked if anyone knew what time the sailors had returned.

No one did.

A bit later someone asked if they actually had returned. A quick look at the shore revealed that the Hobiecat was gone! A check of the bungalows showed that none of their beds had been slept in.

Someone added that winds had come up during the night.

It was panic time on Tetiaroa! We broke out the binoculars, but sighted no trace of boat or people.

Marlon's parting words, "send someone out to rescue us," echoed in my ear. Well, the U. S. Coast Guard was five thousand miles away and no one on Tahiti had ever heard of an air-sea rescue squad. Like everything else, we were our own coast guard on Tetiaroa.

Admiral's hat in hand, I hustled over to the Tahitian worker's camp to start up the Zodiak for a search mission, visualizing the linotype machines banging out the headlines, "Marlon Brando Disappears in the South Pacific - Tetiaroa Coast Guard Launches Massive One Boat Sea Rescue Search."

With Marlon's son, Christian, and my son, Gregory, as crew, our rescue mission pulled out to sea, cutting through the channel between Onetahi and the adjacent islet. Then, just as we entered the lagoon, we spotted the white sail of the catamaran in the distance, headed our way.

A short while later the errant boat reached shore. Out stepped a slightly disheveled pair - Marlon and Reiko. Marlon rather sheepishly explained that they had sailed across the lagoon. The wind had blown up. He and Klaus, being less sober than judges, had lost control of the boat and it had beached on one of the small islets. They had slept the night there on the shore.

Whereas Marlon and Reiko looked weary, Klaus and Puraya stepped off the boat with more spring in their step, Puraya with a contented smile and Klaus with an absolutely beatific expression - known to male teenagers everywhere as "a shit-eating grin."

It seems that a torrid May - December romance had blossomed on the beach. It probably was not quite as white-hot as Lancaster and Kerr amidst the crushing waves of Hawaii, but the thirty-something French Foreign Legionnaire had found himself a sixty-something Tahitian princess.

Thereafter, Klaus could not have cared less that he had lost his job, for his days were filled with chasing around the lagoon in his speedboat or running around Tahiti in his new friend's bright yellow convertible, with the stately Puraya looking very grandmotherly and very blissful, close to his side.

Though she never moved one grain of sand to construct a vacation home on Tetiaroa, she was quite content to spend many evenings there sharing a weathered, beat up, six by eight foot canvas tent.

CHAPTER TWENTY-FOUR

BRANDO, VISIONARY SCIENTIST OR PSEUDO-ECOLOGIST?

During the past twenty years, Brando has come to be regarded as an active, dedicated, and innovative ecologist. He has expounded his views on preservation of the environment to reporters ad infinitum and the press has been a deceitful, albeit unwitting, partner in promulgating the image of Brando - the enlightened conservationist.

While he may be more preserver than destroyer, the reality falls far short of the image.

Brando is a popular target for writers. The combination of his occasional public pronouncements, such as at the Academy Award ceremony and the Dick Cavett Show, his magnetism on the screen, his tempestuous personal life, and his eccentricities off-screen fairly demand the attention of the public. Perhaps occasional forthright interviews would suffice to satisfy the public curiosity. However, Brando's often stated, almost paranoiac, demand to maintain the privacy of his personal life has just the opposite effect; it increases the curiosity. The irony is that if he demanded privacy less, he might be granted more.

In the occasional interview he has granted, Brando has effectively parried reporters' questions on the movie business and on his personal life. Despite their probing, he inevitably manages to turn the conversation to what he wishes to speak about - social injustice, the environment, his philosophy of life.

Consequently, the magazine and newspaper feature writers come away impressed with Brando's knowledge and sensitivity and write their profile pieces. This is something new, an actor not talking about his career, his love-life, his latest movie, or what it was like working with his romantic co-star. Stories of innovative research and development, of magical technology, of a community of artists, scientists, and intellectuals, of paradise itself on a romantic South Pacific island with the mellifluent name of Tetiaroa flow from the mesmerized writers' pens. The words pass from Brando's mouth to the printed page without being investigated in between.

In the occasional magazine piece written about Brando, as well as the biographies, reference was inevitably made to his plans for preserving the ecology of Tetiaroa. While on Tetiaroa, I read of "ecological projects in which a group of scientists are growing fruits and vegetables under specially controlled, non-polluting conditions and raising fish and crustaceans in underwater cages." An interesting concept and, indeed, a Brando vision, but it certainly did not exist.

Subsequently, magazine writers reported that he planned to turn Tetiaroa over to the French government as a bird sanctuary. Another reporter wrote of Brando's plan of "establishing a fish farm and growing flowers and creating a refuge for artists and scientists and intellectuals."

Another article reported on his hopes to "establish a scientific community that will research ways of living in this technological age without subscribing to its demands. The community on Tetiaroa will raise animals, trap methane gas from compost piles for power and test other ways of obtaining power without harming the environment."

Brando frequently was quoted on his plan to use the natural elements of the wind and sun to generate electricity. He inevitably added a reprimand to the rest of mankind for burning polluting fossil fuels. During my first several months with him, this was also one of his favorite topics of conversation, whether with me or with guests on Tetiaroa or at his Beverly Hills home.

The concept of wind generation of electricity on Tetiaroa made a lot of sense. In contrast to Tahiti, where the still, humid days were often stifling, there was an almost constant breeze on Tetiaroa, many days reaching over twenty knots. In fact, the wind was so strong that it would always toss the small planes around as they came in to land. While not normally a white knuckle flyer, I was always considerably relieved to feel the wheels touch down on the grass landing strip.

Not only was the wind available, but traditional generating processes were not particularly attractive, because of the high cost of transporting fuel to Tetiaroa. Brando would often expound on his plans for erecting wind generators, not so much for economy, but to "preserve the ecology and not add to the pollution of the atmosphere of the earth."

He frequently spoke of solar generation, since sunshine was another abundant commodity in the South Pacific. He wanted to use the sun to heat the water that would be required to service the tourists and also spoke of the possibility of solar generation of electricity.

Yet, when I arrived at Tetiaroa, I found a noisy, smoke belching diesel fuel generator and no trace of the wind doing anything but blowing through the coconut palms.

There was, however, a solar heater of sorts. The camp shower consisted of a small hut with a fifty-five gallon barrel on top. The workers manually filled the barrel with water, bucket by bucket, from time to time. A length of black garden hose was connected to the barrel and wound in a coil in the sunshine. The water flowing through this short length of hose was to magically be heated and provide warm water for the shower. Despite the proud proclamations of the resident architectural designer and the warm climate, nobody other than the designer could ever detect the slightest additional heat in the water. Showers were always brief. Our children always preferred bathing in the warmth of the lagoon.

It was apparent that Brando had read widely on wind and solar generation, for his observations had a ring of expertise. His discourse on the pollution caused by fossil fuels - and by mankind in general - had a genuine passion. However, nothing had been done to implement plans to achieve his conservationist objectives for Tetiaroa. In fact, there was a second diesel generator on order.

He continued to talk about wind, sun, and methane power. For the first couple of months, I deferred to him because of his greater knowledge on these subjects. However, he would never make up his mind on which energy alternative he preferred and how to proceed in developing it. He wanted to do something, but he would not commit himself.

While back in the United States, some of my evenings were spent in libraries, doing research on energy topics. One day in the course of conversation with Don Widener, producer of the proposed South Pacific documentary, we began discussing energy generation.

Widener mentioned that he had a friend on the faculty at California Institute of Technology in Pasadena who was an expert on wind and solar energy and proposed a meeting with him. Upon mentioning it to Brando, he agreed to invite Widener and the expert over to the house for an evening discussion.

(During this time period, the French government was testing nuclear weapons in the South Pacific, on the Mururoa Atoll, 700 miles northwest of Tetiaroa. Demonstrators were protesting in Papeete. Brando was concerned about the radiation resulting from the atomic tests. Widener had previously prevailed upon another Cal Tech professor to test a sample of milk Brando had smuggled into the United States from Tahiti for Strontium 90, the dangerous cancer causing residue of atomic blasts. The test revealed an alarmingly high level. Brando uncharacteristically insisted the results of the test be kept secret; he did not want to raise the hackles of the French governmental officials on Tahiti, fearing that might jeopardize an application we had made for a government tourism grant - that's right - Brando requesting government aid.)

Widener set up the meeting at a mutually agreeable time and managed to get a second eminent Cal Tech professor from the energy field and a Professor of Architecture and Urban Planning at UCLA to come as well. We had a meeting scheduled with three top experts in the wind and solar energy generation field. Undoubtedly, the chance to meet Marlon Brando had an influence on their attendance. Regardless of their motives, this was an opportunity to get advice from experts who would normally charge large fees for their consulting services.

On the appointed evening, Widener and the three other guests arrived. I showed them into the library/den, which was also serving as my bedroom, and went to get Brando from his bedroom. He was on the phone, so I told him we were ready to begin our discussion. He replied that we should start and he would be out when he finished his call.

We began and it was soon apparent that the guests were indeed most knowledgeable in their areas of expertise. I wanted Brando to get the benefit of the discussion. The signal light went out on the phone in the den, indicating that he had finished his call. So, when another twenty minutes or so had passed and he still had not entered the room, I excused myself and again went to get him. He was lying on the bed doing nothing. This time he said he would be out in a little while.

The discussion went on and there was still no sign of Brando. I did not try to get him again, having learned by then that he operated by his own clock and his own sense of commitment. If he felt like coming out, he would. If he did not, then nothing could convince him to do so and it really made no difference that his invited guests were waiting for him.

Three hours of discussions brought me more information about the possibilities for generating energy on Tetiaroa than could have been learned from weeks in a library. Our guests finally left without Brando ever making an appearance.

Although it was a productive evening for me, I could not help being annoyed with Brando. He could endlessly pontificate about his pollution-free energy generation plans for Tetiaroa to laymen. Now, when he'd had a chance to try out his ideas on those knowledgeable in the field and to develop the foundation for specific plans for Tetiaroa, he had instead elected to lie on his bed and stare at the ceiling.

There are at least two possible explanations for Brando's action - or, inaction. He may have been reluctant to expose his level of knowledge to people who were truly knowledgeable in the field. Or, he may have been more interested in talking about energy generation and projecting the image of the benevolent concerned protector of Tetiaroa than he was of actually taking action. His subsequent behavior convinced me that the latter explanation had significant validity.

My objective for the evening had been to finally get his commitment to a specific plan of action for Tetiaroa. While this did not occur, at least enough knowledge did emerge to formulate a plan by myself. The conclusion from our meeting was that it would be feasible and economical to use the wind to generate electricity and that solar energy would be an efficient way to heat water. Methane generation was impractical, given Tetiaroa's small projected population and limited amount of source material.

The following day, I discussed the meeting with Brando and suggested how we should begin to acquire equipment to achieve his energy generation objectives, recommending the purchase of wind generators from a source in the United States (found, incidentally, in THE WHOLE EARTH CATALOG) and having simple solar water heaters constructed in Tahiti. Brando, however, wanted to do his own further investigation of wind generators and, in his inimitable rambling way, never did give an affirmation on constructing the solar heaters.

A few days later, I returned to Tetiaroa. The interior plumbing in the bungalows had not yet been completed, so there was sufficient time to acquire the solar heating systems. Despite Brando's lack of direction, we moved ahead and designed a very simple, low cost solar heater consisting of little more than a rectangular box with a glass top and a few pipes running through it and got bids from a couple of Tahiti plumbing shops. A Tahitian bidder was selected and contracted to build two heaters. If they worked well, they could be built for all the bungalows. The plumbing shop promised delivery "in about a week."

When a couple of weeks had passed without hearing anything, a phone call to the plumber brought another promise, "in about a week." An inquiry a week later brought the response that "they are about done and should be ready in a couple of days."

When they still did not arrive, it was time for a trip to the plumbing shop. Nothing had even been started. In fact, the plumber now decided that he really did not want to build them. When I asked why he had said that they were almost finished a couple of weeks earlier, he gave a typical Tahitian response, "I didn't want to disappoint you."

I then pleasantly suggested, with unassailable logic, that he would be disappointing me even more now by not building them at all. He, however, apparently did not find the argument the least bit convincing, for the only response it brought was a pleasant Tahitian smile.

Such was the way of doing business on Tahiti, the land of slow motion. This transaction was not unusual. An almost identical experience occurred in trying to get the furniture for the bungalows produced on Tahiti. A written contract was drawn up by Yvonne Chung with a small wood working shop. Even though this business was run by Chinese, the "efficient" merchant class on Tahiti, there was again delay after delay and then finally a decision not to produce the furniture. They had decided the order was too large.

Periodically, as time went by, I would bring up the topic of the wind generators to Brando, whether we were on Tetiaroa or in Beverly Hills. He continued to equivocate, leaving me totally confused about his desires. Sometimes, he would declare the need for more information on the technology, but more often lament that we were not already in the wind generation business. He said that he could not understand how he had ever agreed to allow Bernard Judge to order a second diesel generator.

After several of these expressions of regret, it became apparent that something would have to be done to get us off dead center. On one of my trips to the United States, I ordered a wind generator. It was a small, quite inexpensive machine, but of sufficient size to produce valuable electricity. More importantly, it would provide the experience and knowledge necessary to eventually install a large scale system.

Action was needed if we were ever to get beyond the talking stage. I felt that Brando, who could procrastinate forever, would be happy that something was finally being done. He indeed seemed pleased and went around proudly telling people that after just talking for years, he was finally doing something - a wind generator would soon be on Tetiaroa.

I went ahead with business, temporarily putting wind generation out of my mind, waiting for the equipment to arrive in Los Angeles for shipment to Tetiaroa. Then, one day on Tetiaroa, a short note arrived in the mail from Alice Marchak saying that Brando had gone to Arizona to visit the factory and had decided to cancel the order for the wind generator because, "We aren't ready for it."

When Brando returned to Tetiaroa a short while later, I asked why he had canceled the order. He tersely said that he was not very impressed with the people at the factory.

From that time on, he never again breathed a single word about wind generation of electricity.

With Brando's disinterest in participating in the energy meeting at his house and his cancellation of the order, and with a thousand other things to do first, I had no further inclination to pursue wind energy generation anymore either.

The second diesel fuel generator arrived and was installed, Tetiaroa adding its full measure of fossil fuel pollution to the atmosphere.

Brando's actions to establish Tetiaroa as a community where artists, scientists, and intellectuals could come to conduct research fell as short of his expressions of interest as did his ecological accomplishments.

During his infrequent interviews with newspaper or magazine writers, he would invariably dwell on his views about the inhumanity of man and the dreadful state of modern society and suggest that Tetiaroa would be a breeding ground for creating new, more humane ways of living.

He had a way of speaking in a self-reproving manner, suggesting that his head had also been in the sand for most of his life and he had only recently become aware of the extent of the problems of modern day society. In a self reproachful manner that would so beguile profile writers, he would say to a reporter, "Hell, I've been as ignorant as anyone about the terrible way we have treated the Indians," or, "How we've polluted the earth with our consumer based society," or some similar expression. This was more effective in convincing the reporter of his sincerity than would have been the strident voice of the militant crusader.

He was a dreamer, that most dangerous and seductive of individuals. In our society, or any other, there are legions of followers - good leaders are rare. Simply through the eminence bestowed by the public upon a prominent movie actor, Brando had the opportunity to assume an important leadership role in those causes he cared about - be they ecology, Indian welfare, scientific research, or anything.

He also had the capacity to assume a leadership role. He had significant knowledge about these topics; he enjoyed reading factual material at times, and there was no shortage of experts willing to give him the benefit of their knowledge. He also had the luxury of time to pursue these interests since he really spent little time on his acting profession. While his financial resources were often limited due to losses on business ventures and his own mismanagement, he had the capacity to raise substantial funds for other individuals and organizations who shared his goals.

Although his interests and compassion were sincere, Brando never sustained an idea or project through to significant accomplishment.

In a one-on-one meeting or with a small group, he would speak softly, yet with a passion and a depth of knowledge about a cause, for example, preserving the culture of the Tahitians. He could be so convincing to those hearing him that they could be moved to make his cause their own. I was as seduced as any listener at first as Brando's descriptions of his plans for Tetiaroa completely captivated me. Like countless others who had succumbed to his seduction, I readily left secure employment for the opportunity to work with such a dedicated person on such important projects. If Brando had been truly ready to devote the effort to match his spoken commitment, then he would have found legions to follow his lead and magnify his efforts with their own.

Indeed, many were convinced to follow only to soon find that their leader would not lead. They would make commitments only to find that he would not follow through with his promised efforts. Sometimes these broken promises were for financial support. Other times only for a phone call, or letter, or personal meeting - things that would require only a minimal amount of effort from Brando, but things that he would, for reasons known only to himself, refuse to do. And, all too often, the committed were to find that he would make himself unavailable to even discuss projects on which he had gotten them started.

A prime interest of one day would be of no consequence the next; he might refuse even to discuss it. As a consequence, his true contributions to his causes - to Indian welfare and to disseminating the true history of the Indian people, to preserving the heritage of the Tahitians, to developing new and creative technologies on Tetiaroa - while they have generated much favorable publicity for Marlon Brando over the years - have been minimal. Moreover, measured against what he was capable of doing, his accomplishments have indeed been disappointing.

Brando's on again, off again interest in creating a community for scientific research on Tetiaroa was just a series of abortive efforts, projects that sometimes started with considerable promise, but ultimately died, usually of simple neglect or inaction on his part.

In addition to the lobster farm, turtle farm and hydroponic vegetable projects, underdeveloped project starts included a bird sanctuary, other aquaculture projects, classification of Tetiaroa's flora, fauna, and marine life, and study and preservation of its primitive archeology.

Only the lobster project required substantial Brando capital, but that had been created as a commercial venture and much of the money had been expended without his having been fully aware of it. Some of the other projects would have eventually required substantial investment, but some would have required little Brando funding, and others only his agreement to open Tetiaroa for study.

But, all were cut off in midstream. The scientists who had committed their time were left, sometimes without reimbursement for promised expenses, and always without an explanation of why his interest had terminated. Their letters to Brando would go unanswered - usually even unread. If they made inquiries through me, my consequent discussions with Brando would meet with only the most laconic of explanations or more often, with a refusal to discuss it. He would ignore even a direct question of whether or not he was willing to let a project continue. His silence meant, "No."

Sadly, the only tangible results that could be shown from several years of effort were a half dozen washtubs full of baby turtles and a couple of short scientific reports. An intangible result was the lost time and effort of the scientists who were cut off in the midst of their research.

During my brief time on Tetiaroa, more than a dozen individual researchers either came or tried to come to the island to study the natural history of the island.

There was also a student group from the University of Hawaii that spent two weeks there engaged in field research on the archeology of Tetiaroa. The archeological expedition was typical of the short term nature of Brando's interest. A year earlier, when Bernard Judge had been in charge of development on Tetiaroa, he had convinced Brando to pay the expenses for a two year study, citing the benefits to the tourist operation.

The project was under the direction of the eminent Dr. Koshiko Sinoto of the Department of Archeology of the Bishop Museum of Honolulu. A check for $6,000 was sent to the Bishop Museum. It was Brando's single non-trivial charitable, tax deductible, contribution for the year. Sinoto and the students arrived on Tetiaroa in midsummer of 1973, at a time when Brando happened to be staying on the island. They set up tents and spent their days searching and digging throughout the atoll and their evenings discussing and cataloging their findings.

Their diligence was impressive; although their camp was within fifty yards of ours, we heard no raucous behavior. In fact, it was hard to believe that a group of college students on a field trip thousands of miles from home could be so quiet.

They found relics from previous island dwellers including a large wall near the air strip, that had once been used as an altar. Dating done later by Sinoto showed that Tetiaroa had been settled as early as the fifteenth century.

Throughout their excursions and digging on Tetiaroa, Brando exhibited no interest in their endeavors. When Judge or I would comment on some discovery, it would bring only a curt response, if any at all. Finally, as their two week stay neared its end, Sinoto asked Judge to invite Brando to join the group at their camp the evening before departure where they would be honored to show him their discoveries. Judge made the invitation to Brando, together with a little gentle persuasion, pointing out how important it would be to the students to have their work acknowledged by their patron. Brando received the invitation with a noncommittal stare.

Evening arrived. Presentation time arrived. Brando did not. It was not that he had anything more important to occupy his time, for he spent the night alone in his bungalow.

After the archeological study group left, Judge attempted to get Brando's confirmation that he would pay the expenses for the second year, as previously agreed. By this time, he again had substantial funds in the bank due to the LAST TANGO income. Brando again followed his habitual practice of not saying yes, not saying no, not saying anything. After several attempts by Judge to get a decision, he concluded that Brando would not commit the funds and reluctantly informed Sinoto that the promised second year expedition would have to be canceled.

Sinoto did compile and publish a report of the findings on Tetiaroa. Over the subsequent years, undoubtedly Brando proudly showed it to many people to demonstrate his cultural interest in Tetiaroa. He showed it to profile writers who have presented it in print as an example of Brando's concern. Indeed, it was a commendable effort by Sinoto and his students; unfortunately, Brando cut off the program in midstream.

This expedition did involve the $6,000 financial contribution by Brando. Most other scientific research undertaken or attempted on Tetiaroa required little or no cash outlay. The results, however, were not markedly different.

At the time of my initial exploratory trip to Tetiaroa, Dr. Jack Randall of the Bishop Museum was there conducting research on the fish life of the atoll. Randall is one of the most distinguished marine biologists in the world. He had been invited by Tap Pryor at Brando's behest, with Brando paying the expenses. Daily, Randall would dive in the lagoon to observe and to gather specimen, equipped with scuba gear and protected by an assistant brandishing a powderhead. The powderhead was a simple gun-like device with a shotgun shell that was deadly when exploded at point blank range against an inquisitive shark.

Part of Randall's research was to take a survey of all the marine life within a specified area of the lagoon. To do so, he proposed spreading a net and gathering up all the marine life within its confines. He hoped to perform a similar experiment every few years at the same spot in order to determine how the marine life was changing over time.

To do the survey, it was necessary to poison a small quantity of fish within the confines of the net and then gather them in for counting, weighing, and classifying. He asked the residents in the camp to assist in the gathering. He purposely did not include any of the Tahitians, believing that their view of fish as a food source would override their sense of scientific inquisitiveness to the point that they might be upset with the experiment.

My swimming style was not that of a fish, or even like a Tahitian, but the water was alluringly warm and crystalline clear and the fish exotic and beautiful, so I grabbed a snorkel and a pair of fins and jumped into one of the boats for the short ride to the center of the lagoon.

After the net was put in place, Randall released a small quantity of rotenone. Within minutes, the aquatic life was dying. A few fish were floating to the surface, but most were staying at their previous swimming depths, in various positions - on the side, head down, etc. We gathered hundreds of specimen.

A few days later, Randall was ready to leave Tetiaroa to return to Hawaii. He was pleased with his field research and planned to return and dive again six months later in August. He noted that it would be expensive in overweight air charges to take his compressor and tanks to Hawaii and then haul them to Tetiaroa again in August.

He suggested a trade. He would leave the compressor and tanks if we would pay for his research supplies, approximately $300 for the rotenone and film. He would then use the compressor and tanks when he would return, but they would remain the property of Tetiaroa. It seemed logical and I readily agreed. We would need such equipment when the tourists arrived.

Weeks later, Randall submitted his expenses, which came to $290. He had been paid in advance for the airfare, from the Mona Mona funds before that project had been terminated. I happened to mention to Brando my request to Brown Kraft to send a check to reimburse Randall. He wanted to know why he should pay for those expenses, since the Mona Mona project had been terminated.

Although I had previously explained the trade to Brando and he had thought it a good deal, apparently he had now forgotten. I explained it again. This time he did not like the idea and told me not to send the check. I argued that we could not back out of an agreement already made, also pointing out that the compressor and tanks were worth the money and that he had invited Randall to come and his continued research there was the kind of thing that he had so often said that he wanted.

I explained that it would be very expensive to pay for the overweight baggage charges twice, and made the crowning argument that Randall had returned an overweight baggage ticket for $212 to Mona Mona since he did not have to pay for bringing the compressor and tanks back to Hawaii. All this was to no avail. With Brando, it was a case of, "That was then, this is now. Don't send the check."

Further beseeching on my part finally elicited a promise that we would talk about it later. Because of circumstances, it was a few weeks before the topic came up again. Brando remained adamant.

Weeks passed; another request for payment arrived in the mail. Brando simply would not okay it. I finally quit bringing the matter up with Brando, made an executive decision that the bill should fall within my purview, and sent the check.

Randall never asked to return.

During my time working with Brando, other scientists made plans to conduct research on Tetiaroa only to find their plans dashed after one trip there. Others were discouraged even before coming. Botanist Dr. F. Raymond Fosberg, and botanist and curator Dr. Marie-Helene Sachet of the National Museum of Natural History of the Smithsonian Institution made a trip to Tetiaroa, funded through Mona Mona. They submitted a report on the plant life and wanted to organize a research program. Brando was not sufficiently interested to issue an invitation.

Dr. S. Dillon Ripley, Secretary of the entire Smithsonian Institution, wanted to stop at Tetiaroa to study the birds on his way to Australia. There would have been no expense to Brando. Ripley was not invited. Others whose associations were perhaps not as imposing, but who nonetheless had demonstrable academic and research credentials would write requesting permission to study the natural history of Tetiaroa at their own expense. Their letters would go unanswered. I was told not to reply.

In response to Brando's expressed interest and request, I had written to several prominent U. S. universities, suggesting the possibility of natural scientists spending portions of sabbatical leaves conducting research on the flora and fauna and on the animal life on Tetiaroa. When inquires came in, Brando decided he did not want such people there after all and I had to withdraw the invitations.

Certainly, there was nothing reprehensible about Brando's lack of interest or support of these scientific research efforts in itself. Given his strong beliefs in his right of personal privacy, it is not surprising that he would be reluctant to have anyone, scientists included, prowling around. If he were simply "Marlon Brando - movie star," who had bought a little island in the sun to escape from the public, then it would be understandable and consistent behavior for him to ignore the scientists.

However, this was the Marlon Brando who would regale friends and acquaintances and profile writers with his interest in scientific research on Tetiaroa and who was so often acknowledged for his enlightened perspective; the man who would tell reporters that Tetiaroa was a place "where scientists can go to discover new ways to feed the earth's masses from the abundance of the seas." Moreover, he was inviting tourists and they would be prowling around and certainly not providing anything of scientific value.

After I left my job with Brando, his supposed interest in the ecology of the South Pacific continued. The results, however, remained disappointing. In recent years, he made plans with Professor Jean Dorst of the Musee d'Homme in Paris, in conjunction with the University of French Polynesia, to allow the Polynesian students to study the history, botany, and ecology of Tetiaroa and the ecology of the lagoon. They gave the project an enticing name, The University of the Sea. The project never materialized.

CHAPTER TWENTY-FIVE

THE BOUNTY

Although Brando was in poor financial condition, he had earned a substantial fortune over his lifetime, once telling me that he had made over thirty million dollars up to that time in 1973. Based on reconstructed information about his income, that was probably a highly inflated figure, though his income has certainly exceeded that amount by the 1990s.

Despite his upper echelon income, he seldom indulged in the typical trappings of wealth. Inside his modest residence, the furnishings were not expensive and there was no art work of any substantial value. His only automobile, a two year old Ford station wagon, was so nondescript that his son, Christian, kept needling him to buy a "sporty" car like my very ordinary two year old Chevrolet Impala.

He did not own a private plane, even though there was an economic justification for having one on Tetiaroa in order to reduce the high cost of chartering planes from Air Tahiti and Air Polynesia.

He kept no fancy automobile on Tahiti, only an ages old Citreon, an automobile correctly described as the ugliest car ever built. Its tiny seating compartment was stretched to its full capacity to hold Brando's considerable bulk. With tires so worn that the fabric windings showed through, it provided less than a safe ride even in the slow Tahiti traffic.

His only real indulgence was Tetiaroa, and even there he lived simply.

On Tetiaroa, there was no speedboat to whisk him around the lagoon, only the inexpensive Hobie catamaran sailboat and the work boats. The jeep he liked to use to ride around the island was of a vintage and condition that left it incapacitated much of the time, despite Klaus Rober's constant ministrations.

In his younger days, Brando had favored motorcycles. They were used as utilitarian transportation, with perhaps a little rebelliousness and publicity-gathering motivation thrown in. He displayed no particular pride in his cycles. On two different occasions, when mechanical problems had occurred, he had simply left the cycle by the side of the road and hitched a ride home. By the time he got around to telling Alice Marchak a few days later to have someone pick them up, they had disappeared - much to Alice's consternation. Brando's response was merely surprise that anyone would bother to take them.

Despite his previous disinclination to rich man's toys, he soon began to express an interest in a very big, and very expensive, toy - the BOUNTY.

Brando described to me his longtime desire to own and sail the movie ship BOUNTY, the replica of the original ship BOUNTY on which Fletcher Christian had led the mutiny against the infamous Captain Bligh. This BOUNTY was a 118 foot three masted vessel constructed in a Nova Scotia shipyard in 1960 at a cost of $750,000.

It was surprising that Brando wanted to acquire a reminder of that earlier period in his life spent making the movie, MUTINY ON THE BOUNTY, when his troublesome behavior had severely tarnished his reputation in Hollywood.

Some nostalgia for his earlier days at the helm must have remained, for Brando now wanted the BOUNTY back from its current resting place as a dockside tourist attraction in Florida and from its owner, which was still MGM. He wanted to use it to ferry tourists back and forth between Tahiti and Tetiaroa.

It was a scheme utterly without practicality. The BOUNTY might have appeared to sail smoothly in the movie, but it would have been folly to operate it daily with a hold full of tourists.

Its authenticity, like that of sound stage structures, was external. It was driven by diesel engines and was outfitted with dressing rooms for actors. It originally arrived in Tahiti in 1960 two months behind schedule after a journey that nearly provoked another mutiny. Two fires broke out, fittings tore loose, and the ship's ballast could not compensate for the top-heavy rigging installed for cameras and other filming equipment. In heavy seas, the entire crew of twenty-five suffered from seasickness as the ship rolled forty degrees. The original BOUNTY of nearly two centuries earlier, with its reeking holds and cramped, spartan quarters, must have been easier to sail.

There were a few problems with Brando's plan. First, the vessel was probably not seaworthy. Its original design was for filming, not sailing. The more than a decade of lying tied up at dockside would likely have rendered the engines and instrumentation inoperable.

Second, there was nowhere to land the ship on Tetiaroa. Brando had refused to blast a passage through the reef to allow boats to bring material to Tetiaroa because of the potential change in the ecology of the atoll. This was an admirable stance. However, the impregnable reef also would keep out the BOUNTY. As I voiced this problem, he remained steadfast in his opposition to tampering with the reef.

It was absurd to consider transferring the tourists to small boats and bring them over the reef that way, given the extreme treachery of such action. He nonetheless continued to urge me to investigate purchasing the BOUNTY. When I would ask him how we would land the tourists on Tetiaroa, I would get the typical Brando silence. Perhaps he thought that if Charlton Heston, whose acting he disdained, could part the Red Sea on command, then Marlon Brando could work the same miracle with a small coral reef.

Third, there was the problem of the money to buy and refit the ship. At that time, Brando still just did not have any.

Given these obstacles, the purchase of the BOUNTY did not go to the top of my "Things To Do Today" list. In fact, I did my best to forget it.

However, Brando would periodically question me on my progress. Finally, I made a few phone inquiries, hoping to simply find it not for sale. Unfortunately, MGM did want to sell it. The

MGM representative gave me the name of Ron Craig. He said Craig could testify to the vessel's seaworthiness.

I contacted Craig. After telling him of Brando's interest, we arranged to meet. His business card identified him as a Director of the American Bicentennial Continental Fleet Commission. He informed me that the BOUNTY was indeed seaworthy and he, in fact, was negotiating to buy it himself. He suggested that Brando join him in the purchase, and also - surprise, surprise - provide the purchase funds.

Upon informing Brando of my findings, I discovered that he knew Craig, having sailed on a ship of his off Tahiti several years earlier. The ball was now in Brando's hands. He knew the ship was available, its price, and that there was an experienced captain ready to take charge.

Brando has depreciatingly described himself as having a short attention span. He says, "I get excited about something, but it never lasts more than seven minutes. Seven minutes exactly. That's my limit."

That, of course, is an exaggeration - by about two minutes.

Such was the case with the BOUNTY. When he now had a chance to take action, even if it was to make a negative decision, he simply dismissed the BOUNTY from his mind. He did not respond to my information and never again mentioned the BOUNTY to me.

Craig continued to phone both Brando and me, offering his services - as consultant, captain, partner - or any thing we wished. Brando refused to take the calls. To my inquiries of whether he wanted me to continue discussions with Craig, I got the familiar Brando silence.

A short while later, a letter arrived from Craig, saying that he had finalized an agreement with MGM and expected to take possession of the BOUNTY within three months. He inquired if we wanted to charter it for Tetiaroa. Brando was completely uninterested. He even asked me not to investigate possible financial terms.

Craig never did complete the purchase.

Some fifteen years later, the BOUNTY was reworked and put back into service. It is now available for charter along the Atlantic coast.

CHAPTER TWENTY-SIX

BRANDO, THE INDIAN GIVER

Between the time of his father's death and the hiring of Brown Kraft, Brando had used another business manager for a brief time. When I began working for Brando, there was one investment that remained from that period, a forty acre plot of undeveloped land in an area called Liberty Canyon. It was located about forty miles northwest of Los Angeles, a few miles south of the Ventura Freeway.

It had been purchased during the time when the top personal federal income tax bracket was a confiscatory ninety percent. In addition, there was the California state income tax. At that time in 1965, Brando's income put him into that highest bracket. Thus, after reaching a certain income level, he paid out about ninety-two cents in taxes on each additional dollar of income.

Schemes for sheltering income abounded. One of the favorite methods used at the time was prepaid interest. Property could be purchased with a nominal or no down payment but with a sum of cash which was attributed to interest payments for several years in advance. The income tax code allowed up to ten years of prepaid interest to be deducted from income in the year paid.

The previous business manager, Guy Gadbois, had arranged the purchase of the Liberty Canyon land by Brando in 1965. It was priced at $318,000. Nothing was paid on the principal, but ten years interest of nineteen thousand dollars per year was paid at closing. Thus, $190,000 was paid out. However, the effective out of pocket cost to Brando was only about $15,000, since writing off

$190,000 of interest saved about $175,000 in federal and state income taxes. It was the kind of deal that made economic sense for someone in Brando's tax bracket - if the land had a value approximating the purchase price.

Over the next ten years, no payment of principal or interest was required. The only additional expense was the property tax, which was also a deduction for income taxes.

On some of my trips back to Los Angeles, I would work on evaluating this investment. The entire principal amount of $318,000 was due at the end of 1975. It seemed prudent to decide what to do about the land well before that time. I drove out to Liberty Canyon and found a hilly, wind-swept piece of ground covered with knee high prairie grass and with gnarled scrub oak trees scattered about. It was well beyond the suburban range of Los Angeles, but there were pockets of development here and there in the area. In fact, nearby was a large development of town house style condominiums selling for prices hard to imagine today in Southern California - $17,500 to $21,000.

Brando's land looked less promising for development because of its very steep terrain. I researched land values. While some easier to develop land was reportedly selling for more than the eight thousand dollars per acre that was the existing balance on Brando's land, the consensus from realtors was that his land would not sell for nearly as much as the existing mortgage.

It was strange that the land should be worth so much less than it was purchased for eight years earlier. That was not the normal pattern for Southern California. I happened to mention the land to Jack Bellin, a friend of Brando's, one day. He told me that Brando had asked him to evaluate the possible sale of the land a couple of years earlier.

Bellin had found out that entertainer Bob Hope owned much of the surrounding land. He phoned Jack Hope, who helped manage his brother's business interests, and inquired about the possibility of Hope purchasing Brando's land. Jack Hope said that they had paid about one thousand dollars an acre and laughed at Brando's asking price of over ten thousand dollars an acre. In looking at plot maps of the area, I found that R. Leslie Hope was indeed the recorded owner of thousands of surrounding acres.

The parcel immediately adjacent to Brando's was for sale at an asking price of one thousand dollars an acre below the amount still owed on the Brando land - with no takers. It appeared economically imprudent for Brando to now pay more on the existing mortgage than the land was worth.

In reading over the original purchase agreement, I determined that it was not absolutely necessary to pay the $318,000 when it came due in 1975. The contract had a *non-recourse* provision. Thus, if Brando would simply allow the land to revert back to the mortgage holder, that is, the previous owner, he would not be liable for any payment. It was a common and accepted real estate practice. Brando's lawyers and accountants confirmed that there would be no adverse legal or tax consequences.

I recommended that Brando hold onto the land until the final payment was due. If the market value should suddenly increase, the land could be sold for more than the remaining payment before its due-date, or the payment could be made and the land held longer as an investment. If the value did not increase, then the land could just be allowed to revert to the previous owner.

Brando accepted my recommendation to essentially do nothing, and wait to see if land values would change. No efforts were made to sell the land.

About a year later, I was watching the television news on the very last day of 1974. There was my old friend and former employer Marlon Brando, presenting his Liberty Canyon land to a group of American Indians.

Brando had informed the press of his intended presentation and brought along Senator John V. Tunney of California. The announced presentation time arrived; Brando did not. The press and the Indians had to wait. His timing had not changed. He finally arrived, attributing the delay to his being unable to find his way. To the roll of tribal drums, he presented a quitclaim deed to Hank Adams of the Survival of American Indians Association (SAIA), a multi-tribe organization headquartered in Tacoma, Washington.

A quitclaim deed is simply a relinquishing of whatever rights one has to a property; it does not mean that the property is free and clear or even that the person signing the deed has any valid claim to the property.

Brando also produced a letter renouncing his rights to the property and said, "I hope with our two hundredth year celebration coming up, this will serve as an example toward righting the long history of wrongs we have committed against the Indian nation."

A newspaper report the next day quoted Adams as saying the SAIA would hold the land while drawing up plans for its use. He said it probably would be given to the Chumash Indians, who had once occupied that area, by 1976.

Brando said he would have "absolutely no objections" to whatever use the Indians decided on for the land. He also was quoted as saying that he intended to donate his other properties to the Indians including his one-third interest in the forty acre family farm in Illinois (owned jointly with his two sisters, Frannie and Jocelyn), the apartment complex in Anaheim, and even his Beverly Hills home.

Brando also said, "I think giving up *all my land* in America will entitle me to ask others to make a contribution, too."

The media was generally laudatory of Brando's humanitarian benevolence.

Having evaluated the economic worth of the land the previous year, the media coverage of the event naturally caught my attention. His action was surprising. There was no doubt in my mind about the depth of Brando's concern for the Indians. However, it had been my experience that he talked a much better game than he played; that he was far better at promising and at chiding others to take action than he was at backing his concern with real contributions of his own. And, since the land was worth less than the previous balance on the mortgage, it did not make economic sense to pay off the mortgage and then donate the land. His contribution would have had greater real impact by simply giving an equivalent sum of cash to the Indians. That, of course would not have had the same symbolic value or publicity impact.

Over the next few days, the media coverage turned sour. First, sister Frannie, who was living on the family farm in Mundelein, Illinois, said she was not planning to move and that "the family homestead" would only be given away "over my dead body."

She said that she had spoken to Marlon when he was first quoted about his plans to donate his properties (and before the public presentation), and he had assured her that he did not intend to include the Mundelein farm in his land giveaway. Yet, Brando did include it in his announcement.

The big surprise came a few days later. The newspapers reported that Brando had never paid a cent on the principal of the land. It was still encumbered by the $318,000 mortgage. John F. Hamilton Jr. of Pacific Palisades, who held the mortgage with his brother and sister, was quoted as saying, "I think that Mr. Brando is doing a terrific job to bring out the plight of the American Indians. But I have talked the matter over with my brother and sister and we are just not in a position to donate the land to the Indians if the mortgage is not paid off."

An unnamed spokesman for the Indians was quoted as saying that the Indians were aware of the debt and had been promised that it would be paid off, although they did not know by whom. However, a couple of days later, Indian spokesperson Hank Adams said that his people might not want the land. He had learned from realtors that the property had a market value between $200,000 and $250,000. He said that, after Brando realized there was a mortgage, he made a personal commitment to come up with the $318,000. However, because of the low value of the land, his group might prefer the money.

The television and newspapers gave the new developments as much attention as the original story of the gift. Art Buchwald devoted his syndicated humor column to the story of a neighbor wanting to deed his mortgage ridden house to the Indians because it was under foreclosure, drawing parallels to the Brando gift. The Los Angeles Times showed a large cartoon with Brando standing in front of the Brooklyn Bridge handing over a deed to an Indian chief in full regalia. The caption was, *"Brando's Last Tango."*

The mortgage on the land remained in limbo for a year. On the last day of 1975, Hank Adams announced that the title had passed unencumbered to the Indians the previous week after Brando's attorney gave a certified check covering the debt to the loan holders.

However, the attorney, Lawrence Kartiganer of Los Angeles, would not reveal whether Brando had paid the $318,000 personally. He would only mysteriously say that the actor "saw to it that the Indian association was able to resolve the matter." He added, "After all, the Indians own the land."

It was several years later when the matter again made news.

The SAIA had not given the land back to the Chumash Indian tribe, as director Hank Adams had originally suggested. The SAIA now proposed to sell the land to a developer for a forty-home, upper-income subdivision. The powerful Sierra Club was opposing the development, contending that the Chumash had never been consulted during development planning; that extensive building there would destroy what was left of the park like nature of the environment; and that fire, landslide, and earthquake hazards threatened anyone who would settle there. Brando wrote to the Regional Planning Commission asking it to allow the development "as the taxes and insurance are posing a real economic hardship for them." (This was the first time I had heard of anyone insuring raw land.)

It was an ironic case of Brando's concerns with Indian heritage and environmental concerns on opposing sides - help the Indians, harm the environment.

Other Indians opposed the sale of the land. Robert Mohawk, a Tuscarora-Mohawk, who said he spoke for a coalition of six native Indian groups, cited their opposition as part of a "500 year struggle for our lands." The development eventually received commission approval and the land was sold by the SAIA.

The whole process by which Brando gave the land and the handling of the mortgage was bizarre. Information obtained from those close to Brando at the time, suggests that he simply made a bad miscalculation, that he did not think that the existence and discovery of the mortgage would result in the rash of bad publicity that followed. Perhaps he recalled that the terms of the mortgage provided that the land could be returned to the mortgage holder without any recourse to himself or to the Indians. Maybe he thought the Indians would just walk away from it a year later when the time came for the payment. Alternatively, he could have thought that the value of the land was large in relation to the mortgage, so that the existence of the mortgage would not be so important - they could sell the land and still have money left over. Or, perhaps he thought that since he had donated the land, his appeal would be sufficient to induce others to raise the money to pay off the mortgage.

Once the implications of the mortgage were uncovered and the bad publicity followed, he must have felt compelled to announce it would be paid off. To do anything else would be as perfidious an act toward the Indians as any of those for which he so often and so publicly chastised his fellow citizens. The money eventually used to pay off the mortgage may have come from him. However, his attorney's statement remains curiously ambiguous. For Brando to have paid the money without a self-serving pronouncement would have been in sharp contrast to his normal pattern. He usually made very public pronouncements, such as his one percent and twelve percent pledges to civil rights, and then did not deliver.

For example, a short time later, when making the film SUPERMAN, he publicly pledged to put his astronomical SUPERMAN salary into a series of thirteen one-hour films about the native American Indians, a project he said he had already started. Nothing ever came of the promise.

Still, such promises must impress the public. In 1975, the NAACP conferred on Brando their Humanitarian Award.

Today, Brando's home in Beverly Hills still remains his place of residence, the promise to give it to the Indians as broken as the many treaties to which he has so often referred.

CHAPTER TWENTY-SEVEN

RATS, PIG FARMS, TUNA BOATS AND HOTELS

M y family and I spent many nights on Tetiaroa, sleeping first on the ground in a tent, occasionally on the beach under the stars, and later in a bungalow on beds crafted from coconut palm lumber. But, no matter how long we had been there, or how exhausted from a hard day's labor in the searing tropical sun, or where we laid our heads down, we were never able to get a single night of completely relaxed, dead to the world, sound, dreamless sleep.

We were afraid of being bitten by rats.

The rat population was enormous, as evidenced by their consumption of virtually the entire crop of coconuts from the thousands of trees on the island. Coconuts were as rare on the trees as icebergs in the lagoon.

The rats were stealthy and rarely seen during the day. By night they were everywhere.

It would seem a simple matter to get rid of the rats. Just poison them. That might be the case if one did not have Marlon Brando, humanitarian and ecologist, to contend with first.

Brando called the rat population an ecological problem. I call it a Brando problem. It is admirable to have a sympathy for one's fellow downtrodden human beings. It is quite another matter to extend that concern to such a useless, downright verminous creature as that voracious, disease carrying creature known as the Norwegian rat. Ah, but according to Brando, the rat was part of the ecology of Tetiaroa, and one must not mess with Mother Nature. So, nothing had been done about the rats in the seven years he had owned Tetiaroa, and he was reluctant to do anything now.

Still, the rats would have to go. Maybe nobody cared to harvest the coconuts, but rats and tourists do not mix. One part tourist and two parts rat does not make a palatable cocktail in the tropics or anywhere else.

The small canvas tent I slept in during my first trip to Tetiaroa by myself appeared to have an intact exterior. It appeared rat-resistant, if not rat-proof. Yet somehow, a single, solitary, beady-eyed little monster of a rat kept getting in. Three different times, I felt it scurry over my body while lying in the dark.

Whether awake or asleep when it happened, the chilling sensation was the same. Jerked awake to a state of combat ready alertness, I would jump up, search around and find nothing. Unable to relax, I would remove all my belongings from the tent, shake them out, remake my bed, and try again to nod off. Logically, the rat was gone, but he had done his damage; sleep was impossible.

Everyone tried to keep the rats out of our food supplies. Provisions were kept in tins or hung from poles. Still, occasionally foodstuffs would be left exposed and the rats would quickly find them. The food provisions were stored in the lean-to attached to the radio shack. This shed was one place where their behavior was not strictly nocturnal, they stopped by for a daytime snack now and then too.

Some of the island guests would sleep in the radio shack, preferring its brighter, more communal atmosphere to the night alone in a dark, solitary bungalow. Nightly, they would hear the rats foraging. On a few occasions a guest experienced that hair-raising sensation of a rat scampering over her body in the dark, with predictable results. A couple of visits were cut short.

The smells and scraps from the camp kitchen particularly attracted the rodents. Although we usually ate outside, occasional rainy weather would bring us in to eat under the roof of the kitchen. We would be sitting there enjoying an evening meal and suddenly see a rat creeping along the window ledge, inches from someone's face and from the food on our plates. Appetites disappeared. Tourists would too.

When we first moved to Tetiaroa, my family and I moved into the same tent where I had been frightened by *the lone ratster*. Fortunately, with five people plus possessions filling every nook and cranny of the six by eight foot space, there was no room for the rat to squeeze in.

While we could hear them outside at night, we felt somewhat safe within. However, the canvas kept out the cooling breezes and the quarters were just too hot and too cramped. Still, we slept there for several weeks and postponed moving to a bungalow just because of our apprehension about the rats.

Finally, we moved. Now, the rats became an unintended substitute for a nightly bottle of *No Doze* pills. The bungalows were built to keep out neither man nor beast. After turning out the light and retiring at night, it was common to hear the rats running across the floor. They seemed to take a particular delight in crawling around in the coconut nieu roof; they could be heard there every night after bedtime. Sometimes, they would grow even bolder. The bungalow roof was supported by a superstructure of poles of about four inch diameter. The poles extended from the perimeter of the walls to the center of the room where they were joined together. We would lie in bed at night before the lights were extinguished, look up and see one rat chase another from the perimeter to the center of the room along one pole and then back to the perimeter along another, directly overhead. Thank god those little suckers had good balance.

In the uniform climate of the tropics, it was always mating season. Fortunately, the females were fast runners.

Somehow, through all this, no one was ever bitten. Since the rats never did bite, one became somewhat accustomed to them eventually. But still, every night the sleep was shallow and interrupted by the slightest noise.

The children were young and adaptable. They were less aware of the menace of the rats and became accustomed to their presence as they might to the presence of squirrels or chipmunks and slept the night away. My wife and I, however, tossed and turned through the night as we worried about the safety of our children in their beds in our little one room bungalow.

The best benefits of my frequent trips to Beverly Hills were a hot bath and a relaxed night's sleep. It was a luxury not available for my family and the primitive and unsafe living conditions of Tetiaroa were doubly hard on them.

Often, I would talk to Brando about the rat population. He had not previously considered them to be a problem, and had made no plans for their elimination. My first job was to convince him that they had to go. It took several discussions before he agreed to the principle of eradication.

The particular method of extermination was the subject of a second series of debates, rivaling Lincoln - Douglas in length and exceeding it in geographic expanse. Lincoln and Douglas merely crisscrossed Illinois; we talked about rats all over the world.

Experts I had consulted in the United States suggested the use of a poison named warfaren. It had minimal effects on the ecology.

One day, Brando was leaving Tetiaroa to return to Los Angeles. Given his particular and inflexible view of design and construction, I went to his bungalow to get his confirmation on my immediate construction plans before he left so that we would not proceed only to have to retrace our steps upon his return. I took Joel House, a young American friend of Brando's who had just come to work on Tetiaroa, along to the meeting.

The first matter on my list was the plan to poison the rats. Because of his sensitivity to ecological issues, I wanted to make sure again that Brando understood what we proposed to do. When I explained the use of the poison for probably the fourth time, he became concerned anew about its effect on the rats. He wondered how much they would suffer from the poison. I described again how my research on the problem had determined that the application of warfaren was the safe, sanitary, and humane method of eradication.

Marlon said, "You know, Roger, I've been giving this a lot of thought since our last discussion. I sure hate to think of how the rats might suffer if you poison them. Instead, I think we should take a bunch of those used diesel barrels, dig holes and sink them in all over the island.

"Then we can place rotting food at the bottom of the barrels. The rats will smell the food and that will attract them. They'll look down over the edge and fall in or they'll jump in to eat.

"We can grease the sides of the barrels so they can't climb out after they eat all the food," he added. "Eventually, they'll starve and die."

Joel said he could not understand how such a lingering death would be more humane than the quick effects of the poison. I expressed apprehension of the sanitation problem of handling and disposing of barrels of rotting rats, shuddering at the thought of thousands of screeching beady-eyed little monsters clawing, chewing, and eating each other.

Nonetheless, it was a plan from which Brando could not be easily swayed. After a prolonged discussion in which both Joel and I displayed a heightened sensitivity to rat welfare, we succeeded in persuading him of the inefficacy of his rat pogrom. However, he was still not ready to give his authorization to the warfaren. He avoided my request for approval.

Rather than responding directly, Brando embarked on a consideration of what had happened to the rats during the fire that had covered several acres on Onetahi the previous year. He reflected upon whether they had fled ahead of the fire and later migrated back to the burned area; he ruminated on whether they had climbed to the top of the trees and crawled in amongst the fronds and were afforded enough protection to ride out the flames; he agonized over whether they had suffered and died in the tops of the trees or succumbed to flames while on the ground.

As if this was not bad enough, Joel, whom I had brought to the meeting for the specific purpose of helping to keep Brando on course, got caught up in the discussion. Together, they taught me more about rat feelings and about rat behavior than I had ever wanted to know.

Despite my attempts to get back to my list of items, the discussion stretched on interminably. Suddenly, the plane arrived from Papeete and it was time for Brando to leave. We never did get beyond the first item on my rather long list of topics and had not resolved even that single issue. Brando, in fact, specifically asked for a postponement of the rat eradication decision while he further pondered the problem.

After Brando left, I reproached Joel for getting involved in the rat discussion and failing to provide the help that he was supposed to provide when recruited for the meeting. He said that he had concluded that it was one of those days when we were not going to get any kind of decision out of Brando no matter what we did, so he finally just decided to sit back and enjoy the conversation.

I suppose he was right.

There were a lot of those days.

After he left, Brando spent the night on Tahiti with Tarita and their children before returning to Los Angeles. That evening, he gave Raiko Sato a list of things he wanted me to accomplish on Tetiaroa before his return. Many of the items on his list were the very same things that had been on my list for discussion with him the day of our *South Pacific International Rat Conference.*

His list also had a few items that mine had not included. His items numbered twenty, including such brand new, never before discussed ideas as:

1. Acquire pigs and build pens for a pig farm;

2. Purchase tuna boats;

3. Buy hotels.

I looked at the list and tried to figure out how and when those ideas had occurred to him. He had just spent two weeks on Tetiaroa during which we had dozens of conversations. None of them dealt with pigs, tuna boats, or hotels.

What would we do with pigs, tuna boats, and hotels? We could not even get one little resort built. How could pigs, tuna boats, and hotels be purchased without money?

By now enculturated to the Brando span of attention, I quickly decided to ignore the list and did none of the above.

Never again was there any mention of pig farms, tuna boats, or hotels.

Nor did Brando ever agree to poison the rats.

CHAPTER TWENTY-EIGHT

REIKO'S STORY

A s time went on, I grew more uncertain about the future of Tetiaroa. Brando still seemed pleased with my efforts. In our day to day dealings, he continued to be solicitous toward me and concerned about my family's comfort and welfare. This concern helped alleviate my increasing apprehension toward the development of Tetiaroa and the job itself.

Since, other than his irrationality in regard to the rats, Brando had done his best to try to provide for our personal comfort, we were amazed at a story that Reiko Sato told about her earlier times there. It was a story almost unbelievable were not aspects of it confirmed by others.

Between the time that Brando purchased Tetiaroa in 1966 and began construction of the airstrip in 1972, he made only a few brief trips to his island. The boat trip from Tahiti and then over the coral reef was difficult, the existing facilities spartan, and the island totally lacking a means of communication with the outside world.

There was nothing of any real value on the island for an intruder to take. While an occasional Tahitian fisherman might make a trip there in an outrigger canoe to fish in the lagoon and sleep on the beach, the island had withstood centuries of such excursions with no adverse effect. Yet, Brando at one point decided that he should have a watchman on the island, or in this case, a watchwoman.

He asked Reiko to go to Tetiaroa to "guard" it. Now, this was about the last job that Reiko would ever have picked for herself. Rating desirable jobs on a scale from one to ten, this would have rated in the minus territory. When she was a little girl and her mother would ask her what she wanted to be when she grew up, she never once answered, "a guard on an uninhabited island in the middle of the ocean."

But, Reiko had a special and long-standing relationship with Brando which made it difficult for her to refuse him. She had at one time been a girlfriend and later a friend of almost twenty years. Beyond that, she had been on his payroll for many of those years. It would be generous to say her work contribution was valuable. While she had functioned as Brando's secretary during periods when Alice was, for one reason or another, on the outs with Brando, she was simply too disorganized to be effective in such a role. Brando felt a friendship and loyalty to her and would continue to find work for her that would somehow justify a salary and living accommodations. She sometimes served as a companion for Tarita and sitter for her children, sometimes in a role as almost a maid for Brando. If not a member of the family, she was at least "a family retainer."

So, although she dreaded staying on Tetiaroa by herself, Reiko was an undemanding person and felt that she owed it to Brando to at least give it a try, or perhaps more accurately, to appear to give it a try. She said that she thought she would go over for a few days, then tell him she could not stand being there alone. Thereupon, she expected the often softhearted Brando would bring her back, grateful for her attempt and sympathetic to her suffering.

She left for Tetiaroa with Brando's blessings and his promise to look in on her. A couple of Tahitian fishermen transported her and a supply of provisions there in their boat.

However, there turned out to be a major flaw in her plan - she was depending on Brando. As anyone who has ever worked with or waited for Brando could testify, his sense of time seldom coincided with the timing of the rest of the world. In this instance, it certainly did not coincide with the schedule that had been in Reiko's mind.

Reiko had expected a boat to be back to check on her in a few days. She planned well her story of lonely days and scary nights on Tetiaroa. She pictured her return to Tahiti to a Brando grateful for her valiant effort and a little contrite for putting her through a gruesome ordeal.

The few days passed and no boat came. A few more days and still no boat. The days were indeed becoming lonely and the nights scary. This was not the girl scout camping trip that she had expected.

Although she had taken a generous supply of provisions, the larder was diminishing. With an occasional coconut washing up on the shore and fish in the lagoon, she was not about to starve, but she began to have other worries. What if she got sick? What if a rat bit her? After a while she began to fear that a boat load of sex starved mercenaries would land on the island to have their way with her.

Weeks passed and no one came to check on her. Soon she almost began to think that it would not be quite so terrible if a boat load of sex starved mercenaries did land on the island to have their way with her. At least they would bring fresh provisions. As she wandered the sunbaked beaches in her pareau and bare feet, she would think of Robinson Crusoe ever searching the empty horizon for signs of a sailing ship.

Her horizon was not empty. The mountainous Tahiti looked so tantalizingly close and yet was so far away. It was not a matter of just picking up a telephone and ordering a boat to take her home. Had that been possible, she would have been long gone. The problem was that there was no means of communication - no citizens band, no short wave, no radio phone, nothing. Brando's priorities had not included Reiko's safety.

As Reiko looked across the ocean to Tahiti in the moonlight, she would think about starting a big fire on the beach. That would bring someone to investigate. She would put off gathering the wood - surely Brando would send someone the next day. Maybe even he himself would recreate his Fletcher Christian role and commandeer a boat to sail to her rescue.

The sad truth was that Brando simply forgot about her. He had left Tahiti and returned to Los Angeles. While he had likely made some arrangement before he left with, perhaps, some Tahitian fisherman to periodically go over to bring supplies and check on Reiko, it had not happened. In the South Pacific, promises to perform work were easily forgotten.

So, though the plan was made, Brando had not followed up to confirm its execution. Since this was in the years before there were others working for Brando on Tahiti or Tetiaroa, nobody else checked on her either.

Of course, eventually Brando did remember to check and eventually a boat did come. It was probably not as many weeks as Reiko remembered, but it was a thoroughly demoralized guard who was rescued from the island paradise. There had been no life threatening events during that time, but the experience had left a lasting impression on Reiko. She would say, "You have to be careful about Marlon's promises. You cannot rely on them. Sometimes, I think he forgets a promise just as soon as he makes it. Maybe he does not even mean it when he says it."

The subsequently unguarded island collected no visible scars from any visitors who might have set foot on it over the next few years.

Many years earlier, Brando had described to Truman Capote, in their late night vodka enhanced discussion, how he made friends. He said, "I go about it very gently. I circle around and around. I circle. Then, gradually, I come nearer. Then I reach out and touch them - ah, so gently... Then, I draw back. Wait a while. Make them wonder. At just the right moment, I move in again. Touch them. Circle. They don't know what's happening. Before they realize it, they're all entangled, involved. I have them. And suddenly, sometimes, I'm all they have. A lot of them, you see, are people who don't fit in anywhere; they're not accepted, they've been hurt, crippled one way or another. But I want to help them, and they can focus on me; I'm the duke. Sort of the duke of my domain."

Brando had made that statement while intoxicated and he was infuriated when Capote printed it. It was, however, a quite revealing and accurate description of his behavior. It was also an accurate description of ACOAs; they are attracted to weakness in others and live life from the viewpoint of helping, in love or in friendship relationships.

Reiko was a perfect example of someone who had felt the effect of Brando's seductive process. Brando was all she had. He liked her dependence. Others, who had similarly succumbed to that mesmerizing charm, fared less well than Reiko. Bernard Judge could not hide the pleasure he enjoyed because of his association with Brando. Marlon would take advantage of his dependence on him in many ways, even on occasion, cursing and swearing at him and calling him stupid and lazy.

Brando was a master manipulator. By surrounding himself with those who were "crippled one way or another," he did indeed control their behavior. He truly enjoyed being the duke of his domain.

Observing this, I hoped to never be so pliable. On the same evening that Reiko told her story of guarding the island, she also reminisced on her relationship with Brando over so many years. She knew how much she was under his spell and how he could manipulate her.

She finished the evening by issuing a warning to me. She said, "You must watch out, Roger. Be wary of Marlon. He is spending a great deal of time trying to figure you out. The other night he talked to Tarita and me about you for more than an hour. He said that he knows how to control everybody else on the island, but he hasn't figured out how to control you yet. It bothers him."

CHAPTER TWENTY-NINE

AN ISLAND HOME FOR MARLON

I had begun searching for a resident manager to take over management of the tourist facility when it was completed. Finding such a person and bringing him or her on staff during construction would benefit our project in several ways. The resident manager could become familiar with the island and the facilities, assist in developing the tourist programs, and help in supervision during construction, particularly in the communication aspects that were so difficult for me because of my French and Tahitian language limitations.

Over several months, I hired three different candidates for the position - two men and one woman. All proved to be hard working, conscientious people with experience, interest, and competence. All had lived in Tahiti for several years. The first was American, the second French, and the third Chinese. But, no matter what their nationality, they had one thing in common - they failed to please the Godfather of Tetiaroa.

For one reason or another, Brando did not like them.

There seemed to be an inverse relationship between competence and being accepted by Brando. The better someone performed his job, the less Brando seemed to approve of him. And, he made his disapproval very clear. Compared to some of the staff previously on the payroll, these new supervisors were miracle workers, yet Brando remained quite content with the old retainers, even if, like Reiko, there was little benefit ever accruing from their employment.

The only conclusion that could be drawn was that he wanted his own person in the resident manager's position. The three candidates I had hired all looked to me for direction and were content to report to me. They exhibited none of the "movie star" enthrallment of working for Marlon Brando and really paid little attention to him when he was on the island, since he, in turn, give them little attention.

His objections were based on personality, not on performance. In the short time they were employed on Tetiaroa, each of the three provided valuable assistance in supervising the Tahitian workers, and helped to plan for the tourist programs. When I would point out to Brando the value we were receiving, he would always come back to the kind of personality that the resident manager of Tetiaroa should have. He seemed to want a hale-fellow-well-met type, the kind who could sit around the bar swapping stories with the tourists. Imagine Don DeFore in the role, or maybe Brando would have preferred Alan Hale from Gilligan's Island. I wanted the type of manager who made sure that supplies were purchased, beds were made, and the food coming from the kitchen was tasty. If he or she was also a marvelous host, so much the better, but a clean bed and good food were the first essential requisites for a successful tourist operation.

Brando often referred to an American women he knew who had lived on Tahiti for the previous twenty years, whom I will call Myrtle Magee. He described Myrtle as the kind of person who would see that everyone who came to Tetiaroa would feel warm and cozy and welcome. Now, Myrtle had never run a hotel or restaurant or even had any experience working in one. So, she hardly met my criteria for a manager. Finally, after another round of Brando's complaints about my latest selection, I suggested he ask Myrtle to come to Tetiaroa so I could meet her.

From Brando's descriptions, I was expecting a rather vivacious attractive middle-aged woman with a personality that combined the repartee of Johnny Carson with the understanding of Dr. Joyce Brothers. I also suspected she was another girlfriend from long before. If Myrtle was all Brando had described, perhaps she could become the resident manager primarily responsible for hospitality and promotion, while my most recently hired managerial candidate could supervise the operational end.

The Myrtle that arrived at Tetiaroa did not have quite the expected combination of characteristics. She instead paired the unkempt appearance of Marjorie Main with the brash personality of Joan Crawford.

As Brando showed her through the tourist facilities, his ears were blistered by her scornful comments on the primitive nature of the tourist facilities. She was down-to-earth, for she certainly was not the least deferential to the resident movie star. It was hard to imagine that this was Brando's choice for a manager. Attila the Hun would have been charming by comparison.

Like many of the other people who Brando brought to Tetiaroa, Myrtle probably had no idea why she was there. Ten minutes with her on the island was enough to assure that I would never suggest to her the possibility of her working there. It is unlikely that Brando did either.

After her departure, Brando said, "Roger, you know, a person can be outstanding at one thing and be a complete failure at another. Nobody does every job in life well. I guess this shows me that I should never be a casting director."

He never brought Myrtle Magee's name up again.

Like his earlier pursuit for the perfect wave to film for the now aborted travel documentary, his standards for the perfect resident manager could be satisfied by no mortal. Ricardo Montalbon and Tattoo would have been lucky to pass Brando's first qualifying screen for manager of his very own Fantasy Island.

Usually, within two or three weeks of his arrival on Tetiaroa, Brando would become afflicted with the restlessness that affects most people when they try to do nothing and he would return again to Beverly Hills. Though he would do little more there, at least he was getting a change in locale. His return to Beverly Hills followed a pattern. He would stop in Tahiti for a day or two with Tarita and the children and then head back to the northern hemisphere. Rather than taking the direct flight to Los Angeles, he would stop over in Honolulu for a night, thereby adding three hours of flight time, but avoiding the long non-stop nine hour Tahiti - Los Angeles stretch.

However, before long he would be back on Tetiaroa again. In fact, he talked earnestly about the possibility of selling his Beverly Hills home and moving there permanently. He had his eyes on something more than a tourist bungalow; he wanted to build a large, comfortable house.

It was his planning for his home on Tetiaroa, as much as any other single factor, that led me to question the entire viability of the tourist operation. Since he was always dissatisfied with my latest candidate for resident manager, he was beginning to insist that I stay on Tetiaroa beyond the completion of construction and run the tourist operation myself. I was seriously questioning the value of my efforts in what was looking more and more like an aging actor's unrealistic, almost surrealistic pipedream.

The house itself was not a problem. He had in mind a modest home in a very open Tahitian style. Building it would not be difficult.

It was, however, Brando's idea for locating his house and its relationship to the tourist facilities that seemed completely irrational.

When he first mentioned his house plan, he said that he wanted to begin building as soon as the tourist facility was substantially completed. That seemed reasonable.

"Which island do you plan to build it on?," I asked him. (Although the technically proper term for each of the thirteen separate pieces of land that make up the island of Tetiaroa is "islet," we were accustomed to calling them islands.)

"On Onetahi, right down at the end of the point toward Tahiti," he replied.

That was the last place I would have expected him to choose. Onetahi was the islet on which the tourist development was located. We were expecting forty to a hundred or so tourists on the islet every day. Brando had said repeatedly that he was not going to associate with them. It would be the best possible thing for the business if he would mingle with the tourists, but that was so completely out of character that it was totally unrealistic to expect it to happen.

The point of land he was describing jutted into the lagoon so that the broad white beach provided a two hundred and seventy degree expanse. The island of Tahiti lay close on the horizon. The smooth and rhythmic beat of the waves breaking on the nearby reef would provide nature's perfect backdrop for tranquil sleep. However, this site was only a hundred yards or so from the airstrip and another fifty yards from the heart of the tourist village. Any tourist could saunter down the beach from his bungalow to Brando's prospective house location in two minutes.

It was a beautiful site, but there were also dozens of other beautiful sites on other islets. Some were fully as lovely, if not even more beautiful.

"But Marlon," I said, "All the tourists are going to be here. You don't want them constantly bothering you. There'd be someone at your house all hours of the day and night.

"Why don't you pick a spot on one of the other islands? There are some terrific sites on Rimatuu, near the old plantation. You can see Tahiti. It would be nice to look out at night over the lagoon and see the lights of the tourist village. Besides, it's only a five minute boat ride."

"No, I don't want to be on any other island," he replied. "I want to be here. We'll just put up a sign at the airstrip saying that tourists aren't allowed on that side of the island."

"If you do that, you're putting two-thirds of the island off-limits," I said. "All that's left is the tourist village and the worker village. It's unreasonable to expect the tourists to stay so confined when you've got this big island."

"We'll make a big sign so they can't miss it."

"But Marlon, some of them would just ignore the sign. You can't keep your house a secret. Everybody is going to know. The tourists will go there anyway, sign or not. Even when you're not home, they're still going to want to look at your house."

"Well, what if they do? When I'm down here, I'm just relaxing. This isn't like LA."

"Yeah, I can imagine you saying that the first time you're sitting there having your morning coffee and some blue-haired little old lady from Peoria saunters in to tell you how cute you were in GUYS AND DOLLS."

"No, no, we'll prevent that from happening. You know, I don't want to be way over there. I want Christian and Miko to stay with me and they're going to want to mingle with the tourists. They're not going to want to keep taking a boat back and forth all the time."

It was somewhat surprising that he was now concerned that Christian and Miko stay with him. Up to then, each had always stayed in his own bungalow on Onetahi because their father preferred to reside alone.

Brando came up with a new idea, "I'll put guard dogs around the house. A couple of Dobermans will keep the woods clear of tourists."

"For God's sake, Marlon, you can't do that. Just imagine the kind of publicity you would get the first time a dog bit a tourist. I can see the headlines, '*Marlon Brando Invites Island Tourists; Then Releases Attack Dogs.*' The newspapers would have a field day."

Marlon gave me his slow concentrating stare as the implications of the Dobermans chewing on a tourist sank in. When he was concentrating, he would furrow his brow, producing a washboard of wrinkles that were interrupted only by a dime-sized island of smoothness incongruously remaining just to the right of the middle of his forehead. After a bit, he said, "Maybe that's not such a good idea. Instead we'll put up a chain link fence through the woods just beyond the airstrip. We'll run it all the way across the island. Roger, why don't you start checking into the cost of putting up about an eight foot fence?"

"Marlon, they'll just wade out into the lagoon and walk around the fence."

"Then we'll run it out a hundred yards into the water - on both ends."

"Then look what you're going to have. Think about it. You keep saying you want a primitive natural Polynesian island atmosphere for the tourists, right?" I asked.

"Yeah, that's right."

Well, they'll get off the plane to find themselves fenced in, like in a Japanese island concentration camp. It's a scene straight out of an old World War II movie."

"Hmmm," said Marlon as he seemed to be picturing the scene in his mind. He was probably casting himself as the Japanese commandant.

"Even if they didn't think the fence was strange," I went on, "you still have them confined to a tiny little area. People are on vacation. They want to get out and look around. That's what *you* want them to do - enjoy the natural splendor. They're not going to just sit around the bar all day.

"And you know," I added, "even with a fence, there would still be somebody coming over it. I bet a week wouldn't go by without some guy sitting in the bar, bored and half loaded, deciding, 'Hey, let's go over and see what Marlon Brando is doing tonight.' To make your fence work, you'd have to add barbed wire on top and electrify it. Then you'll have yourself a real concentration camp."

"Hmmm. Well, maybe we *should* add barbed wire. A couple tourists get hung up in that and they'll soon stop trying to climb over."

I had no response to that.

In the silence, the absurdity of his last comment seemed to sink in. He ran out of ingenious ideas for keeping the tourists away from his doorstep. "Maybe you're right," he said. "Maybe I should think about putting my house on one of the other islands."

Then he added, ominously, "Sometimes I don't know why I ever started building this damned tourist operation. It looks like I can't even live on my own island now."

Our conversation about where to put his house ended. But, a couple of weeks later he was back to the same topic. Again, he wanted to build on Onetahi. We once more covered much of the same ground. He remained fixed on the preposterous idea of building a chain link fence across the width of the island and out into the lagoon. Nothing anyone said would discourage him; his mind was made up. That is where he wanted his house and that is where it was going to be.

Sometimes, I prayed the actor would return to acting. It had been twenty years since Brando had appeared in JULIUS CAESAR, playing Marc Antony in one of the strongest performances of his career. I thought it time to return to Shakespeare - perhaps MACBETH. I would have liked to feed him a line from Act I, Scene III, "Have we eaten of the insane root that takes the reason prisoner?"

CHAPTER THIRTY

HOLLYWOOD JACK

On Tahiti, I was often asked, "Have you met Hollywood Jack yet?" sometimes in a rather cryptic manner.

My answer was a simple, "No."

My negative response was sometimes met by a comment such as, "He's quite a character," or "You're in for a real treat," or "Wait til you do."

Naturally my curiosity was roused. A hazy picture began to emerge. It seemed that Hollywood Jack's colorful appellation was as much a reflection of his rather uncommon personality as it was a result of his previous association with the motion picture industry.

His rightful name was Jack Bellin. The story was that he had unsuccessfully tried to become a movie actor and had later come to the South Pacific where he had built and now owned the Safari Club resort on the nearby island of Moorea. He had previously been a friend of Brando when he had lived in Hollywood and was now a well-known personality in Tahiti. Apparently, he had frequently come over to Tetiaroa to visit Brando.

However, our paths did not cross for some time. On my occasional trips back to Los Angeles, even some of Brando's friends there inquired about Hollywood Jack. Strangely, they did not seem to wonder about Jack himself as much as about my reaction to Jack. The question was not, "How is Jack?", but rather, "What do you think of Hollywood Jack?" They were always disappointed to hear that I had not yet met him. It seemed as though Hollywood Jack was more a character than a person.

Brando would sometimes go to the Safari Club to visit Bellin and stay for a day or two. He, too, seemed to exhibit a fascination with the Hollywood Jack character and kept urging me to meet him, adding that Hollywood Jack had construction knowledge that could be valuable to Tetiaroa.

One Saturday, Brando was expected to return to Tetiaroa from such a visit. The supply plane made an extra viewing circle around the island before landing, the loop an aerial signal that Brando probably had guests on board. Two couples deplaned along with him. The face of one of the males was easily recognizable to movie fans and his young female companion looked vaguely familiar. The man was actor Leslie Nielsen, who was fresh from his starring role as the Captain in THE POSEIDON ADVENTURE.

Upon returning to Los Angeles a few days later, I saw the front-page feature article in the National Inquirer proclaiming that the late Peter Lawford and his thirty year younger actress wife had settled the problems in their rocky marriage and were now happier than ever. If so, they must have preferred being happy apart because his wife was then on Tetiaroa with another matinee idol.

The second woman was an attractive Polynesian school teacher in her mid-twenties. Her companion was a well-tanned Caucasian some ten years older. Brando, whose social graces were a sometime thing, did not bother to introduce his guests to any of us meeting the plane. He sometimes seemed to enjoy a little mystery among the denizens of the island. He sauntered off toward his bungalow, leaving the four newcomers to fend for themselves. While he could be a most charming host at times, on other occasions he would completely ignore his guests.

However, the identity of the remaining gentleman was no mystery. The long purposeful stride from the tall muscular body and the loud take-charge voice left no doubt that I was finally in the presence of the local legend - Hollywood Jack. The big planter's hat with a broad white band settled solidly on his head somehow confirmed it.

It turned out that Brando had just met Nielsen. He and his companion had been guests of Bellin at the Safari Club. Meeting Brando there had led to their invitation to Tetiaroa.

As the unofficial mayor of Tetiaroa, I welcomed the visitors and got them settled into bungalows. Bellin threw his suitcase down and immediately demanded a tour of the Tetiaroa construction. We gathered up Brando and set off.

It took no time at all to comprehend why people kept wondering about my reaction to Hollywood Jack. He went through the island like a typhoon: he was as full of energy, as difficult to track, and would, in the end, be just as disruptive to Tetiaroa.

Every single thing that had been constructed on the island had been built wrong. If he examined a hundred items, then he found a hundred things wrong. No, more like two hundred, because most things had more than one problem. All this was accompanied with a profanity-sparkled diatribe aimed at Bernard Judge, who was away staying in Papeete that weekend. Bellin's ultimate conclusion was quite simple - everything should be torn down and we should start over from scratch.

Hollywood Jack's distinctive reputation derived primarily from two characteristics - he was decisively opinionated and completely outspoken. On most topics, he knew everything and no one else's opinion was worth hearing. He used absolutely no diplomacy. He bluntly told everyone about everything they did which he thought was incorrect. Unfortunately, he would not stop there, but would go on to suggest they were stupid because they did something differently than he would have done. You did not have to worry about Hollywood Jack talking behind your back. He would tell you that you were an idiot straight to your face. Though Judge was not present that day, Bellin repeated every single criticism and aspersion to Judge when he returned two days later.

Some people regarded Bellin as a blowhard and disliked him intensely, although many had a grudging respect for his abilities. Initially, I found him refreshing. He set high standards and did not tolerate shoddiness. Many of the things he criticized in the construction were indeed badly done. Working on Tetiaroa with native material had resulted in primitive looking buildings. The unskilled workmen had sometimes done shoddy work.

However, Bellin had worked with similarly inexperienced Tahitians over several years in building the Safari Club and had learned how to overcome some of those difficulties. When I later went Moorea and saw the Safari Club, the construction was impressive. His buildings were simple, but solid, and had far more appeal for the tourist than those on Tetiaroa. While Brando doggedly stuck to the concept that everything that could possibly be built with native material would be built that way, Bellin realistically recognized that one could use plywood for sub-flooring or a screen to keep out mosquitoes and still retain a Polynesian ambiance.

In a world of too many wishy-washy irresolute personalities, there can be a great deal of surface appeal to someone who sees everything as black or white and speaks and acts decisively. All too often, however, such an individual's initial brilliance fades upon more lengthy exposure. Such was the case with Hollywood Jack.

Bellin's construction knowledge was impressive. Several of the suggestions made in his whirlwind tour of the island resulted in improvements.

The group of visitors stayed on Tetiaroa for the weekend. From our conversations, it became apparent that Bellin knew his way around Tahiti. He had been dealing with the local governmental officials, airlines, travel agents, suppliers, and others for several years and had learned much about the work culture of Tahiti that was still a mystery to me.

Over the next few weeks, Bellin introduced me around Tahiti to people who could assist the Tetiaroa project. As we made our way through the government offices, he liked to invoke an occasional Bogart imitation, tossing off a "Here's looking at you, kid," to the responding giggles of the female Tahitian and French clerks.

He taught me a lot about how to operate on Tahiti. I reciprocated by offering him some ideas on managing his resort. My main project, however, was to try to get him to tone down his abrasiveness. My efforts met with little success. A certain amount of bureaucratic delay and officiousness exists in all governments and the French influence in the carefree world of the Tahitians led to an abnormally high level of such aggravations. These irritations had caused Bellin's irascibility to boil over to the extent that he had alienated some of the government tourism officials whose cooperation he needed most in order to make a success of his resort. There were rumors that the government was trying to get his visa revoked.

Bellin's Safari Club Resort was an outgrowth of work he had done in Los Angeles. He had tried his hand as an actor. Like the vast majority of those with such aspirations, he encountered little success, never obtaining a role of sufficient importance to be mentioned in the movie credits. His self-declared crowning achievement was a role as a nameless barbarian, marauding alongside Telly Savalas in TARUS BULBA. He had a print of the movie and liked to invite people over to watch it.

Meeting little success as an actor, he next had ambitions to work as a cameraman and carried a bitter grudge against the cinematographers' union for allegedly freezing him out of his desired profession. To make ends meet, Bellin did construction work between his infrequent movie jobs. He had, in fact, converted Brando's Beverly Hills garage into its current status as a guest room/den. Eventually, Bellin started buying houses that needed rehabilitation, fixing them up, and reselling them. He started with a twenty thousand dollar home and, as he profited from his part-time work, took on larger homes until the last one was near the million dollar price range.

His method of buying a house to remodel was effective and illustrative of Bellin's boundless energy. He would go to a realtor's office and have a sales agent show him twenty or more homes in a day. Then he would make ridiculously low offers on almost all of them. He said the realtors hated to see him walk in. They would spend a day with him, followed by reams of paperwork and then have to submit offers that irritated most of the owners to the point where they sometimes heaped verbal abuse upon the realtors.

Usually all the offers would be rejected and the realtor would end up without a commission. However, once in a while someone would accept an offer or counter at a still absurdly low price and Bellin would have a terrific buy. After a few years, he had made enough money to move to Moorea, buy land, and build his resort.

Although Bellin was never successful in the movies, he would eventually play a major cinematic-like role on Tetiaroa.

CHAPTER THIRTY-ONE

BROKEN PROMISES

Initially, Brando accepted my advice on financial matters without debate and I was able to quickly improve his financial status. As time went on, however, many events began to raise concern about my future with him. With money again beginning to accumulate in his bank account from his share of the gross revenue from LAST TANGO IN PARIS, his attitude toward my advice was changing. He was reverting to his prior habit of following his own dictates in financial matters. That had never been successful before. There was no reason to expect it would be now.

His earlier statement to me, "Now that I have you taking care of my finances, I don't think I should ever have to worry about money again," still echoed through my head. However, it was beginning to feel as though I was no longer the one taking care of his finances; he was.

With Brando now increasingly backing out of arrangements and agreements we made for Tetiaroa, I would often think of that earlier discussion. This was one time when I did not want to be right.

My relationship with him was changing, not in a personal sense, but rather in the business and decision making dimension. We remained friends. His concern for my personal comfort and well-being did not diminish. But, the value he placed on my advice did.

Earlier, when I suggested something about financial matters, he generally agreed to it. Now, he would appear to accept my judgment and then take action to revoke or change my decision later - often without telling me about it.

After the agreements with UTA French Airlines, *Islands in the Sun*, and documentary producer Don Widener had been made, the stage was set for successful operation of the tourist facility. But, before long, Brando was backing out of all these agreements.

Although for many weeks he kept going back and forth about signing the commitment letter to formalize his verbal agreement with Widener, finally he announced that he had made up his mind and was not going to consider it further. He asked me to inform Widener the deal was off. He still spoke uncertainly of producing the documentary himself, but I knew it was just smoke to obscure his decision to pull out.

Since he had failed to mention Tetiaroa or the South Pacific when appearing on the Dick Cavett show, and with his disinterest in appearing on other talk shows to promote the South Pacific, the agreement with UTA was also caving in.

Following our agreement with *Islands in the Sun*, Ted Cook revised his tour packages and schedules and made a substantial investment in new brochures for promotion. He then made a short two-paragraph announcement in one of the travel industry trade magazines that *Marlon Brando's Tetiaroa* would soon be included on the *Islands in the Sun* tours. It was a simple low-profile trade industry announcement, completely free of superfluous fanfare.

Rosette Valente, Brando's regular travel agent, telephoned Marlon and mentioned seeing the announcement. Brando telephoned Cook. He was upset with the announcement and repudiated the agreement.

Cook telephoned me. His announcement had been in full compliance with the limitations that Brando had placed on him. He could not understand Brando's reaction.

My discussions with Brando concerning these matters led nowhere. He could not explain why he had canceled the *Islands in the Sun* agreement.

He remained in search of that sparkling personality for his manager of Tetiaroa and indifferent to the tribulations imposed on the several people who had been hired and then abruptly fired, because of indefinable personality shortcomings.

In contrast to the first several months when progress had been made, I was beginning to feel as though I was walking in quicksand. Day by day, the job grew more frustrating.

Other events, such as Brando's irrational plan to build a fence across Onetahi, and his refusal to eradicate the rats, strengthened my feeling that the Tetiaroa tourist operation was heading for disaster.

Apprehension about my future grew. If I could not work in an environment in which my efforts would lead to positive results, there was little point in staying on the job and ending up as bitter as some of the people who worked for him - on the payroll for years, but frustrated every day and uttering the lament that was now becoming a refrain, "If only Marlon wouldn't…"

I was beginning to think the same way and did not like it. There were productive things in life to do; I could not imagine staying in an unproductive job - no matter how attractive the fringe benefits or how prestigious it might look to an outsider.

We had originally agreed to a one year trial period, after which my responsibilities and compensation would be redefined. I began to think about finishing out the one year term and moving on to something else. Brando would still need financial advice - to keep him out of bad investments as much as anything - but I was not sure I wanted to be so closely dependent on his increasingly impractical and shifting whims on an everyday basis.

As Brando now broke many of his financial and personal commitments to others, I also became concerned about the financial agreement he had made with me. Because of his promise of the rental income from building a house on Tetiaroa, I had drawn only a moderate salary. The house arrangement could compensate me for a lower salary several times over. Now, even that promised income was becoming doubtful.

The others were broken business agreements. However, I had thought our relationship extended beyond business. Certainly everything in Brando's personal behavior pattern and our interactions had led me to believe that we were friends as well as employer and employee; that he was committed to my well being just as I was committed to his.

Now, as the cases of broken promises and commitments began to pile up like cordwood, I saw them extend to people who were his personal friends as well as his business contacts. It was disconcerting to see him cast them aside, seemingly without concern for their welfare and the commitments he had made.

Joel House was one such victim. An American in his mid-twenties, Joel had once lived on Tahiti and had married a Tahitian woman. At Brando's request, he had earlier moved to Hawaii to join the Mona Mona lobster project. Joel was a bright, gregarious fellow with a marvelous sense of humor. I first met him when the three of us had dinner together one evening in Hawaii. Joel had a gentle way of ribbing people and he found a perfect foil in Brando. They bantered through the evening, each drawing out the best in the other as they traded good-natured insults back and forth. It was an enjoyable evening, and afterward Brando said he really liked Joel and would like to get him to move to Tetiaroa.

A month or two later, Brando told me that he had again seen Joel in Hawaii, where Joel had continued to work for Tap Pryor after Brando had terminated his financial support of the lobster project. Pryor had not paid Joel his salary for a few months. (Hmmm, that sounded familiar.) Brando said he had invited Joel to move back to work on Tetiaroa. Joel soon moved his wife and baby daughter back to Tahiti and then to Tetiaroa.

Joel had learned to speak both French and Tahitian. He worked hard and got along well with the Tahitian workers. His language talents, all-around knowledge, and enthusiasm would have been valuable in a broad supervisory role. However, he preferred to work with a small crew rather than take on the larger responsibility. Still, he was an excellent addition to the work crew and to our island community. Having a second real family there was a good morale booster for my wife.

Joel was broke and had borrowed money to finance his move. He said that Brando had promised to make up his back salary from Mona Mona as well as to pay his moving expenses. In total, it was a matter of less than twenty-five hundred dollars. He had not been highly paid.

Joel's story sounded true. But, since two people sometimes interpret a conversation differently, it seemed appropriate to find out from Brando precisely what he had promised. In the meantime, I advanced Joel one thousand dollars to cover his immediate needs.

When I later asked Brando about his promise, he evaded my questioning. Despite several efforts, he would not directly respond when asked if Joel should be paid the remaining fifteen hundred dollars. Instead, he would complain about Tap Pryor and how he had mismanaged the Mona Mona project.

I reported my lack of results to Joel and suggested he ask Brando directly. Joel had a non-demanding nature and did not want to. I tried again and again with Brando. He just would not admit promising to pay Joel the money. He would not deny it either and his manner left no doubt in my mind that he had promised.

To a broke young man with a wife and new baby, fifteen hundred dollars was a large sum of money; to Brando, it was the income from five minutes of work.

Everyone backs out of commitments and changes his or her mind time and again throughout life. Courts are filled with stories of broken promises. It would be foolish to suggest that Brando was unique in this regard. What was most dismaying, however, was his cavalier way of letting his friends down. It was done without regard for the cost, both financial and emotional, to the other person and without providing so much as a reasonable explanation. Indeed, he often would hide and refuse to face the other person, just as he did with Billy, the son of his former employee.

Although I was giving Brando one hundred percent of my effort and my loyalty, the way he was now discounting most of my advice made me wonder if the time was fast approaching when none of my efforts would be appreciated, and I wondered if any of my loyalty would be returned. This question loomed larger as Brando displayed his "I'll hide and you can seek" behavior toward a couple of other people who had previously been very helpful to him.

It has been widely documented how Francis Ford Coppola fought the top executives at Paramount Pictures in order to cast Brando as

Godfather Don Corleone when he had been all but unemployable. Coppola's action had rescued his career. Coppola was now casting GODFATHER II and appealing to Brando to act in it. Brando refused to return his calls and ignored his pleading letters. (Robert DeNiro later played the role.)

Even Sacheen Littlefeather, who had gracefully withstood the criticism aimed at Brando when he sent her to read his Academy Award speech castigating the movie industry and all of America for the treatment of the Indian, found her letters and messages unreturned.

CHAPTER THIRTY-TWO

HIGH TIDES AND LOW LOYALTY

A rchitect Bernard Judge worked long and hard for Brando, with low pay, and under difficult circumstances. Yet when his work was finished, he was rebuffed and never received the major reward of the income from a house on Tetiaroa that he had been promised. Moreover, he was even denied permission to display his work to the architectural profession.

Since the promised house income reward was virtually identical to the pledge that Brando had made to me, the circumstances surrounding Judge's situation disturbed me greatly.

Judge and I never had a relationship of mutual admiration. Until my arrival on Tetiaroa, he had been in complete charge of development. Then, one day, I suddenly showed up and his world changed. His contact with Brando was reduced. The expenditure of money was removed from his control. He lost the prestige he had enjoyed as head of the operation and as Brando's man on Tahiti.

It was not surprising that he resented my arrival. Brando had only briefly described Judge and his work before my first trip to Tahiti, although he did say that he would be relieving him of his duties. Similarly, Judge himself said that he could now return to his life in Los Angeles. He wanted to finish his drawings and then planned to leave the job within a couple of weeks. Since he was planning to be there just a short time, it seemed prudent to leave him in charge of construction until his departure.

Time passed but Judge did not leave. The weeks ran into a month, then two, and then three. As the intolerably slow pace of construction continued under his management, it finally became necessary to remove him from overall supervision and take over that position myself. While Brando had expressed disappointment with Judge's accomplishments in construction, he spoke highly of his earlier efforts, of how he had gone to Tetiaroa and started the whole project when others hired before had failed to do anything. George Pakkala had spoken of earlier Brando employees who had been sent to Tahiti and had never ventured farther than a hundred feet away from the Hotel Tahiti bar.

Judge did indeed deserve Brando's gratitude. He had worked on Tahiti and Tetiaroa for over a year. He had completed the airstrip and made a start on construction of the tourist village. While some of the ideas for the tourist operation were impractical, they had been as much a product of Brando's imagination as of Judge's.

Moreover, during this time, Judge had worked at a minimal salary. He was billing Brando an hourly rate less than half what an architect might normally charge and billing for only forty hours a week although he was actually working about sixty. And, while a portion of the time he stayed in a hotel room in Papeete, the vast majority of his evenings were spent in a small uncomfortable tent on Tetiaroa. He would go months at a time without seeing his wife in Los Angeles.

Throughout that time, Judge had kept announcing his plans to leave. His departure date proved to be a constantly moving target, always a week or two ahead. Many of his construction ideas were impractical, he was inconstant in his planning and supervision, and could never seem to get any single project completed before moving off in a half dozen other directions. He played favorites and his relationship with some workers was such that the place sometimes seemed more like Club Med than a work camp. Overall, his presence was disruptive rather than helpful and a deterrent to building a work oriented organization. Still, with his announced departure date always only a short time ahead and in consideration of his earlier service, it seemed prudent to just wait, rather than to insist on his leaving.

After aborting several announced departure dates, he finally purchased an airline ticket. The Judge clique held a going away party. He was clearly leaving this time.

I looked forward to his departure, believing that it would provide the opportunity to build a more effective work organization, without divided responsibilities and divided loyalties. Brando agreed, also feeling that Judge's presence was now a distraction, notwithstanding his earlier valuable contributions.

Construction had been limping forward, progress as distressingly slow and awkward as the halting movements of the baby turtles. Work had been done on all the bungalows - doors, walls, and windows had been added in some, bathrooms in some, electricity in others. A portion of the furniture had been constructed. Still, none of the bungalows were ready for tourist occupancy. Major plumbing deficiencies remained. The toilets and clam shell sinks had not yet arrived and the water system remained inoperable.

The day of Judge's departure from Tetiaroa dawned clear and warm - another typical South Pacific day. There was a stiff wind, but that was not unusual on Tetiaroa. The sun was bright overhead. The moon was also in the sky. Although not visible, it was in a troublesome spot, aligned with the earth and the sun. The confluent effect of the gravitational forces of sun and moon pulling on the earth were creating the extreme *spring* tides - the highs higher than normal and the lows lower.

Although neither the wind nor the waves were abnormally heavy, by noon the wave action had moved up toward the bungalows. Twenty feet of sandy beach had disappeared. With each incoming wave, salt water was lapping at the trees. Before long, inland puddles were forming and remaining as they were refreshed by subsequent waves. Judge scurried around with a worried expression, assuring Brando that the tides would come no further. Despite his assurances, we moved everything from our bungalow floor onto the beds.

Jean Mercier's earlier warning that the tides would wash away the tourist village leaped into my mind.

I knew that the closer to the equator, the smaller the tide fluctuations and that the forty foot tides of places like Alaska are unheard of in tropical areas.

Still, I had passed Mercier's earlier prediction on to Judge. He had scoffed at Mercier's warning, dismissing it as folklore. He said that, as an architect, he was accustomed to looking at tidal fluctuations. He had evaluated the effect of the tides on Tetiaroa and the tourist village was perfectly safe where he had located it. If a major typhoon hit, we could be in trouble, but he said the village was well above the extreme high tide line.

(The subject of typhoons was an occasional dinner topic on Tetiaroa. Though infrequent, they did occur in that part of the Pacific. Since the highest point on Onetahi was only about sixteen feet above sea level, there was always speculation of what might happen in the event of a major typhoon. Legend had it that when such tropical storms hit low lying atolls, the natives would climb up the coconut palms and tie themselves to the trees to wait out the storm. Water might surge over the whole island, wiping out the manmade structures. Some trees would be uprooted and swept away, but others would ride out the storm. It did not sound like much fun, but I had my eye on five strong looking trees.)

Before long, waves were lapping at the bungalows, then washing through them, depositing a film of sand on their way. All the bungalows on the row nearest the lagoon soon had several inches of water flowing in and out.

Brando took it in stride, disgusted more than upset. Viewing the damage, he said, "Some architects build for the hundred year flood. Some build for the fifty year flood. It looks like Bernie builds for the six month flood."

As the tide retreated, the chartered plane from Tahiti arrived. Brando and Judge left on it - Judge to return to Los Angeles the next day and Brando to spend two days with Tarita before also returning to Los Angeles.

After the water had receded, I surveyed the damage. It was not severe. We had piled furniture up or moved it ahead of the advancing tide. The concrete floors of the bungalows were not hurt by a little water. The sand in the drains could be flushed away. The walls, built of the coconut palm trunks and woven fronds were an indistinguishable drab color to begin with, and were not appreciably discolored by the salt water nor damaged by the wave action.

The worker's village, located by the contractor Tapituri on the leeward side of Onetahi, had remained untouched by the tide.

The next day, Yvonne Chung made her usual morning radio phone call from our office in Papeete. She said that there was a change in plans; Brando had told her that Judge was going to come back to work on Tetiaroa.

After the many previous postponements, I had finally been able to bid Judge farewell and did not plan on doing it again. I asked Yvonne to send another plane to Tetiaroa and took it back to Tahiti that afternoon.

Taking a taxi to Tarita's, I found Brando on the bed playing with his daughter Cheyenne in Tarita's new house, where construction had now been completed.

"Roger, what're you doing here? I didn't expect to see you till next week in L A. What's going on?"

"Marlon, there's something I had to come in to talk to you about. Yvonne said Bernie's coming back to work. Why?"

Brando had been lying on his back, one leg cocked in the air with Cheyenne playing *horsy*. He put her down and sat up. "Well, when Bernie saw all the water coming into the bungalows, he really felt bad about screwing up. I felt sorry for him and asked him if he wanted to stay and keep working."

I had expected some such answer and had planned my response. "Marlon, we both agreed that, as long as he was here, it was going to be tough to build an efficient organization. We've been waiting for him to leave for months now and postponing making the organizational changes and we can't wait any longer. You've said a dozen times that Bernie should go back to L A."

"Well, I know," he said. "It's just, you know, he feels bad."

"Well, if you feel that it's important that Bernie stay because he feels bad, then I hope that you've got his plane ticket I can use it. Because, if you want Bernie here, then you don't need me. So, if he's not going to be on the plane, then I'm going to be on it."

Knowing I would likely end up issuing a no-retreat ultimatum, I had been wary of this conversation and was now apprehensive of Brando's response. However, he did not seem to need to even think it over, replying without a moment's hesitation, "Bernie will just have to leave, then. Right now, you're more important in my life than Bernie is."

Knowing Brando's aversion to rejecting anyone face to face, I volunteered, "If you prefer, I can stop by the hotel and tell him there's been a change in plans."

I was pleasantly surprised by Brando's response. "No, I created this mess. I'll take care of it myself."

By the time I left, Cheyenne was back in daddy's arms.

Yvonne later told me that she had been the one to actually "take care of it myself" - at Brando's request.

So, Judge returned that day to Los Angeles to try to build up the business he had abandoned more than a year earlier. We made the planned organizational revisions and the work continued.

My next contact with Judge was several weeks later in Beverly Hills, when he came to Brando's house one day. He asked me to intercede on his behalf with Brando in regard to the Tetiaroa master plan, the large document he had developed under contract to Brando before Marlon hired him to go to Tetiaroa. He wanted to enter his Tetiaroa plan in an architectural competition. Although there was no financial reward, winning the competition would enhance his professional reputation.

I asked Judge, "Why don't *you* ask Marlon? I can't imagine he'll have any objection to you entering it."

"I asked him before I left Tahiti. He put me off. He said he'd let me know. I've been calling him for the last couple of weeks. I've also asked Alice to ask him. He won't give her an answer and he won't return my calls."

"Wait a minute," I said. "He's in the bedroom. I'll go get him right now."

I went to Brando's room and said, "Bernie's here waiting for your approval on submitting the Tetiaroa master plan to that architectural competition. He said you were going to let him know. He's waiting to talk to you."

"Just tell him I haven't had a chance to think about it yet," Brando replied.

"Marlon, there really isn't much to think about. The recognition would mean a lot to him if he wins. I have no idea what the competition is, but it's a nicely presented document and he may have a good chance. Besides, if it won, it would be nice publicity for the tourist operation and for you."

"No, no. Just tell Bernie I'll think about it and let him know. I'm not so sure I want him to. After all, I paid for the work and I'm not sure I want anybody else using it."

"Marlon, I can't imagine anyone else using it. It's of no value to anyone else. How many people do you suppose there are out there trying to develop atolls like yours?   Bernie has done a lot for you, it only seems reasonable to allow him to get some recognition for his own work."

"I just haven't had time to think about it. Tell Bernie I'll let him know."

"When?" I asked.

"I'll let him know."

"When shall I tell him you'll let him know?"

Brando did his impersonation of a hearing-impaired, academy award winning middle-aged actor.

I told Judge of our conversation, suggested he try calling Brando in a week and promised to also keep on him for an answer.

A few weeks later, back in Los Angeles again, I returned a waiting phone message from Judge. Brando had not responded. I tried again with him and could not extract a response. He wouldn't say yes, but he didn't say no either.

I reported my unsuccessful attempt to Judge and suggested that he just go ahead and submit it. There had been plenty of time for Brando to respond and since he had not denied permission, I told Judge that it would not be unreasonable to submit it.

Judge responded, "No, I guess I'll just forget about it. You know Marlon as well as I do. If he didn't mind my submitting it, he would say so. Obviously he doesn't want me to. If he doesn't want me to, then I'm not going to do it."

"Bernie, it's your work," I said, "not his. I'm not sure what is ethical in your profession, but an architect must have the right to show his work. There's no practical reason for confidentiality. He's never asked you to keep it confidential. If it was mine, I'd send it in. It could mean a lot to you."

"No. Thanks for your help, but just forget about it", Bernie said.

Then he added words that made a little chill run through me. "Marlon doesn't seem to want to talk to me anymore. I suppose that he's not going to honor his promise to let me build my house there either. I might as well just forget about that, too."

I do not know whether Brando, in the end, refused Judge's request to build there, ignored it, or if Judge just decided it was useless to ask.

The house was never built.

CHAPTER THIRTY-THREE

CONTRACT, CONTRACT WHO'S GOT THE CONTRACT?

R *ight now,* you're more important in my life..." Brando's words sent me a message. The time I would not be important in his life might lie just around the corner.

My work grew increasingly frustrating. Hopes for financial reward were dimming. Although Tetiaroa could be a very profitable venture with proper management, I began to wonder if it would ever even open. Brando kept imposing design changes. The closer we came to completion, the faster the changes would come. At the same time, he aborted our promotional plans and continued talking about building his chain link fence.

Because of the royalties arriving every month from Brando's LAST TANGO IN PARIS revenue share, his back bills and taxes had been paid and he once again had money in the bank. It was no longer necessary to defer my salary; my back pay was brought up to date.

Still, in everyday conversation, Brando kept optimistically making plans for Tetiaroa. He kept urging me to stay on Tetiaroa and manage the resort. He wanted to start the construction of a school. He encouraged me to hire a tutor for our children; he would pay the salary. They had missed the last two months of the prior school year and the new fall term was approaching.

The work was not developing the way it had so promisingly begun. I had expected to be dealing with investments and with new innovative technology. Now, Brando expected me to operate a poorly built, rat infested little tourist resort, handicapped by his unreasonable operating restrictions and his reluctance to deal with bona fide experts in science and technology.

How long would I last as resort manager if the resort was the failure I foresaw? As Brando's broken commitments accumulated, it seemed prudent to protect the house income promise that he had so generously made to me in the beginning.

When Brando had promised to give me land on Tetiaroa on which to build a house, lend the money to build it, and the income from renting it out, he had forecast a rental rate of one thousand dollars per week with the income in perpetuity, even if I was no longer his employee. It looked like a near fifty thousand dollar a year annuity. His spur-of-the-moment offer had seemed an unbelievable windfall, almost like winning the lottery. Since fifty thousand dollars was less than his daily compensation when acting, it might not have seemed extravagant to him, but to a university professor, it was better than an endowed chair at Harvard.

I was working for Brando without a written contract. That may have been naive, but I had always previously gotten along fine without a written employment agreement. My employers had been pleased with my performance and had provided the pay and benefits they had promised. Besides, if my employer was dissatisfied with my performance, then I would rather find another job, written guarantee or not.

However, those employers had been universities, not Marlon Brando. I realized now that our agreement should be written and signed. After all, in the movie industry, *"Verbal agreements aren't worth the paper they're written on,"* according to a Goldwynism. From time to time, we had discussed the house arrangement, establishing that it had not been just a passing and hastily forgotten thought, but I wanted to make sure that he did not conveniently forget it in the future. I had taken no action to begin construction, giving priority to completing and opening the tourist facility.

I typed up a one page agreement, signed it and gave two copies to Brando, one for him to sign and return to me and the other to keep or to file with Brown Kraft. It was not the kind of long drawn-out document covering all the imaginable contingencies that

Brando's high priced lawyers at Rosenfeld Meyer and Susman would have written, but it covered the essential terms of our respective obligations.

Even though he still seemed pleased with my work, I wanted to ensure that there would be nothing in the contract to which he could reasonably object. So, I somewhat reduced the housing benefit to me by putting in a provision whereby he would get back my first year's thirty thousand dollar salary from the house rental income before it switched to me. I even reduced my projected income by deducting the operating expenses, even though he had specified that the tourist operation would absorb them.

Trapping Brando in his Beverly Hills bedroom one day, I presented the written agreement to him, explaining what it was and why it should be formalized on paper, and requested that he read it.

He glanced at it without any perceptible emotion and put it alongside his bed with a promise to read it "later."

A couple of days later, I asked him if the agreement was all right.

He had "forgotten" about it, but would read it "tonight" and let me know.

The next day, he "couldn't find it" and so had not read it. I walked to the table at the other side of his bed, pulled it out and said, "Marlon, it's one page. Read it now."

He read it once and then a second time and asked a couple of questions to clarify points. Finally, he put it back on his table and tried to change the topic.

I interrupted, "Before we go to that, if that contract is all right then, would you please sign it?"

He picked it up again, looked at it without reading, put it back and said, "I guess it's all right, but I should have Nortie Brown look it over first."

It was approaching the time for my scheduled return to Tetiaroa. I squeezed out a promise to have Brown read it and then mail a signed copy to me - if Brown had no changes.

The agreement never arrived in Tahiti. Upon my next return to Los Angeles, I asked Brown if he had read the agreement.

He knew nothing about it.

Back to Brando's sanctum sanctorum, "Marlon, the last time I was here, you promised to have Norton read that employment agreement and have it signed and mailed to me if it looked all right to him. I never got it."

"I'll ask Nortie about it. He must've forgot," Brando said from his recumbent position.

"I already talked to him. He doesn't know anything about it," I replied.

"Oh? I must've given it to George (Pakkala) then."

"No, he doesn't know anything about it either." I did not know that to be the case, but figured it was worth the bluff. "Let's take a look and see if it's still around here." With Brando looking on, I rummaged through a stack of material on his bedside table and found the two copies near the bottom of the pile.

"Is there anything wrong with this agreement?" I asked. "Is there anything you would like to modify? Is there any reason you can't just sign it now?"

I tried sneaking in a little underhanded appeal to Brando's fatherly instincts. It was the kind of thing that often worked with him. "It's important to me. My family's on your island. With all this flying and traveling that we both do, suppose something happened like that plane that crashed off of Tahiti and we both went down. They'd be stuck down there on Tetiaroa without anything."

Until that point in our conversation, his eyes had been evasive. This argument did cause him a bit of a pause, and he looked at me at length as though trying to decide if I was being honest or if my argument had just been an attempt to manipulate him. Then, in an unemotional flat voice, he said, "It looks all right, but I still want Nortie to look it over."

Time went on. Despite further similar efforts, the contract never left Brando's bedroom.

One might question my competency because of my inability to get an answer or some action from Brando in such situations. Sometimes I wonder myself about being unable to extract a simple yes or no from him. Perhaps, after all the years in the halls of academe, I was too much the mild mannered professor and not enough the hard driving executive. Yet, I was up against a formidable adversary. Some say that Brando is the greatest actor of our century. I say that he deserves the same ranking when it comes to evading a question and a commitment. Indeed, that skill is an extension of the prodigious acting talent.

This conversation was just one that illustrates scores of such perversely unproductive conversations we had. The words, after all these years, may not be precisely accurate. Memories do fade. Yet, the denials, the avoidance, the excuses were all part of a pattern that Brando would repeat, time and again, when faced with a problem he did not want to resolve.

In the end, it came down to this: He was the boss; I was powerless.

Brando never did sign the agreement.

CHAPTER THIRTY-FOUR
A NEW PARTNERSHIP
BACK HOME IN THE GOOD OLD USA

A s the summer months passed, my three sons, twelve-year old-Gregory, ten-year-old Eric, and five-year-old David, enjoyed their unusual vacation. They were outside from dawn to dusk, luxuriating in the warmth of the lagoon, playing their own made up island games, feeding the turtles, or riding their bicycles around visiting with the workers. It was refreshing to see three inveterate television watchers get along just fine without a set. They became friends with Brando's outgoing fourteen-year-old son Miko, but fifteen-year-old Christian did not often participate in their games.

One afternoon, when my son David was swimming in the lagoon, Christian was fishing from shore nearby, using a small fish as lure to catch a larger fish. Either the erratic movement of the hook-pierced bait fish or David's splashing somehow drew the attention of a shark. Christian was the one to spot the telltale triangular dorsal fin of a the shark ominously passing back and forth ever nearer to the splashing five-year-old. Instead of yelling out hysterically, he had the composure and courage to calmly walk out and bring David to the shore.

Miko had learned a broad vocabulary of cuss words in the Tahitian language. He took a perverse delight in standing back and cursing insulting names at the workers, questioning their origins and their sexual orientation, until they got riled up. He would then run off, while they gave chase. He would gather up my sons before these performances. He liked an audience.

Christian hung back more from the frolicking and games. His quiet personality was in sharp contrast to half-brother Miko's carefree and adventurous nature. While Miko would roam around the island from one spot to another, always looking for action, Christian spent most of the day alone, disappearing into his bungalow for hours at a time. When he did emerge, he was more likely to follow me as I went around the island from one work group to another, than to play with Miko or with my children. He found it more difficult than did his father to accept the Tahitian work culture. He would complain daily that the workers were lazy and urge me to fire them.

In Anna Kashfi's 1979 book on her marriage to Brando, she told stories of cruel and perverted treatment of Christian by Marlon. I find them unbelievable. In all the time I spent living in Brando's Beverly Hills home or with Marlon and Christian on Tetiaroa, Marlon never exhibited overtly cruel behavior toward his son. He could be accused of a lack of attention toward Christian - they would reside in separate bungalows on Tetiaroa and spend little time together, even though there was little else to occupy Marlon's time - but none of the blatant viciousness that Kashfi described.

When Brando and I would carry on a normal pass-the-day, non-business conversation over a cup of coffee in the morning or a rum punch before dinner, the topic would often drift toward bringing up our children, directed there as often by Brando as by me. It was clear that one of his major concerns in life was Christian's upbringing.

Like so many adults who were brought up in a home where there was an alcoholic parent, Brando had a deep desire to provide a more stable and less traumatic childhood for Christian than his own had been. However, he did not seem to know how to do that. His own upbringing did not prepare him to be a loving, nurturing parent. In Anna Kashfi, he married a person who had alcohol and drug dependency problems of her own and they together formed a parent team incapable of providing a loving, nurturing, stable family environment. Consequently, Christian's upbringing had been far more unstable and traumatic than had Marlon's.

Writings of others and even court records establish that the emotionally charged confrontations between his father and mother regularly occurred in Christian's presence. The fights included screaming obscenities, shoving and hitting, and even brandishing of knives and threats to kill one another. Christian was not only present at the fights, he was the subject of many of them.

Christian outwardly seemed to be a well adjusted, if somewhat withdrawn, teenager. But, all the turmoil must have affected him in unseen ways.

The exercise and fresh air of Tetiaroa had an unexpected benefit for my sons. All three had suffered from various allergies throughout their lives. Gregory, the oldest, had hardly gone a week without breathing difficulties. The constant breeze that washed over Tetiaroa reached its shores after traveling thousands of miles over open ocean. It was completely free of pollen. The rashes, the itching, sneezing, and wheezing disappeared without a trace for all of them. It was the first time in David's life that his skin was free of raw allergy caused sores.

While Tetiaroa could quickly become boring for an adult, the children loved it and wanted to remain there through the next year. I thought they would benefit more from regular schooling and friends their own age. When school would begin in the fall, Christian and Miko would be gone for the year and the tourists would not be bringing children.

Brando still wanted me to manage the tourist operation. With my reservoir of misgivings, I was uncertain what to do and postponed making a decision on schooling - I was catching the Brando disease. Meanwhile, we did advertise for tutors in Los Angeles and had received a few promising looking applications.

Since he wanted the Tahitian workers, who would work for the tourist operation, to live on Tetiaroa with their children, Brando would inevitably want a voice in approving the tutor. If we did hire someone and bring him or her half way around the world, Brando might not approve of our choice in the same manner he had rejected my choices for resident manager of the tourist operation. I did not want to be responsible for someone giving up a regular job and then have to listen to Brando's complaints for months or even have to send the tutor back because Brando did not want him or her on his island.

We also gathered information from correspondence schools. As August drew to an end, we had not hired a tutor and seemed to have decided, almost by default, to stay for the year and teach the children through a correspondence program. Even with the rats and the boredom, my wife enjoyed the island and was content to spend the next year there.

One day, our middle son Eric developed a stomach ache. When it persisted for a couple of days, my wife, children and I flew into Papeete to take Eric to see a doctor. Parents often have difficulty judging the seriousness of childhood complaints as vague as "a stomach ache." On the short flight to Tahiti, however, there was a litmus test on Eric's health. In the casual world of the South Pacific, a couple of the Air Tahiti pilots would allow the passengers to fly the planes - even those not tall enough to see through the windshield. It was an adventure Eric loved. When he turned down the pilot's offer this time, we knew he really was ailing.

The doctor, a Frenchman, mentioned several possible causes of the stomach pain including food poisoning or some kind of virus. He finally settled on a diagnosis that it was Eric's appendix that was causing the problem.

He did not prescribe immediate surgery, but suggested we watch the symptoms for a few days. When we told him of our location on Tetiaroa and the impossibility of coming to the hospital immediately in the event of an acute attack after dark, he then advocated surgery for removal. Since his diagnosis appeared to us like randomly picking one of the alternatives in a multiple choice exam question, we thought it a drastic action.

It happened that there was another French medical doctor on Tetiaroa at the time, having arrived on the coattails of a government biologist, who was there for a couple of days to do a government mandated report on the birds of Tetiaroa. Since the doctor was going to be there for a few days and had even brought his black bag with him, we decided that it would not be unduly risky to take Eric back to Tetiaroa.

On the flight back and into the next day, the pain persisted, so the island-visiting doctor examined him. He too was quite uncertain, but said that appendicitis was a reasonable diagnosis. Given our remote location and the continued pain, it was necessary to take some action, either move Eric to Tahiti for a while for observation or have the surgery to remove the appendix.

Brando was on Tetiaroa at the time. When I discussed the situation with him, he suggested that I fly back to Los Angeles with Eric and take him to the Medical Center at UCLA for treatment. He insisted that he would not allow any of his children to be treated in Papeete if it could be avoided and he did not think Eric should be treated there either. Without a second's hesitation, he said that he would pay for the trip.

Brando had learned to avoid the Tahiti physicians some twelve years earlier. During the filming of MUTINY ON THE BOUNTY, he had issued an ultimatum one day that he would not work unless his personal physician, Dr. Robert Kositchek, was flown in from Beverly Hills to treat his upset stomach. MGM was forced to fly him to Tahiti where he examined Brando, diagnosed him as overweight, and prescribed a diet. Dr. Kositchek flew back to Beverly Hills and presented MGM with a bill for ten thousand dollars.

Strange tales of misdiagnoses by local doctors and of patients being bitten by rats in the Papeete hospital had circulated through the island, so we had similar misgivings about surgery there. Since there was always Brando business to do in Los Angeles anyway, I decided to take Eric there almost immediately.

It was the end of August, after the shipment of material and supplies had arrived at Tetiaroa aboard the landing craft Meherio. Since it would be several months before we could again schedule the Meherio, the cargo had also included part of the opening inventory including fifty cases of beer, six cases of wine, and eighty cases of liquor, all of which was placed under lock and key.

My family and I left for Papeete. Yvonne Chung had made reservations for Eric and me to fly to Los Angeles the next afternoon. The rest of the family was going to stay in a Tahiti hotel for a few days as a break from the boredom of Tetiaroa. Brando decided to return to Los Angeles too.

The next morning, a radio-phone call arrived at the Papeete office from Thomas Roura, the Tahitian storekeeper on Tetiaroa. Immediately after we had all left the island the previous day, chief of construction, Jean Mercier, had appropriated part of the Meherio shipment - a case of wine and several cases of beer. Most of the workers began drinking in the early afternoon and continued until nightfall. In the evening, Mercier had demanded the key to the storeroom from Roura and expropriated several cases of liquor. Joel House attempted to retrieve the key and the liquor, but was pushed around by Mercier, who by now was intoxicated. House used the radio phone to request assistance from the police on Papeete. When the *gendarmes* arrived by plane early the next morning, the liquor and key had been returned.

Things seemed to be back under control, but the absence of authority on Tetiaroa was alarming. We had discovered that even the more responsible Tahitians would display a tendency to play when the boss was away. The last time that Mercier had been left in charge on construction, he had more than doubled the size of the work force in my absence.

With this new liquor problem astir on Tetiaroa, I was reluctant to leave Mercier in charge, while I returned to the USA. A promising solution lay near at hand though. Brando retained his high opinion of Hollywood Jack Bellin's ability to get things done. I had also been impressed with the quality of construction of his *Safari Club* and felt that Bellin's high energy style might stimulate more activity among our workers. Also, Bellin had frequently been vocal about how much better he would run things if he were in charge on Tetiaroa, stating his opinion almost as a challenge. So, in the few hours remaining before our flight back to Las Angeles, Brando and I decided to talk to him about supervising construction during my absence.

With my family in the Tahiti hotel, Brando and I took the fifteen minute plane ride to Moorea to meet with Bellin. Moorea has been described as one of the most beautiful places on the earth. It was used as the site for the fictitious island of Bali Hai in the movie SOUTH PACIFIC.

Bellin was having his own problems with *The Safari Club*. It was suffering from one of the most debilitating of business ailments - no customers. He had a pleasant and comfortable facility in a lovely setting. The food was good, the help attentive; everything required for success was present except customers. Consequently, he was losing money.

His several outside investors from the United States, all Pan American Airline pilots, had become disenchanted and he was running out of funds to keep going. He had recently managed to get actors Glenn Ford and Leslie Nielson to visit *The Safari Club* on separate occasions, but had not convinced either to invest in his business.

(When Brando heard that Ford was on Moorea, he expressed a strong personal dislike for Ford. When I asked why, he said, "The man has absolutely no humanity. We worked together on a movie in Japan once (TEAHOUSE OF THE AUGUST MOON). They'd serve tea and these little cookies every afternoon. There were always little kids around. I gave my cookies to the kids. That guy always ate his.")

Our discussion with Bellin soon took on a broader context than originally anticipated. We got into a discussion of Bellin's problems with *The Safari Club* and the long range future of Tetiaroa.

Out of the discussion, we developed a major realignment of operations and an agreement which had benefits for all three of us.

It was a broad restructuring and a drastic revision of plans for Tetiaroa, *The Safari Club*, and for all of us as individuals. Under the agreement, Bellin would supervise construction on Tetiaroa. Brando would allow *The Safari Club* to be promoted under his name. I would move back to Los Angeles and set up promotional programs with airlines, tourist boards, and travel agents for both *The Safari Club* and Tetiaroa and handle all the stateside arrangements for both enterprises. Bellin would handle promotion in Papeete. I was also to look into the possibility of buying another resort on Tahiti so that we could offer a complete island package tour of our own with a variety of locations and styles. There was even to be a three-way sharing of profits in this joint venture between Bellin, Brando, and me.

Although Brando had earlier repudiated the Islands in the Sun, UTA French Airline, and South Pacific documentary agreements, he was enthusiastic about the possibilities under the new organization. He committed to reinstating the agreements during our meeting. I tried to believe him.

I was apprehensively pleased with the agreement; it seemed the only way to be able to move my family back to Los Angeles. Had there not been the fear that Brando would soon back out of this agreement, I would have been ecstatic. It again had all the ingredients for success and I was even to have a share of the profits.

Brando's name attached to *The Safari Club* also enhanced Bellin's chance of reviving the economic health of his business. A few weeks earlier when Brando had been staying at *The Safari Club* for a couple of days, he had stepped behind the bar to mix a few drinks one night. The only customers were two couples from a nearby Club Med resort. It was a typical week-night crowd for *The Safari Club.* The very next evening, the bar was packed with tourists from the Club Med, hoping to catch a glimpse of the South Seas most famous relief bartender.

Brando's arm did not have to be twisted to come up with our new plan of organization. He seemed the most enthused of any of us.

Following our meeting, I flew from Moorea to Tahiti for the trans-Pacific trip to Los Angeles. It had been planned that only Eric and I were going. When Brando saw my wife's tears at seeing her ill son leave without her, he had Yvonne Chung immediately purchase three more tickets for the rest of the family. Maybe I could not get his name on a contract, but you could count on him to be the first one in line to help if a child was suffering.

(Alice Marchak once told me of Brando having seen a small girl on Tahiti with a facial deformity. He paid for the child and mother to be flown to the United States for corrective surgery and even put them up in his home in Beverly Hills. Touched by Brando's kindness in her story, I asked whether he frequently performed such humanitarian acts. The only other example Alice could relate was when Brando had presented a large console stereo set to Elizabeth Taylor and Richard Burton when Brando and Taylor were shooting REFLECTIONS IN A GOLDEN EYE in Italy. That particular act of benevolence did not seem to fall into quite the same category.)

So, off the five of us went to Los Angeles in search of a doctor in whom we might have confidence - with little more than the clothes on our backs.

We took Eric to the UCLA medical center the next morning. The doctor who examined him declared that there was absolutely no sign of any problem with his appendix. When he found out where we had been, he said the most likely cause of the problem was food poisoning. Eric had been in the habit of making daily excursions to the workers' village where the food was typically handled without the sanitary precautions necessary in such a warm climate.

On two subsequent occasions during the next two years, Brando would also fall victim of the same malady and be rushed to Los Angeles for treatment, one time resulting in his hospitalization there for a couple of days.

With each day, Eric's stomach got better and the problem completely disappeared within a week. We were thankful that he had not been exposed to unnecessary surgery in Tahiti and grateful to Brando for his help.

ANARCHY ON TETIAROA
CAN IT BE MUTINY
IF IT IS ON AN ISLAND?

I t had been a last minute decision for the whole family to return to Los Angeles. Regardless of the reason, we were now there. Schooling for the children and some of the creature comforts were again available. We temporarily moved into a hotel in Los Angeles. When five-year-old David got into his first hot shower in months, he could not be dragged out for an hour and then it took a promise of a chocolate malted milk. It was nice to be back to the good old U. S. of A.

Brando was also back in Los Angeles. Bellin had assumed charge of construction on Tetiaroa. I plunged into Brando's stateside business again. If the new partnership agreement among the three of us would work out as we had verbally agreed, my job could mostly be done stateside. Brando and I discussed the new arrangement during the first few days back in Los Angeles. I proposed that we continue to search for a resort manager in Tahiti. I would go to Tetiaroa as required to check on construction and later to provide supervision of the tourist operation. We forecast a tentative schedule of a week or two on Tetiaroa every couple of months. Brando agreed with the arrangement, although he was already beginning to grumble about Bellin's ability to handle things there.

Although he was an articulate person, Bellin would never pronounce Tetiaroa correctly. He would add an extra R, making it Tetiarora. Brando took this mispronunciation as an insult. He would constantly correct Bellin and it seemed to be Bellin's obstinate refusal to bother with the correct pronunciation as much as anything that riled Brando. He would repeatedly say, "If we can't even get him to say Tetiaroa right, I don't know how we can depend on him to do anything right over there."

I was immensely relieved to be out of the obligation of day-to-day management of the resort that Brando had been trying to hand me. As a university graduate student, I had managed a motel for a year and had experienced enough of twenty-four hour a day problems and nights of interrupted sleep to know that was not what I wanted to do with my life. Besides, I was not very good at sitting around making small talk with the tourists, and a lot of that would be necessary for the kind of operation which Tetiaroa would be.

We hurriedly looked for a house to rent in Los Angeles so the children could get enrolled for the start of school. We found a nice house just off Mulholland Drive and Laurel Canyon, not far from Brando's home. However, realtor-owner Harold Starr did not want to rent to us when he found out I worked for Brando. He'd had previous bad experience with renters from the entertainment business. It was rather ironic that when he discovered that I knew George Pakkala, he changed his mind and enthusiastically leased the house to us.

During the following week I went about my business in Los Angeles, blissfully ignorant of a major uprising taking place on Tetiaroa. At the end of the week, Yvonne Chung frantically called with a report of multiple confrontations on Tetiaroa between Hollywood Jack Bellin on one side and fifty Tahitians on the other.

There had been a complete cessation of work and mass exodus of the workers. The Tahiti newspapers were providing full coverage and the Labor Department of the government was up in arms for alleged contravention of the labor laws. News of the problem soon reached the United States. A reporter from the NATIONAL INQUIRER began phoning for my comments.

Diplomacy not being Bellin's strong suit (or even one of his weak suits), it was clear the conflict would not be resolved without intervention. It was time for me to return to Tetiaroa.

Back across the Pacific I flew to Tahiti. It was time to listen to fairy tales. As with most second hand accounts, the report of what had happened on Tetiaroa depended on who was doing the telling. While certain facts were incontrovertible, part of the following account is based on my best interpretation of various statements from the participants in the drama.

Brando and I had left Tahiti on a Saturday. At noon the next Tuesday, Bellin flew to Tetiaroa and spent about two hours there, which was sufficient time to stir up the initial level of chaos. He concluded that few of the workers possessed sufficient skills and dedication and ordered Mercier to cut the work force from fifty people down to the best twelve. He ordered everyone else off the island.

This pronouncement met with immediate opposition. Had it been made tactfully, perhaps the transition could have been peacefully accomplished. However, tact was not a Bellin characteristic. You could say the two parties were not even acquainted. His order was accompanied by character aspersions on the workers who were to be eliminated.

Mercier voiced his objections. Bellin and Mercier were both big tough outspoken men. The ingredients were there for a physical confrontation. While it did not quite reach that stage, apparently it came quite close. Bellin soon flew away from Tetiaroa with the work force reduction issue unresolved.

Over the next two days, little work was accomplished. Bellin returned Thursday morning, again giving orders to reduce the work force to twelve. Mercier insisted that either everyone would stay and work or else nobody would work. Various threats were exchanged between Mercier and Bellin. Workers also reported being threatened with physical beatings from Bellin if they did not leave and from Mercier if they did. One even provided a written statement that Bellin had threatened to kill him.

Bellin had earlier secretly smuggled a twelve gauge shotgun into Tahiti and then to Tetiaroa for Brando. Somehow, word of its presence on the island escaped and rumors were rampant that Bellin was threatening people with the gun, although this apparently did not actually occur.

The level-headed Chung was summoned from Papeete to try to restore peace. While Bellin retreated to a bungalow, she gathered the workers together at the airstrip and told them that those who wanted to work could stay and those who wanted to return to Papeete could do so. Many wanted to stay, but Mercier again invoked various threats, thereby succeeding in persuading them all to return to Papeete. Thereupon, five airplanes were ordered to return the workers.

By the time I returned to Tetiaroa a week or so later, Bellin had transported about ten new workers from Moorea to Tetiaroa and work was back in progress. The Tahiti newspaper was running daily stories on the Tetiaroa drama. A front page cartoon showed Bellin with a gun aimed at three natives dressed only in loincloths. The natives were in turn throwing knives at Bellin.

The government did not find the situation nearly so amusing. The Labor Department Inspector for French Polynesia had a letter waiting for Brando deploring the "anarchy" on Tetiaroa and demanding that Bellin be removed of all authority whatsoever on Tetiaroa and that all the workers be rehired or paid for the month of September.

Naturally, the stories I heard from both Bellin and Mercier were that each was the perfect embodiment of misunderstood innocence and "it was all his fault."

The workers Bellin had imported from Moorea were, on the average, better than those we had previously employed. However, he had hired them at about three times the wage rate we had been paying. They were not three times as productive.

The problems with the Labor Department were smoothed over without undue difficulty. This was one instance when my inability to speak French seemed to pay off. We had two conferences in which Yvonne Chung acted as interpreter. I acted particularly dense until the French labor inspector just gave up trying to communicate with me and forgot the complaint. I had learned something from the master.

With only ten workers, work had slowed to an intolerable level. With Bellin's concurrence, I hired back about fifteen of the best workers from the previous crew and we returned to smooth operations. We now had a two-tier pay system with vastly different wage scales. It seemed to work without causing any complaints from the lower paid workers. This was the crew that remained working for the balance of my time on Tetiaroa.

A small incident which occurred after my return to Tahiti illustrates one of the many differences between Tahitian and North American workers. While walking down the street in Papeete, I saw one of the former workers approaching from the opposite direction. On his feet were the rather distinctive running shoes that had walked away from my bungalow during my absence. After we exchanged a few pleasantries, I casually mentioned that his shoes looked remarkably like a pair of mine. Without a change in expression, he took them off, handed them to me, bade me a pleasant good-bye and walked off barefoot down the street.

Bellin continued to supervise construction on Tetiaroa. He worked without pay to fulfill his part of our recently negotiated agreement. He was only one of several people, including me, who worked with dedication for Brando at lower than normal or even no pay. Brando's celebrity status was certainly part of the appeal that drew people to do that. However, I believe that just as influential in their motivation was the fact that Brando's disorganization and lack of direction were so extreme that they somehow felt compelled to help him.

Construction continued on Tetiaroa with Bellin shuttling back and forth from Moorea a couple of days a week. I packed up most of our household effects and arranged for their shipment back to the states. With the worker conflict now resolved, I was pleased with Bellin's supervision. He was far more experienced in construction, particularly with the unique problems of working in Polynesia. I knew that he was capable of doing a good job. However, with his no-nonsense attitude, I did wonder if he would be able to tolerate some of Brando's impractical ideas. With construction again moving smoothly, I returned to Los Angeles.

I continued to work out of Brando's home. There were still matters to resolve with his cattle investment. I was also investigating alternative uses for his Liberty Canyon land, including building houses on it, and evaluating the possible sale of his Anaheim apartment complex. In addition, there were still many Tetiaroa matters to deal with stateside.

Based on several discussions with Brando and with George Pakkala, I began looking at real estate investments for Brando. Income property such as apartments, shopping centers, and so on would be good investments for some of the excess funds he was now accumulating from LAST TANGO. By now it appeared that he would be receiving about three million dollars within the first year. With part of it tucked away in long term real estate investments that were not so liquid, perhaps he could now begin to build an estate and a stable income.

After locating a couple of good properties, I found that Brando did not want to even look at them or at my analyses. He decided he did not want to invest in real estate after all. Considering the enormous increase in real estate values in southern California since then, it was an unfortunate decision.

It was apparent that Brando no longer recognized me as his financial guru. I thought back to our long past conversation when I had asked him if he might not always find some way to lose his money and he had responded that he should never have to worry about that again with me managing his funds.

With my financial advice on hold and with Bellin's management assistance on Tetiaroa construction, for the first time since starting the job, I did not have to put in twelve-hour days or seven-day work weeks. Also, with the children in school and a real house to live in, our family life was getting back to a comfortable pattern.

With construction moving closer to completion, Brando again began to express uncertainty about the operation and about Bellin. I interpreted this as the same anxiety which had caused him to interpose design changes before in order to delay opening. From his comments, it appeared the time was fast approaching for him to retreat from the agreement with Bellin. Every time I tried to discuss drawing up a contract to formalize our three-way agreement, Brando's response was a litany of complaints about Bellin's abrasive style. He was already hinting that I should return to Tetiaroa to manage the tourist operation.

He would not agree to talk to Don Widener about reinstating the South Pacific documentary or do anything else to promote the South Pacific, so the UTA French Airline agreement also remained in an inactive status.

He had found so many excuses to avoid signing my contract containing the Tetiaroa house income commitment that I had given up asking.

Under ideal conditions, I did not want to manage the Tetiaroa tourist operation. With Brando's destroying the lucrative financial and promotional arrangements that had been arranged, with his disapproval of the people I had hired, with his hare-brained scheme to build a chain link fence across the island, I fairly cringed at the thought of it.

I concluded that permanently working full time for Brando would be a world of frustration that could lead to an early grave. Yet, despite his broken promises to me, despite the frustration and the profound disappointment, I retained an affectionate feeling for him. On a day-to-day personal level, he still treated me kindly. And, he would always need financial help - badly.

Catching him in what seemed to be a conciliatory mood one day, I made a proposal. "Marlon, Hollywood Jack's taking care of construction now. We'll be able to find a good resort manager sooner or later. You know, your financial situation here is straightened out somewhat and you've got a healthy bank account. Maybe you don't have the kind of need for me that you once did. I was thinking that we should change my job."

"I don't know about Jack. We can't trust him. You know how he is," he said. "But, what are you talking about?"

"You could still use somebody to watch your finances - to keep expenses down, to keep an eye on things you have now, to maybe help find some safe investments for the money that is coming in and help keep away the people with the imaginary cattle and salted gold mine deals."

Brando's frown showed he did not like my comments about the cattle and gold, but I'd learned long before that it did no good to beat around the bush with him.

Ignoring his frown, I went on, "Why don't I go on a kind of consulting arrangement with you, instead of working as a full-time employee. You'd be rid of my thirty thousand dollar salary and I could still do most of the same things for you I've been doing. I just wouldn't get involved in all the details of day-to-day operations."

Brando's expression did not show enthusiasm, but he did seem to exhibit at least mild interest. "How will we run Tetiaroa?" he asked.

"We'll hire an on-site manager like we're planning anyway. I'll work with whoever we hire for a couple of months and then go back there to oversee operations for a week or so every month until things are operating smoothly and then as often as necessary thereafter."

"Well, that might work, if your sure you'll go over there when I need you."

"Absolutely," I said. "And while I'm here, I'll set up the office to handle stateside promotion and train somebody to run it." I had mentally given up all idea of buying another resort on Tahiti or even pulling *The Safari Club* fully into the fold. Brando might be a terrific movie actor, but I was not buying his act that our three-way partnership would ever really get out of the starting gate.

Brando seemed to be giving my proposal favorable consideration. While in so many respects, money was not important to him, he was bothered if people were making more than he thought they were worth. He called Alice into the room and asked, "What kind of salary do you think those guys get over at MCA that manage things?"

"What do you mean, Marlon?" she responded to that question that no one could answer. "What kind of guys are you talking about?"

"Ah, you know. Like Jay Kanter (his former agent), do you think he makes more than $30,000?"

"Marlon, do you realize what year this is? Have you looked at salaries lately? Of course, Jay makes a lot more than $30,000." Although Alice was sometimes deferential with Brando, she did not hesitate to tell him when he was wrong.

"Marlon," I interrupted, "I'm not talking about that kind of a salary. I'd be satisfied to handle the routine investment work here for a thousand dollars a month, besides all those things I was talking about before. For those extra trips to Tetiaroa, you could pay me a daily rate.

"I just don't want to stay working full-time if it means I have to take my family back to live on Tetiaroa. At the age our kids are now, I think it's important that they get regular schooling and grow up in the United States with other kids their ages."

"Well, how can you support your kids on a thousand dollars a month?"

I told him my plans. "I thought I might try to pick up a few more entertainment industry clients to assist with investments or do some business consulting."

Knowing how contrary Brando could get when he thought he was being pressured into a decision, I suggested, "Why don't you think about my ideas and we can talk about it in a few days."

I thought my proposal was reasonable and realistic and went home happy with our conversation.

As I was working at his home the next day, Alice said that Brando wanted to talk to me in his bedroom. Without any preamble of normal conversational pleasantries, he said, "Roger, I thought over what you suggested yesterday. If you don't want to live on Tetiaroa, then I don't know that you can be much help to me. That's where all of the action is going to be."

Under the terms of our recently negotiated partnership arrangement, we had mutually decided that I was not going to live there. I had been correct in anticipating that he was ready to do a one hundred and eighty degree turn on Bellin.

He continued, "I don't think that Jack can handle things there. He's too hot-headed and he's got enough troubles of his own with *The Safari Club*. I can understand that you don't want to raise your kids there. I guess I wouldn't be ready to keep Christian down there either. But, if you can't work for me full time, then I don't see any point in you working for me at all.

"I've spoken to Nortie (Brown) about this already. Why don't you go down and work something out with him," he said, referring, apparently, to some kind of severance arrangement.

So, as abruptly as my job had begun when Brando had made the offer I could not refuse, it ended.

Another classic behavior pattern of ACOAs is their struggle with limit setting and personal boundaries. They view limit setting by others as rejection. Brando's response to my proposal illustrates that pattern. As long as I give him my full attention, he treat me as more than an employee, certainly as a friend. His earlier described concern for my comfort, his sharing of personal confidences, indeed his sharing of his home, all illustrate this. Now, I proposed carrying out my job to the full extent that was required, but giving him less than one hundred percent of my time. He saw me rejecting him and responded in kind.

For, as far as Brando was concerned, I had been dispatched to oblivion as surely and efficiently as the fictional Godfather had dispatched his discarded minions to "sleep with the fishes," for I never saw him face to face again.

CHAPTER THIRTY-SIX

RETURN TO PARADISE?

For the first time in my life I had been fired and I liked it. My immediate reaction to the dismissal was relief. I would not have to apologize to anyone again when Brando broke an agreement.

Over the last few months, he had disappointed me profoundly. Yet I could not be angry at him. That's Marlon Brando. No one had ever caused him to change and no one ever would.

The next morning I went down to the Brown Kraft offices on Wilshire Boulevard to see Norton Brown. This conversation was as brief as the one of the prior day.

"Marlon asked me to settle up on your pay," said Brown. "Did you have any kind of an employment agreement with him?"

"Well, we did have an agreement...," I replied, deliberately leaving the sentence hanging.

"Marlon said he never signed it."

"That's true," I said, surprised that Brando had even acknowledged its existence.

"Well, let's make this simple. You had six months left on the contract. How about if we pay you for three months?"

"Done."

While I felt justified to press for the whole six month's pay, I was happy to return to a life of sanity and normality and satisfied to receive any compensation. Frankly, I had not expected anymore than a chorus of SO LONG, IT'S BEEN GOOD TO KNOW YOU - played on Brando's drums.

I was out of a job. It was a new experience. George Pakkala intercepted me on the way out and invited me to lunch. He expressed condolences, but added that maybe I was the fortunate one. He still had to deal with Brando.

Pakkala had handled the account on Brown Kraft's most troublesome client for a decade and had done a creditable job, considering the constraints imposed by Brando. He was more familiar than anyone else with the difficulties of handling finances for the inconstant actor. For me, George had been an island of sanity and tranquillity in an otherwise storm-tossed sea of turmoil and irrationality. More than anyone else, he had helped me perform my job and had carried me through difficult situations. For that, he had earned my undying gratitude.

More than once, I had suggested to Brando that Pakkala's advice was always worth strong consideration. Yet, because Pakkala was an accountant, Brando thought that he somehow lacked the vision necessary to understand his needs and motivations.

Pakkala has by now added another twenty years on the Brando account. It is his calm Finnish demeanor, soothed by the tranquilizing effect of daily running, that keeps him smiling as he talks about Brown Kraft's number one problem child.

At lunch that day, George boosted my spirits and helped lift a bittersweet mood. In his kind way, he told me that it was Brando, not I, who was the loser by my leaving. He said that Brando had spent over three-quarters of a million dollars on Tetiaroa with almost nothing to show for it before the last year. The expenditures during my tenure amounted to less than one hundred and fifty thousand dollars. Despite our many problems and setbacks, there had been substantial progress on construction during that time. (The resort was opened a short time later.) Pakkala said it was the first time that Brando had hired someone to work on Tetiaroa and gotten his money's worth.

I decided that was worth a second martini. I did not have to work that afternoon.

Before we left, Pakkala made a final comment and a prediction. He said, "Roger, you know, you haven't heard the last of Marlon. Even though you are leaving, he still thinks you've done a good job. He said so."

"Thanks George, that makes me feel better, anyway. Maybe he and I can at least remain friends then."

"It looks to me like he's going to get rid of Jack pretty soon," I added. "Nobody else really knows what's going on down on there. If he does fire Jack and gets stuck, maybe I can give him a hand if he'd want. That's if you don't want go there instead."

That comment caused George to cast his eyes to the heavens, emit a barely audible groan, and say, "Please, don't even say that out loud."

He then added, "You know Marlon, he is not going to change; he won't listen to our advice. Within two years, he is going to be broke again."

"Roger, you've seen how Marlon is, he may even avoid talking to you now. But, I'll make a prediction. One day you'll pick up the telephone and there he'll be on the other end, asking you to come back to work for him."

"I can't imagine that happening."

In the days before I received my walking papers from Brando, he had asked me to investigate selling his Anaheim apartment house. I had produced an analysis for him with a recommended selling price. He had not looked at it.

Now, out of a job, I decided to make a purchase offer on the property myself. It was badly in need of repair and renovation. By fixing it up and increasing the rents, the value could be increased enough to make a fair profit. I put my offer on paper and left it at his home. Over the next couple of weeks, I stopped by or phoned several times. Brando was always "too busy" to talk to me. Finally, one day Alice said he had asked her to tell me he was not interested in selling the building. When I asked for his reason, she said that he did not want to talk about it.

It was my turn for the Brando brush-off.

I went on with my life. A few months later, there was a phone call at home from Pan American Airlines. Our household effects from Tahiti were sitting in their baggage claim room. The airline representative chastised me for not picking them up earlier. He had sent notices to the address and left messages at the phone number listed on the boxes - namely Brando's - on numerous occasions. He said he had talked to "somebody by the name of Alice" there at least three times, the last time telling her that they would throw the boxes away if they were not picked up within three days. When that time had passed, he had made one last try before disposing of them and had found my phone listing from directory assistance.

Alice had both my phone number and address. Even if they had been misplaced, it would have been a simple matter to find me. We lived, as she knew, only a mile away. The palace intrigue continued. I decided it was time to reread Machiavelli.

In December, 1973, two months after I last set foot on Tetiaroa, the tourist operation opened for what was later described as a trial run. The operation closed ten days later. It reopened again in six months, only seven bungalows ready for tourist use. From Bernard Judge's original two week time estimate for completion, construction had now stretched to more than a year and a quarter and there were still only a third of the bungalows ready for occupancy. By December, 1974, twelve bungalows were finished.

Reiko Sato happened to be caught by a reporter while in a talkative mood. All was not paradise on Tetiaroa. Reiko said, "It is all becoming a bad dream. Marlon is totally unbusinesslike. He has no idea for figures. He's impulsive. If he wants something, he goes and gets it - without analyzing the best way to do it.

"He's a dreamer, but his dreams are totally unworkable. He wants to eliminate anything that might cause just one ounce of pollution. For example, he refuses to allow us to spray for flies and mosquitoes. He refuses to treat the coconut palm roof of the bungalows even though termites chew through a roof every twelve months. He's so unrealistic."

As for the tourists, she reported, "Marlon detests having them here. It burns him up inside."

By 1976, TIME magazine reported the grandiose failure of Tetiaroa. From the beginning, storms and high tides washed through the huts, causing constant need for repairs. The resort never approached making a profit. Brando suggested, "It was a bad idea, and it was badly managed."

Still, periodically, it would reopen in the summer tourist months.

In 1975, Brando went back to acting. From 1975 through 1980, he appeared in THE MISSOURI BREAKS, APOCALYPSE NOW, SUPERMAN, and THE FORMULA. He was now able to command salaries of up to $3.7 million per movie for supporting roles requiring as few as twelve days of shooting, thereby earning more for each hour than my annual salary with him had been. His reviews varied from bad to dreadful for all these performances.

Over the years, I occasionally thought about my conversation with George Pakkala. When two years passed and it was announced that Brando was acting in a movie, I realized that half of his prediction had come true - Brando was broke again. But, I received no call to the rescue.

Several years after leaving the job, I read in the paper of a lawsuit filed by Jack Bellin against Brando. Bellin had lost *The Safari Club*. He alleged in his suit that Brando had failed to pay him for his work on Tetiaroa and had failed to provide promised help in promoting *The Safari Club*.

I was reminded of a rhyming couplet attributed to an earlier Brando associate:

While Marlon Brando bleeds for the masses,
the people he works with get kicked in their asses.

Another paper reported that he had successfully eliminated alimony payments to Movita, convincing the court that she was living as the wife of another man.

With Christian finally reaching the age of majority, the eighteen years of conflict and lawsuits with Anna finally came to an end. Christian was married and worked as a fisherman and tree surgeon, not seeing his father for months at a time. Brando bought the newlyweds a house, but their marriage was a turmoil with Christian suffering from alcoholism and an explosive temper. The union soon ended in divorce.

Miko became a bodyguard for singer Michael Jackson.

Teihotu and Cheyenne grew up on Tahiti. Like many young Tahitians, they found the United States alluring and wanted to stay, but Brando limited their visits to brief duration. Cheyenne had grown into a lovely young woman. During a 1989 visit to Tetiaroa, she was driving the jeep that Klaus could never keep running and ran into a coconut palm tree. She was thrown through the windshield, severely cutting her face. After emergency treatment on Tahiti, Brando had her flown to the UCLA medical center where several lengthy sessions of plastic surgery were necessary to restore her beauty.

Alice Marchak retired, whether by her wish or Brando's, it is difficult to say.

Over the years, many of the people close to Brando died, with three deaths in 1982 leaving him feeling ever more alone. Reiko Sato suffered a seizure when Brando was at her home. He called an ambulance, but Sato died in the hospital. Brando's long time girlfriend Jill Banner was tragically killed when a truck hit her car on the Ventura freeway. After I departed the job, attorney Norman Garey took over many of the management and financial advisory duties I had performed. He became a companion and confidant to Brando. Two weeks after Banner's death, Garey committed suicide, shooting himself in the head. He was in his mid-forties.

Two of Brando's closest friends from his early acting day also died; Carlo Fiore succumbing to his lifetime of drug addiction, Sam Gilman from cancer.

There were reports of Brando secluding himself at home for weeks at a time, brooding and eating, his weight climbing to three hundred and fifty pounds. An occasional photograph would reveal his Orson Welles-like shape.

He put his beloved Tetiaroa up for sale. When an offer came in, he refused to look at it.

In 1988, the announcement came that he was returning to the screen after an eight year absence to film a screenplay titled JERICO, which he had written himself. It had been a full fifteen years since his triumphant performances in THE GODFATHER and LAST TANGO IN PARIS.

Like most of his projects, Brando never got this one off the ground, thereby continuing to exhibit another classic ACOA behavior pattern, the difficulty of following a project through from beginning to end. He has talked about and worked on making various Indian movies for decades without anything to show for it. Nor was any part of the Tetiaroa development for tourism, aquaculture, hydroponics, or energy generation ever truly completed.

However, in 1989, he did accept offers to appear in two other movies, A DRY WHITE SEASON, a South African anti-apartheid film, and THE FRESHMAN, shot in Canada. In preparation, he went to an Australian fat farm to try to trim his girth. He lost some weight, but still returned at a full three hundred pounds.

He received generally good reviews for his brief appearance in the South African film, but became incensed at MGM/United Artists, the distributing studio, for what he regarded as massive artistic blunders and a financial double cross. He complained to reporters that he had acted an Academy Award deserving performance, but most of it had been left on the cutting room floor because MGM/UA was afraid to alienate the South African government. The alleged financial betrayal so disturbed him that he gave a television interview to Connie Chung, his first in the sixteen years since the 1973 Cavett show.

In the interview, he stated that he had pledged his entire salary of $3.3 million dollars plus 11.3% of the gross revenue, a total he estimated at ten million dollars, to an anti-apartheid organization. This was for a role so brief that, prior to production, a studio official had estimated that only about three days would be required to shoot Brando's part. Brando said that MGM/UA had promised to match that amount but had reneged on its agreement. He stated that Jeffrey Barbakow, CEO of MGM/UA and a former investment banker from Merrill Lynch, had reported to the police that Brando had threatened to shoot him and blow up his family. Brando said Barbakow's story was a lie and merely an attempt to discredit him before he had a chance to bring the alleged MGM/UA financial transgression to the attention of the public.

Amidst Brando's on camera conversations with his dog and his numerous references to the money he had made in movies, the interview was filled with the Brando homilies on life. He met Chung's inquiries about his acting with denigration of the profession, calling acting "a waste of time, odious, unpleasant, not stimulating, and not satisfying." Acting on the stage had been the worst experience of his life. There had never been any great movies, or great artists in the movies, only "people like you and me who make money."

Since my time with him, he continued to seclude himself in his bedroom; he stated that he spent hours and hours watching the ants crawl up and down his sink. He also confessed to having nine children, now including a new born baby daughter. He refused to identify the mother.

Although many hours of conversations were edited down to thirty minutes for telecasting, the general consensus of reports from viewers could be summarized in one word - boring. Even Chung faked falling asleep and snoring loudly.

On May 16, 1990, tragedy occurred in the Brando family when son Christian, then 32, shot and killed Dag Drollet, the boyfriend of his half-sister Cheyenne, in the den of Brando's Beverly Hills home. Christian pleaded guilty to voluntary manslaughter and was sentenced to ten years in prison. Marlon emotionally and tearfully testified in court at the pre-sentence hearing, pleading for leniency for Christian and confessing to his own shortcomings as a father. Christian was released from prison in 1995, his sentence cut short for good behavior.

Cheyenne suffered mental instability and spent the years after 1990 in and out of institutions. After at least two unsuccessful suicide attempts, she took her own life by hanging in her mother's house on Tahiti on Easter Sunday, 1995, at the age of 25.

On several occasions over the years, as business took me to Los Angeles, I would telephone on the business line to Brando's house, his personal number having been changed. Alice would answer the phone. I would tell her I was in town and would like to say hello to Marlon, if he was available. Even though it was sometimes obvious that he was home, she would always take my phone number and promise to give him the message. My calls were never returned.

It saddened me that Marlon would never call back. I had not been disappointed to lose my job. I was disappointed to lose contact with a man whom I had considered a friend.

Still, Brando did not disappear from my mind. In the twenty plus years since I last saw him, hardly a week has gone by without some reminder in the newspapers, magazines, books, radio, or television of my erstwhile friend and employer, whether it be a direct reference to him or merely the use of his name as a point of reference in a report on another actor or another topic.

Now and then, whenever I caught a whiff of lime, a vision from the depths of my memory would resurface, recalling the rum punches which were our nightly ritual before dinner on beautiful Tetiaroa.

One day, a full five years after I had left my job with Brando, I picked up my ringing telephone at home, twelve hundred miles from Los Angeles in Bellingham, Washington. A voice said, "This is Alice Marchak. Marlon would like to speak to you."

Brando came on the phone. "Hello Roger, how are you doing?"

"Just fine, Marlon, I'm doing just fine. It's nice to hear your voice again, it's been a long, long time. How have you been?"

"Well, I guess I'm still kicking. Things are pretty quiet around here now. Say, Roger, I was wondering about something."

"What's that?"

"How would you like to strap your harness back on and move down here and take charge of everything again?"

"Marlon, you have got to be kidding. I think one time in paradise is enough for anybody."

This time, the Godfather's offer was easy to refuse.

―――――――

In 1983, a series of typhoons struck Tetiaroa, splintering the palms and flooding and ripping apart the bungalows. The tourist operation was mercifully closed permanently.

Brando still owns the island.

THE END